Lucia Förthmann

CROCHET FOR PLAY

90 PATTERNS FOR FOOD AND KITCHEN

STACKPOLE
BOOKS
Guilford, Connecticut

Published by Stackpole Books
An imprint of The Rowman & Littlefield Publishing Group, Inc.
4501 Forbes Blvd., Ste. 200
Lanham, MD 20706
www.stackpolebooks.com

Distributed by NATIONAL BOOK NETWORK
800-462-6420

© Edition Michael Fischer GmbH, 2015, www.emf-verlag.de
This edition of *Spiel Mit in Meiner Häkelküche* first published in Germany by Edition Michael Fischer GmbH in 2015 is published by arrangement with Silke Bruenink Agency, Munich, Germany.

Cover design: Silvia Keller and Sally Rinehart
Layout: Verena Raith
Editing: Charlotte May
Typesetting and production: Claudia Weyh
Styling: Natascha Mössbauer and Saskia Wedhorn
Translation: Katharina Sokiran

Photography:
Lucia Förthmann: pages 8–20
Ziska Thalhammer: pages 1, 3, 4, 5, 6, 27, 28, 52, 68, 88, 100
Natascha Mössbauer and Saskia Wedhorn: all other photographs

British Library Cataloguing in Publication Information available

Library of Congress Cataloging-in-Publication Data available

Names: Förthmann, Lucia, author.
Title: Crochet for play : 90 patterns for food and kitchen / Lucia Förthmann.
Other titles: Spiel mit in meiner häkelküche. English
Description: Lanham, MD : Stackpole Books, 2020. | First published in Germany by Edition Michael Fischer GmbH in 2015. | Summary: "Crochet cupcakes, teapots, ice pops, pizza, cucumbers, lettuce, a mixer, measuring cups, food scale—if it's in the kitchen, you can crochet it with the instructions in this book. Patterns are provided for 90 foods and kitchen items to make a child's dream play kitchen come true"— Provided by publisher.
Identifiers: LCCN 2020010915 | ISBN 9780811738606 (paper : alk. paper) | ISBN 9780811769778 (electronic)
Subjects: LCSH: Crocheting—Patterns. | Miniature craft. | Miniature food. | Miniature objects.
Classification: LCC TT820 .F68313 2020 | DDC 746.43/4—dc23
LC record available at https://lccn.loc.gov/2020010915

First Edition

CONTENTS

AT THE MOM-AND-POP STORE 101

My career as a "toy elf" for my children started with a simple ball and led me through an array of baby toys to realms I would never have dreamed of. During the last few years, I've churned out crocheted blood pressure cuffs, IV bags, cupcakes, tools, make-up sets, and other everyday objects almost at production-line speed, since my daughters are always coming up with something still missing from their crocheted world. As a mother, I am equally delighted: Not only can I indulge in my passion—crocheting—but it is also easy on the wallet. In this book, I want to whisk you away to the world of the kitchen and the store and show you what can be magically accomplished with a simple crochet hook, a bit of yarn, and stuffing. With just a few basic skills, even absolute beginners can try their hands at our starter projects, creating something pretty and useful right away. Fast results will inspire further practice, so that, piece by piece, more complicated and time-consuming objects can be tackled. If you're like me, you'll end up putting down your hook only reluctantly!

Have fun crocheting!

Lucia Förthmann

MATERIALS

YARN

Except for the cook outfit from pages 48–51, the crochet projects in this book are worked using a thin cotton yarn (yardage about 131–142 yds per 1.75 oz/120–130 m per 50 g). I will often use Schachenmayr Catania yarn (137 yds per 1.75 oz/ 125 m per 50 g), washable at 104°F (40°C), and 100% cotton. It can be substituted by any of these good and affordable alternatives in a wide range of colors:

- Rico Design Essentials Cotton DK, 142 yds per 1.75 oz (130 m per 50 g), washable at 86°F (30°C), 100% cotton
- ONline Linie 165 Sandy, 131 yds per 1.75 oz (120 m per 50 g), washable at 104°F (40°C), 100% cotton
- Lang Yarns Quattro, 131 yds per 1.75 oz (120 m per 50 g), washable at 104°F (40°C), 100% cotton
- Schewe Baumwolle Classic, 137 yds per 1.75 oz (125 m per 50 g), washable at 104°F (40°C), 100% cotton
- Wolle Rödel Millefili, 142 yds per 1.75 oz (130 m per 50 g), washable at 86°F (30°C) in the delicates cycle, 100% cotton

THE GAUGE SWATCH

Every crocheter has their individual way of crocheting. Some crochet more densely, others more loosely. Most crochet patterns, especially for garments, where fit really matters, will have a gauge listed, which shows how many rows and stitches are in a crocheted square measuring 4 x 4 in (10 x 10 cm). Depending on your personal crocheting style, when your individual gauge differs from the one listed in the instructions, you will have to use a smaller or larger crochet hook, or crochet more densely or more loosely. If, for instance, your crocheted swatch has fewer stitches than required, you have to either crochet more densely or change to a smaller hook. If your swatch has more stitches, it will be the other way around—in that case, you need to either crochet more loosely or use a larger hook.

I will often state the length and width for a sample piece of 10 rows in height and 10 single crochets in width. This can yield a more precise gauge swatch. The gauge for the crocheted finished objects in this book is:

10 rows = about 1.6 in (4 cm), 10 sc = 1.9–2 in (4.8–5.0 cm)

For most of the items, an exact gauge match is not necessary, as long as they are crocheted not too loosely, to ensure that the objects retain their shape, and the stuffing does not show through the stitches. Gauge does, however, matter especially for finished items featuring incorporated sticks or stems. Cardboard components are usually individually matched to the item worked.

CROCHET HOOK CASE

SCHACHENMAYR CATANIA YARNS

CRAFT FELT

POLYESTER FIBERFILL

CROCHET HOOKS (2.5 MM [US B-I OR C-2] AND 6.0 MM [US J/IO])

CARDBOARD

SNAPS

BUTTONS

POPSICLE STICK, 4.5 IN [II.5 CM] LONG

PEN

GLUE

TAPESTRY NEEDLE

THIN WOODEN DOWEL, 4 IN [IO CM] LONG, APPROX 3 MM DIAMETER

WOODEN DOWEL, IO IN [25 CM] LONG, APPROX 7 MM DIAMETER

CAKE POP STICK OR LOLLIPOP STICK, 4 IN [IO CM] LONG

RICO DESIGN
BASTELKLEBER
HOBBY GLUE
COLLE BRICOLAGE

TOILET PAPER CORE

PIPE CLEANERS OR CRAFT WIRE

SEWING NEEDLE AND SEWING THREAD

ROW COUNTER

COMPAASS

SCISSORS

YARN

WOODEN BEADS

WASHI TAPE

SEED BEADS (ROCAILLES)

CROCHET BASICS

HOW DO I BEGIN?

Depending on the pattern, you will start with either a crocheted chain (foundation chain, beginning chain) or an adjustable magic ring.

CROCHETED CHAIN

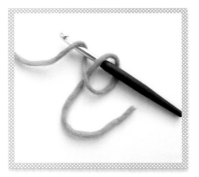

1. Make a loop at the tail end of the yarn. Insert the crochet hook through this loop.

2. Draw the working yarn through, and pull it through this loop.

3. Pull at the yarn tail to cinch the loop smaller.

4. Now lead the hook under the strand of yarn, draw the working yarn through, and pull it through this loop on the hook. You have crocheted a chain.

5. Repeat step 4 as many times as needed for the required number of chains stated in the instructions. This is how the beginning chain looks.

6. To continue in rows of single crochet, insert the hook into the second chain, counted from the hook. When using half double crochets, insert the hook into the third chain, and for double crochets, into the fourth.

1. For an adjustable magic ring, make a loop as for the beginning chain, and pull the yarn through. Here, however, do not cinch the loop smaller, but crochet a chain instead.

2. Insert the crochet hook into the center of the ring, draw the working yarn through, and pull it through the ring, securing the loose tail within. You now have two loops on the hook.

3. Draw the working yarn through once more, and pull it through both loops on the hook at once. Your first single crochet has been completed!

4. Work five more single crochets into the ring the same way.

5. Now pull on the loose end to cinch the loop closed.

6. Insert the crochet hook into the first stitch, draw the working yarn through, and pull it through the stitch and the loop on the hook. You have just worked a slip stitch.

7. The adjustable magic ring is now finished.

IMPORTANT: If working an adjustable magic ring with double crochets, start the first round with 3 chains. These replace (and count as) the first double crochet. At the end of the round, join with a slip-stitch into the third chain of the three chains in place of the first double crochet.

When learning the adjustable magic ring, you have killed four birds with one stone: chains, single crochets, slip stitches and the magic ring. For later reference, all these stitches are explained in detail below.

CHAIN (CH)

Draw the working yarn through with the hook, and pull it through the loop on the hook.

SLIP STITCH (SL-ST)

1. Insert the crochet hook into the stitch.

2. Draw the working yarn through, and pull it through the stitch and the loop on the hook at once.

SINGLE CROCHET (SC)

1. Insert the crochet hook into the stitch, draw the working yarn through, and pull it through the stitch. There are two loops on the hook now.

2. Draw the working yarn through again, and pull it through both loops at once.

JOINING NEW WORKING YARN

1. Insert the hook into the stitch, draw the new working yarn through, and pull it through the stitch.

2. Draw the working yarn through again, and pull it through this loop on the hook. The loose end of the new working yarn has to be securely woven in with a tapestry needle when you finish the crocheted piece.

DOUBLE CROCHET (DC)

I. Lead the working yarn over the hook once. This procedure is called "yarn over hook."

2. Now insert the hook into the stitch, draw the working yarn through, and pull it through the stitch.

3. There are 3 loops on the hook now.

4. Draw the working yarn through once more, and pull it through the first 2 stitches on the hook at once. Two loops remain on the hook.

HALF DOUBLE CROCHET (HDC)

5. Now draw the working yarn through a last time, and pull it through the remaining 2 loops on the hook at once.

I. As done for a double crochet, lead the working yarn over the hook once (one loop on the hook).

2. Insert the crochet hook into the stitch, draw the working yarn through, and pull it through the stitch. This yields 3 loops on the hook. Now draw the working yarn through again, and pull it through all 3 loops on the hook at once.

3. The half double crochet has been completed.

TREBLE CROCHET (TR)

1. Lead the working yarn over the hook twice.

2. Insert the crochet hook into the stitch, draw the working yarn through, and pull it through the stitch. You now have 4 loops on the hook.

3. Draw the working yarn through, and pull it through the first 2 loops on the hook. There are 3 loops on the hook now.

4. Draw the working yarn through once more, and pull it through the first 2 loops on the hook at once. Now only 2 loops remain on the hook.

5. Draw the working yarn through a last time, and pull it through the last 2 loops on the hook at once.

BOBBLE (BB)

1. Begin as for a double crochet: Lead the working yarn over the hook once, and then insert the hook into the stitch, draw the working yarn through, and pull it through the stitch. Draw the working yarn through once more, and pull it through the first 2 loops on the hook. 2 loops remain on the hook. Do not finish the last step of this double crochet ("unfinished double crochet").

2. Work 5 more unfinished double crochets into the same stitch. There are now 7 loops on the hook.

3. Draw the working yarn through, and pull it through all 7 loops on the hook at once.

COLOR CHANGE

1. First, work the last stitch of the row in the old color, except for the very last step.

2. Work the last step of the stitch in the new color and continue in the new color.

INCREASING (INC)

Work two stitches into the same stitch of the previous row or round. This increases the stitch count by 1.

DECREASING (DEC)

Decreasing is achieved by crocheting two stitches together. This decreases the stitch count by 1.

FOR SINGLE CROCHET:

1. Insert the hook into the first stitch, draw the working yarn through, and pull it through the stitch. Insert the hook into the second stitch, draw the working yarn through, and pull it through the stitch. You now have 3 loops on the hook.

2. Draw the working yarn through, and pull it through all 3 loops on the hook at once.

FOR HALF DOUBLE CROCHET:

Lead the yarn over the hook once, insert the hook into the first stitch, draw the working yarn through, and pull it through the stitch. Lead the yarn over the hook again, insert the hook into the second stitch, draw the working yarn through, and pull it through the stitch. There are 5 loops on the hook now. Draw the working yarn through once more, and pull it through all 5 loops on the hook at once.

FOR DOUBLE CROCHET:

1. Lead the working yarn over the hook once, insert the hook into the first stitch, and draw the working yarn through.

2. Lead the working yarn over the hook once, insert the hook into the second stitch, and draw the working yarn through. This yields 5 loops on the hook.

3. Draw the working yarn through, and pull it through the first 3 loops on the hook, leaving 2 loops on the hook.

4. Draw the working yarn through a last time, and pull it through the remaining 2 loops.

FRONT POST DOUBLE CROCHET (FPDC)

1. Lead the working yarn over the hook once. Insert the hook not as usual under the top loop of the stitch, but below, from the front, to the right of the post of the stitch. Lead the hook in the back around the post of the stitch, emerging in the front again, but this time to the left of the post of the stitch.

2. Draw the working yarn through, and lead it back all the way around the post of the stitch again.

3. Yarn over hook and pull through 2 loops on the hook; then yarn over hook and pull through 2 loops again to finish the double crochet.

FRONT POST SINGLE CROCHET (FPSC)

Work the same way as for a front post double crochet, but work only a single crochet instead of double.

BACK POST DOUBLE CROCHET (BPDC)

1. Lead the working yarn over the hook once. Insert the hook not as usual under the top loop of the stitch, but below, from the back, to the right of the post of the stitch.

2. Lead the hook from the front around the post of the stitch, then insert the hook from the front to the left of the post of the stitch, and lead it through to the back again. Draw the working yarn through, and lead it all the way back around the post of the stitch again.

3. Yarn over hook and pull through 2 loops on the hook; then yarn over hook and pull through 2 loops again to finish the double crochet.

BACK POST SINGLE CROCHET (BPSC)

1. Back post single crochets are especially well suited for prominent divisions and edges within a crocheted piece. Insert the hook not into the stitch proper, but instead from the back and to the right of it.

2. Lead the hook in the front around the post of the stitch, and insert the hook through to the back again.

3. Draw the working yarn through, and lead it all the way around the post of the stitch back again. Finish the single crochet as usual.

DOUBLE CROCHET POPCORN (POP-DC)

1. Work 5 double crochets into the same stitch.

2. Remove the hook from the working loop, and pull the working loop slightly longer. Insert the crochet hook into the first one of the 5 double crochets, and afterward into the loop that was just pulled longer.

3. Pull the working yarn slightly taut again. There are 2 loops on the hook. Draw the working yarn through, and pull it through both loops at once. This has created a pocket-like extension, which bulges out to the front of the work.

SPIKE STITCHES

I. Spike stitches are worked into the stitch one row or round below the current one.

2. This is how a spike stitch looks.

3. If the stitch has to be worked even deeper than 1 row or round below, this will be explicitly stated in the pattern. Make sure that the stitch is worked loosely enough to prevent the crocheted fabric from puckering.

TULIP STITCH (TULIP-ST)

Lead the working yarn over the hook once, insert the hook into the stitch, draw the working yarn through, and pull it through the stitch. You now have 3 loops on the hook. Repeat the steps 2 times more. This yields 7 loops on the hook. Now draw the working yarn through, and pull it through all 7 loops on the hook at once.

INSERTING THE HOOK FROM THE BACK

Insert the crochet hook from the back to the front into the stitch, and finish the stitch as usual.

WORKING THROUGH THE BACK LOOP OF THE STITCH ONLY (BLO)

Insert the crochet hook only through the back one of the two loops, and then work the stitch as usual.

WORKING THROUGH THE FRONT LOOP OF THE STITCH ONLY (FLO)

Insert the crochet hook only through the front one of the two loops, and then work the stitch as usual.

ABBREVIATIONS

Since many instructions are repeated throughout, the following abbreviations are used:

bb	bobble
bpsc	back post single crochet
ch	chain
ch-sp	chain space (around the chain)
dc	double crochet
dec	decrease
fpdc	front post double crochet
fpsc	front post single crochet
hdc	half double crochet
hdc2tog	crochet 2 half double crochets together (2 bases, 1 shared top)
inc	increase
pop-dc	popcorn from double crochet
prev	previous
rep	repeat
rnd(s)	round(s)
RS	right side
sc	single crochet
sc3tog	crochet 3 single crochets together (3 bases, 1 shared top)
sc4tog	crochet 4 single crochets together (4 bases, 1 shared top)
skip	skip the stitch and work in the next
sl-st(s)	slip stitch(es)
st(s)	stitch(es)
tr	treble crochet
WS	wrong side

DIFFICULTY LEVELS

Difficulty levels are indicated as below.

    EASY

    MEDIUM

   ADVANCED

FINISHING OFF AND BREAKING THE YARN

To secure the yarn before cutting it from the skein at the end of a piece, work 2 chains. Now cut the yarn, leaving an end of about 6 in (15 cm). Thread it through the last chain, and pull it taut.

WEAVING IN ENDS

Loose ends are woven in with the help of a tapestry needle. Weave the yarn tail carefully and as invisibly as possible through the stitches of the final row or round.

HOW DO I WORK A ROUND?

At the end of a round, join with a slip stitch into the first stitch of the round to close the round. Chain 1 ("height-adjustment chain"), and continue without turning. If the first stitch of the new round will be a double crochet, chain 3 for height adjustment instead, and for half double crochet, chain 2 to reach the required height for the new round.

HOW DO I WORK A SPIRAL ROUND?

At the end of a spiral round, work is not joined into the round with a slip stitch, but instead continued without joining. Since the beginning of the round is not easily recognizable in continuous rounds, it is recommended to place a marker on the first stitch of the round. This will eliminate the need for time-consuming stitch counting later.

HOW DO I WORK A ROW?

At the end of a row, a "turning stitch" is always worked, after which work is turned. Sometimes, instructions will state to work an additional slip stitch into the first stitch of the row. Here, too, you will still work in back-and-forth rows with turning, not in rounds. If the first stitch of the new row will be a double crochet, chain 3 for height adjustment instead, and for half double crochet, chain 2, to reach the required height for the new row.

SEAMING PIECES AND SEWING ON EMBELLISHMENTS

For sewing crocheted pieces together and attaching crocheted appliques, always use the project yarn and a tapestry needle. Sewing thread would be too thin and not elastic enough for this purpose. Non-crocheted embellishments such as woven ribbon, bows and buttons, however, are sewn on using a sewing needle and sewing thread.

WARNING

Children may inadvertently swallow small parts! To prevent small components from becoming loose, sew over them two or three times, and then securely fasten the tail and hide the end. Very small pieces should only be given to children age 4 and older.

BASIC INSTRUCTIONS FOR A CIRCLE

Some of the patterns start out from a crocheted circular piece. Since a circle is always worked the same way, you will find basic instructions to make one here. The individual pattern will later contain only the required number of rounds to be used from the basic circle pattern following here.

Work in rounds. Begin every round with 1 chain, and end every round with 1 sl-st into the first stitch of the round. Do not turn work.

Rnd 1: Work 6 sc into an adjustable magic ring. (6 sts)

Rnd 2: Inc 1 st each, 6 times in all. (12 sts)

Rnd 3: * 1 sc, inc 1 st *, rep from * to * 5 times more. (18 sts)

Rnd 4: * 2 sc, inc 1 st *, rep from * to * 5 times more. (24 sts)

Rnd 5: 1 sc, inc 1 st, * 3 sc, inc 1 st *, rep from * to * 4 times more, 2 sc. (30 sts)

Rnd 6: * 4 sc, inc 1 st *, rep from * to * 5 times more. (36 sts)

Rnd 7: 2 sc, inc 1 st, * 5 sc, inc 1 st *, rep from * to * 4 times more, 3 sc. (42 sts)

Rnd 8: * 6 sc, inc 1 st *, rep from * to * 5 times more. (48 sts)

Rnd 9: 3 sc, inc 1 st, * 7 sc, inc 1 st *, rep from * to * 4 times more, 4 sc. (54 sts)

Rnd 10: * 8 sc, inc 1 st *, rep from * to * 5 times more. (60 sts)

Rnd 11: 4 sc, inc 1 st, * 9 sc, inc 1 st *, rep from * to * 4 times more, 5 sc. (66 sts)

Rnd 12: * 10 sc, inc 1 st *, rep from * to * 5 times more. (72 sts)

Rnd 13: 5 sc, inc 1 st, * 11 sc, inc 1 st *, rep from * to * 4 times more, 6 sc. (78 sts)

Rnd 14: * 12 sc, inc 1 st *, rep from * to * 5 times more. (84 sts)

Rnd 15: 6 sc, inc 1 st, * 13 sc, inc 1 st *, rep from * to * 4 times more, 7 sc. (90 sts)

Rnd 16: * 14 sc, inc 1 st *, rep from * to * 5 times more. (96 sts)

Rnd 17: 7 sc, inc 1 st, * 15 sc, inc 1 st *, rep from * to * 4 times more, 8 sc. (102 sts)

Rnd 18: * 16 sc, inc 1 st *, rep from * to * 5 times more. (108 sts)

Rnd 19: 8 sc, inc 1 st, * 17 sc, inc 1 st *, rep from * to * 4 times more, 9 sc. (114 sts)

Rnd 20: * 18 sc, inc 1 st *, rep from * to * 5 times more. (120 sts)

RUNNING STITCH

Insert the tapestry needle from the back, and then insert it again from the front at a small distance and pull the yarn through. Now insert the needle at the same distance and repeat the previous steps.

BACK STITCH

Insert the tapestry needle from the back, and pull the yarn through. Now insert the needle again at a small distance (about 3 mm) to the right of the exit point, and pull the yarn through. Now insert the needle from the back, about 3 mm to the left of the first exit point, and pull it through to the front again. Repeat the previous steps.

WHIPSTITCH

This stitch is worked over two open edges. Insert the tapestry needle from the back to the front through the edges of both layers. Lead the needle back over the work, insert it, slightly offset to the side, again through the edges of both layers, and pull it through to the front. Repeat these steps as often as needed.

CHAIN STITCH

1. Insert the tapestry needle from the back to the front through the fabric and then in the same spot from the front to the back again. Pull the thread until a loop has formed. Now insert the needle from the back to the front, going through this loop, and then insert it, slightly to the side of the exit point, again from the front to the back.

2. Leave a loop again, and repeat the previous steps.

MATTRESS STITCH

Use this stitch to seam the edges of two pieces invisibly.

1. Insert the tapestry needle from the back to the front through one of the two edges and then back down from front to back, about 3 mm away, taking a small stitch.

2. Lead the needle from the back perpendicular to the other edge and insert the needle again on the same side of the edge, offset about 3 mm, from the front to the back.

3. Now bring the needle again perpendicular to the other edge. Repeat these steps throughout.

FRENCH KNOT

Insert the tapestry needle in the desired spot from the back to the front through the crocheted fabric. Wrap the yarn around the needle two times, close to the fabric. Insert the needle into the same spot again, and pull the yarn through.

Finished!

KITCHEN EQUIPMENT

Up-and-coming masters need proper tools–with these, the tasty dishes from our play kitchen will turn out just perfectly! Equip your little chef with apron, chef's hat, pots, dishes, and flatware, and let the fun begin!

PORTABLE CROCHET KITCHEN

MATERIALS

- crochet hook, 2.5 mm (US B-1 or C-2)
- tapestry needle
- sewing needle and thread
- Schachenmayr Catania (100% cotton): 2 skeins (3.5 oz/100 g) in Kiwi; 1 skein (1.75 oz/50 g) each in Black (Schwarz), Silver (Silber), Signal Red (Signalrot), Anise (Anis), Pastel Blue (Hellblau), and Orange; 0.5 oz (15 g) each in Apple (Apfel), Pink (Rosa), Regatta (or any other shade of Blue), May Green (Maigrün), White (Weiß), Coffee (Kaffee), and Mimosa (Mimose)
- polyester fiberfill
- white craft felt and glue
- 2 buttons

INSTRUCTIONS

KITCHEN SURFACE MAT

Work in rows. At the end of every row, chain 1, and turn work.

Using Black yarn, crochet a chain of 46.

Row 1 (RS): Work 1 sc into the 2nd stitch from the hook, 1 sc each in every following ch. (45 sts)

Rows 2–44: 1 sc each in every st of the prev row. (45 sts)

Change color to Silver.

Rows 45–88: 1 sc each in every st of the prev row. (45 sts)

Break the working yarn, and secure the end.

OUTSIDE POCKET

Work as before for Kitchen Surface Mat, but this time, use only Kiwi.

Now place the 2 crocheted pieces together, wrong sides facing each other, and crochet them together evenly by working sc through both layers at a rate of 1 sc into every st and 1 sc into every end of the row. At the corners, work 2 sc each into each one of the 4 corner sts.

Break the working yarn, and secure the end.

FIRST HANDLE

Hold the crocheted-together kichen surface mat with the kiwi-colored side facing you (with the Silver part of the mat located in the back), and join new working yarn in Anise to the first stitch of the narrow edge. Work in rows. At the end of every row, chain 1, and turn work.

Row 1: 1 sc each in every st of the prev row. (45 sts)
Row 2: Dec 1 st, 41 sc, dec 1 st. (43 sts)
Row 3: Dec 1 st, 10 sc, ch19, skip 19 sts, 10 sc, dec 1 st. (41 sts)
Row 4: Dec 1 st, 9 sc, 19 sc in ch-sp, 9 sc, dec 1 st. (39 sts)
Row 5: Dec 1 st, 1 sc, ch3, skip 3 sts (1st buttonhole), 27 sc, ch3, skip 3 sts (2nd buttonhole), 1 sc, dec 1 st. (37 sts)

Row 6: Dec 1 st, 3 sc in ch-sp, 27 sc, 3 sc in ch-sp, dec 1 st. (35 sts)
Row 7: Dec 1 st, 31 sc, dec 1 st. (33 sts)

Break the working yarn, and secure the end.

SECOND HANDLE

Now work the second handle at the opposite narrow edge of the kitchen mat, kiwi-colored side facing you. Work Rows 1–7 as for the 1st handle, except for the buttonholes: Instead of 3 chains, work 3 sc, skipping no sts.

OUTSIDE POCKET

Work in rows. At the end of every row, chain 1, and turn work.

In Orange, crochet a chain of 34.

Row 1 (RS): Work 1 sc into the 2nd stitch from the hook, 1 sc each in every following ch. (33 sts)
Rows 2–21: 1 sc each in every st of the prev row. (33 sts)

Change color to Apple.

Row 22: Ch3, 1 sl-st into the 1st st of the row, * 1 sl-st into the next st, ch3, 1 sl-st into the same st as the last sl-st had been worked *, rep between * and * to end of row.

Break the working yarn, and secure the end.

KITCHEN SINK

Work in rows. At the end of every row, chain 1, and turn work.

In Pastel Blue, crochet a chain of 25.

Row 1 (RS): Work 1 sc into the 2nd stitch from the hook, 1 sc each in every following ch. (24 sts)
Row 2: Inc 1 st, 22 sc, inc 1 st. (26 sts)

Rows 3–27: 1 sc each in every st of the prev row. (26 sts)
Row 28: Dec 1 st, 22 sc, dec 1 st. (24 sts)
Row 29: 1 sc each in every st of the prev row. (24 sts)

Do not turn at the end of the row. Work sc edging evenly around the rectangle to the 1st st of the last row. Work 1 sl-st into this 1st st.

Break the working yarn, and secure the end.

FAUCET

PART 1

Work in rounds. Begin every round with 1 chain, and end every round with 1 sl-st into the first stitch of the round. Do not turn work.

Rnd 1: In Silver, work 6 sc into an adjustable magic ring. (6 sts)
Rnd 2: Inc 1 st each, 6 times in all. (12 sts)
Rnds 3–13: 1 sc each in every st of the prev rnd. (12 sts)

Break the working yarn, and secure the end.

Now stuff the faucet with polyester fiberfill.

PART 2

Work in rounds. Begin every round with 1 chain, and end every round with 1 sl-st into the first stitch of the round. Do not turn work.

Rnd 1: Work 6 sc into an adjustable magic ring. (6 sts)
Rnds 2–8: 1 sc each in every st of the prev rnd. (6 sts)

Break the working yarn, and secure the end.

Lightly stuff the part with polyester fiberfill.

Sew on Part 2 in mattress stitch at the level of Rnds 6–8 of Part 1.

DIAL

Work in rounds. Begin every rnd with ch1, and end every rnd with 1 sl-st into the 1st st of the rnd. Do not turn work.

Rnd 1: In Signal Red, work 6 sc into an adjustable magic ring. (6 sts)
Rnd 2: Inc 1 st each, 6 times in all. (12 sts)

Change color to Silver.

Rnd 3: 1 sc each in every st of the prev rnd. (12 sts)
Rnds 4 and 5: Working through the back loop of the st only: 1 sc each in every st of the prev rnd. (12 sts)

Stuff the dial with polyester fiberfill.

Rnd 6: Working through the back loop of the st only: dec 1 st each, 6 times in all. (6 sts)
Rnd 7: * Skip 1 st, 1 sl-st *, rep from * to * 2 times more. (3 sts)

Break the working yarn, and secure the end.

Make a second dial the same way, but working the first two rnds in Regatta instead of Signal Red.

BURNER (MAKE 2)

Using Signal Red, crochet a circle from Basic pattern (Rnds 1–11, see page 23).

Break the working yarn, and secure the end.

TEMPERATURE DIAL

Work in rounds. Begin every round with 1 chain and end every round with 1 sl-st into the first stitch of the round. Do not turn work.

Rnd 1: In Pink, work 6 sc into an adjustable magic ring. (6 sts)
Rnd 2: Inc 1 st each, 6 times in all. (12 sts)
Rnd 3: Working through the back loop of the st only, 1 sc each in every st of the prev rnd. (12 sts)
Rnds 4 and 5: 1 sc each in every st of the prev rnd. (12 sts)

Break the working yarn, and secure the end.

Stuff the temperature dial with polyester fiberfill.

FINISHING

Sew the burners to the black surface staggered, using Black yarn

MATERIALS

- crochet hook 2.5 mm (US B-1 or C-2)
- tapestry needle
- Schachenmayr Catania (100% cotton): 1 skein (1.75 oz/50 g) each in Jeans and White (Weiß)

INSTRUCTIONS

POT

In Jeans, crochet a circle from Basic pattern (Rnds 1–10, see page 23).

Rnd 11: Working through the back loop of the st only: 1 sc each in every st of the prev rnd. (60 sts)

Rnds 12–22: 1 sc each in every st of the prev rnd. (60 sts)

Rnd 23: 4 sc, inc 1 st, * 9 sc, inc 1 st *, rep from * to * 4 times more, 5 sc. (66 sts)

Rnd 24: 1 bpsc in every st of the prev rnd. (66 sts)

Change color to White.

Rnd 25: 5 sc, dec 1 st, * 9 sc, dec 1 st *, rep from * to * 4 times more, 4 sc. (60 sts)

Rnd 26: * 8 sc, dec 1 st *, rep from * to * 5 times more. (54 sts)

Rnds 27–37: 1 sc each in every st of the prev rnd. (54 sts)

Rnd 38: * 7 sc, dec 1 st *, rep from * to * 5 times more. (48 sts)

Rnd 39: 3 sc, dec 1 st, * 6 sc, dec 1 st *, rep from * to * 4 times more, 3 sc. (42 sts)

Rnd 40: * 5 sc, dec 1 st *, rep from * to * 5 times more. (36 sts)

Rnd 41: 2 sc, dec 1 st, * 4 sc, dec 1 st *, rep from * to * 4 times more, 2 sc. (30 sts)

Rnd 42: * 3 sc, dec 1 st *, rep from * to * 5 times more. (24 sts)

Rnd 43: * 2 sc, dec 1 st *, rep from * to * 5 times more. (18 sts)

Rnd 44: * 1 sc, dec 1 st *, rep from * to * 5 times more. (12 sts)

Rnd 45: Dec 1 st each, 6 times in all. (6 sts)

Rnd 46: * Skip 1 st, 1 sl-st *, rep from * to * 2 times more. (3 sts)

Break the working yarn, and secure the end.

Turn the white part into the blue part, so that Rnd 24 forms the top edge of the pot.

LID

In Jeans, work Rnds 1–10 as in instructions for pot. (60 sts)

Rnd 11: 4 sc, inc 1 st, * 9 sc, inc 1 st *, rep from * to * 4 times more, 5 sc. (66 sts)

Break the working yarn, and secure the end.

In White, work Rnds 1–10 as in instructions for pot. (60 sts)

Rnd 11: 4 sc, inc 1 st, * 9 sc, inc 1 st *, rep from * to * 4 times more, 5 sc. (66 sts)

Place the blue circle RS up onto the WS of the white circle, and crochet them together in Jeans in sc, making sure to only work through the back loop of the st for the sts in Jeans.

Break the working yarn, and secure the end.

Work an additional rnd of sl-st through the front loops of the sts of Rnd 11 of the blue circle.

---

and working in backstitch along the last row of the burner. Next to them, sew the temperature dial onto the mat. Embroider a curved "S" to the center of the burner in backstitch.

In May Green and working in backstitch, embroider the digital clock face.

In Pastel Blue and working in backstitch, sew the kitchen sink to they gray mat. Centered above the kitchen sink, first sew on Part 1 of the faucet, and then, next to it, the red and the blue dials.

The buttons are sewn on the inside of the handle without buttonholes, matching the spot where the buttonholes are on the other handle.

In Orange and working in backstitch, sew the orange edges of the outer pocket to the kiwi-colored kitchen mat base (on the buttonhole side). Do not sew on the edge with green border. To divide the pocket into two partitions, place a vertical seam in Orange in backstitch, which attaches the outer pocket to the mat base. The right one of the two partitions should be narrower than the left one (10 sts wide).

Embroider the name of the restaurant (for instance, "Chez Jasper") in White and Coffee in chain stitch (see page 25) onto the outer pocket, making sure to not accidentally attach the outer pocket to the kitchen mat! In Mimosa, embroider 5 stars. Using the template from page 128, cut a chef's hat from white craft felt, and glue it onto the outer pocket below the 5 stars.

HANDLE (MAKE 3)

In Jeans, work 6 sc into an adjustable magic ring. Join into the round with 1 sl-st into the 1st st of the rnd. Chain 9. Work 6 sc into the 2nd chain from the hook. 1 sl-st into the first one of these 6 sc. Work as follows into the 7 remaining chains: 2 sl-st, 1 sc, 1 hdc, 1 sc, 2 sl-st. Work 1 sl-st into the adjustable magic ring.

FINISHING

Sew one of the handles centered onto the topside of the lid, and the other two to the outsides of the pot, attaching them with a stitch placed between the crocheted chain and the circle.

FRYING PAN

MATERIALS

- crochet hook, 2.5 mm (US B-1 or C-2)
- tapestry needle
- Schachenmayr Catania (100% cotton): 1 skein (1.75 oz/50 g) each in Black (Schwarz) and Silver (Silber)
- polyester fiberfill
- thin wooden dowel

INSTRUCTIONS

FRYING PAN

In Silver, crochet a circle from Basic pattern (Rnds 1–10, see page 23).

Change color to Black.

Rnd 11: Working through the back loop of the st only: 4 sc, inc 1 st, * 9 sc, inc 1 st *, rep from * to * 4 times more, 5 sc. (66 sts)

Rnds 12 and 13: 1 sc each in every st of the prev rnd. (66 sts)
Rnd 14: * 10 sc, inc 1 st *, rep from * to * 5 times more. (72 sts)
Rnds 15 and 16: 1 sc each in every st of the prev rnd. (72 sts)
Rnd 17: 1 bpsc in every st of the prev rnd. (72 sts)
Rnd 18: * 10 sc, dec 1 st *, rep from * to * 5 times more. (66 sts)
Rnd 19: 1 bpsc in every st of the prev rnd. (66 sts)
Rnds 20 and 21: 1 sc in every st of the prev rnd. (66 sts)
Rnd 22: * 9 sc, dec 1 st *, rep from * to * 5 times more. (60 sts)
Rnd 23: 1 sc in every st of the prev rnd. (60 sts)
Rnd 24: Working through the back loop of the st only: * 8 sc, dec 1 st *, rep from * to * 5 times more. (54 sts)
Rnd 25: 3 sc, dec 1 st, * 7 sc, dec 1 st *, rep from * to * 4 times more, 4 sc. (48 sts)
Rnd 26: * 6 sc, dec 1 st *, rep from * to * 5 times more. (42 sts)
Rnd 27: 2 sc, dec 1 st, * 5 sc, dec 1 st *, rep from * to * 4 times more, 3 sc. (36 sts)

Rnd 28: * 4 sc, dec 1 st *, rep from * to * 5 times more. (30 sts)
Rnd 29: * 3 sc, dec 1 st *, rep from * to * 5 times more. (24 sts)
Rnd 30: * 2 sc, dec 1 st *, rep from * to * 5 times more. (18 sts)
Rnd 31: * 1 sc, dec 1 st *, rep from * to * 5 times more. (12 sts)
Rnd 32: Dec 1 st each, 6 times in all. (6 sts)
Rnd 33: * Skip 1 st, 1 sl-st *, rep from * to * 2 times more. (3 sts)

Break the working yarn, and secure the end.

Don't stuff the frying pan. For shaping, turn the crocheted piece from Rnd 19 on into the remaining work so that Rnds 17 and 18 form the rim of the pan.

HANDLE

Work in rounds. Begin every round with 1 chain, and end every round with 1 sl-st into the first stitch of the round. Do not turn work.

Rnd 1: In Black, work 6 sc into an adjustable magic ring. (6 sts)
Rnd 2: * 1 sc, inc 1 st *, rep from * to * 2 times more. (9 sts)

Rnds 3–19: 1 sc in every st of the prev rnd. (9 sts)

Stuff the handle with polyester fiberfill.

Change color to Silver.

Rnd 20: Working through the back loop of the st only: * 1 sc, dec 1 st *, rep from * to * 2 times more. (6 sts)
Rnds 21 and 22: 1 sc in every st of the prev rnd. (6 sts)
Break the working yarn, and secure the end.

FINISHING

Shorten the wooden dowel to a length of 1.8 in (4.5 cm). Slide one end into the opening of the handle, and add more stuffing. Push the other end into a stitch of Rnd 17 of the frying pan (pan rim). In Black and working in mattress stitch, sew the handle to the pan rim. To prevent the dowel from shifting, sew the layered pan sides together in back stitch to the left and right of the dowel.

TOASTER

MATERIALS

- crochet hook, 2.5 mm (US B-1 or C-2)
- tapestry needle
- Schachenmayr Catania (100% cotton): 1 skein (1.75 oz/50 g) each in Capri, Violet (Violett), Apple (Apfel), and Cyclam; and 0.5 oz (15 g) each in Pastel Blue (Hellblau) and Black (Schwarz)
- polyester fiberfill

INSTRUCTIONS

INNER POCKET

First, work in rows. At the end of every row, chain 1, and turn work.

Row 1: In Apple, crochet a chain of 23, work 1 sc into the 2nd chain from the hook, 1 sc each in every following ch. (22 sts)
Rows 2–4: 1 sc in every st of the prev row (= 22 sts), ch1, do not turn work.

Now work an edging of 1 rnd sc (22 sc into the long sides, and 3 sc into the short sides = 50 sts), 1 sl-st into the first stitch of the rnd. From here on, work in rounds. Begin every rnd with ch1, and end every rnd with 1 sl-st into the 1st st of the rnd. Do not turn work.

Rnds 1–19: 1 sc in every st of the prev rnd. (50 sts)

Break the working yarn, and secure the end.

In Cyclam, work a second inner pocket following the instructions listed above.

TOPSIDE OF TOASTER

Work in rows. At the end of every row, chain 1, and turn work.

Row 1: In Violet, crochet a chain of 31, work 1 sc into the 2nd chain from the hook, 1 sc in every following ch. (30 sts)
Row 2: 1 sc in every st of the prev row. (30 sts)
Row 3: 4 sc, ch1, and turn work. (4 sts) Leave the remaining sts unworked for now.
Rows 4 and 5: 1 sc in every st of the prev row. (4 sts)

Break the working yarn, and secure the end.

Row 3: Now return to Row 3, and skip 22 sts, and then work 4 sc. (4 sts)
Rows 4 and 5: 1 sc in every st of the prev row. (4 sts)
Row 6: 4 sc, ch22, 4 sc (into the first 4 sts of Row 5). (30 sts)
Row 7: 4 sc, 1 sc in every ch of the chain, 4 sc. (30 sts)
Row 8: 1 sc in every st of the prev row. (30 sts)
Rows 9–14: Repeat Rows 3–8. (30 sts) Chain 1, turn work.

From here on, work in rounds. Begin every rnd with ch1, and end every rnd with 1 sl-st into the 1st st of the rnd. Do not turn work.

Rnd 1: Work sc edging evenly around the whole piece, working 1 sc in every st widthwise and every row heightwise. (30 + 14 + 30 + 14 = 88 sts)
Rnd 2: 1 bpsc in every st of the prev rnd. (88 sts)

TOASTER BODY

Change color to Capri.

Rnds 3–24: 1 sc in every st of the prev rnd. (88 sts)
Break the working yarn, and secure the end.

BOTTOM OF TOASTER

Work in rows. At the end of every row, chain 1, and turn work.

Row 1: In Capri, crochet a chain of 31, work 1 sc into the 2nd chain from the hook, 1 sc in every following ch. (30 sts)
Rows 2–14: 1 sc in every st of the prev row. (30 sts) Chain 1, turn work.

Work sc edging evenly around the whole piece, working 1 sc in every st widthwise and every row heightwise. (30 + 14 + 30 + 14 = 88 sts)

HANDLE

From here on, work in rounds. Begin every round with 1 chain, and end every round with 1 sl-st into the first stitch of the round. Do not turn work.

Rnd 1: In Pastel Blue, crochet a chain of 7, work 1 sc into the 2nd chain from the hook, 5 sc, 2 sc into the same st, and then continue in the ch-sp, around the chain: 5 sc, 1 sc into the st into which you had previously worked the first st. (14 sts)
Rnd 2: 5 sc, inc 1 st, 6 sc, inc 1 st, 1 sc. (16 sts)
Rnds 3 and 4: 1 sc in every st of the prev rnd. (16 sts)
Rnd 5: 7 sc, inc 1 st, 5 sc, inc 1 st, 2 sc. (18 sts)
Rnd 6: 1 sc in every st of the prev rnd. (18 sts)
Rnd 7: 7 sc, inc 1 st each twice, 7 sc, inc 1 st each twice. (22 sts)

Break the working yarn, and secure the end.

FINISHING

In inner pocket color, sew the last rnd of each inner pocket in whipstitch to one opening of the toaster topside. To do this, slide the inner pocket into the toaster body. After having sewn on both inner pockets, stuff the remaining gaps in the toaster with polyester fiberfill, taking care to avoid overstuffing, which would distort the toaster and close up the bread slots.

Now, in Capri, wrong sides facing each other and working in mattress stitch, sew the bottom part of the toaster to the last rnd of the toaster body.

Stuff the handle with polyester fiberfill, and sew it in mattress stitch to the side of the toaster. In Black, working in backstitch and starting at the handle, embroider a vertical line.

SPATULA

MATERIALS

- crochet hook, 2.5 mm (US B-1 or C-2)
- tapestry needle
- Schachenmayr Catania (100% cotton): 1 skein (1.75 oz/50 g) in Black (Schwarz), and approx. 0.5 oz (15 g) in Silver (Silber)
- flat wooden spatula
- cardboard

INSTRUCTIONS

Work in rounds. Begin every rnd with ch1, and end every rnd with 1 sl-st into the 1st st of the rnd. Do not turn work.

Rnd 1: In Black, work 6 sc into an adjustable magic ring. (6 sts)

Rnd 2: * 1 sc, inc 1 st *, rep from * to * 2 times more. (9 sts)

Rnds 3–27: 1 sc in every st of the prev rnd. (9 sts)

Rnd 28: Inc 1 st, 4 sc, inc 1 st, 3 sc. (11 sts)

Rnd 29: 4 sc, inc 1 st, 5 sc, inc 1 st. (13 sts)

Rnd 30: 5 sc, inc 1 st, 6 sc, inc 1 st. (15 sts)

Rnd 31: * 4 sc, inc 1 st *, rep from * to * 2 times more. (18 sts)

Rnd 32: 7 sc, inc 1 st, 8 sc, inc 1 st, 1 sc. (20 sts)

Rnd 33: 8 sc, inc 1 st, 9 sc, inc 1 st, 1 sc. (22 sts)

Rnd 34: 9 sc, inc 1 st, 10 sc, inc 1 st, 1 sc. (24 sts)

Rnds 35–38: 1 sc in every st of the prev rnd. (24 sts)

FINISHING

Slide the flat wooden spatula into the handle of the crocheted spatula. Using the template from page 128, cut a piece of cardboard, and insert it into the top part of the crocheted spatula, so that the increases of Rnds 33–35 end up at the side edges. Sew the remaining opening along the edges closed in whipstitch. In Silver and in chain stitch, embroider 3 vertical lines on both sides as pictured.

SOUP LADLE

MATERIALS

- crochet hook, 2.5 mm (US B-1 or C-2)
- tapestry needle
- Schachenmayr Catania (100% cotton): 1 skein (1.75 oz/50 g) in Silver (Silber), and approx. 0.5 oz (15 g) in Black (Schwarz)
- polyester fiberfill
- wooden dowel

INSTRUCTIONS

Work in rounds. Begin every rnd with ch1, and end every rnd with 1 sl-st into the 1st st of the rnd. Do not turn work.

HANDLE

Rnd 1: In Black, work 6 sc into an adjustable magic ring. (6 sts)
Rnd 2: * 1 sc, inc 1 st *, rep from * to * 2 times more. (9 sts)
Rnds 3–5: 1 sc in every st of the prev rnd. (9 sts)
Rnd 6: 1 sc, dec 1 st, 6 sc. (8 sts)
Rnd 7: 1 sc in every st of the prev rnd. (8 sts)

Stuff with fiberfill up to Rnd 6.

Rnd 8: 4 sc, dec 1 st, 2 sc. (7 sts)
Rnd 9: 1 sc in every st of the prev rnd. (7 sts)
Rnd 10: Dec 1 st, 5 sc. (6 sts)

Change color to Silver.

Rnd 11: Working through the back loop of the st only: 1 sc in every st of the prev rnd. (6 sts)
Rnds 12–22: 1 sc in every st of the prev rnd (through both loops of the stitch). (6 sts)

Break the working yarn, and secure the end.

Insert the wooden dowel into the handle. It will stick out a little bit.

BOWL

Rnd 1: In Silver, work 10 sc into an adjustable magic ring. (10 sts)
Rnd 2: Inc 1 st each twice, 3 sc, inc 1 st each twice, 3 sc. (14 sts)
Rnd 3: Inc 1 st, 2 sc, inc 1 st, 3 sc, inc 1 st, 2 sc, inc 1 st, 3 sc. (18 sts)
Rnd 4: 1 sc, inc 1 st, 2 sc, inc 1 st, 5 sc, inc 1 st, 2 sc, inc 1 st, 4 sc. (22 sts)
Rnd 5: 2 sc, inc 1 st, 2 sc, inc 1 st, 7 sc, inc 1 st, 2 sc, inc 1 st, 5 sc. (26 sts)
Rnds 6–8: 1 sc in every st of the previous rnd. (26 sts)
Rnd 9: Working through the back loop of the st only: 2 sc, dec 1 st, 2 sc, dec 1 st, 7 sc, dec 1 st, 2 sc, dec 1 st, 5 sc. (22 sts)
Rnds 10 and 11: 1 sc in every st of the prev rnd. (22 sts)
Rnd 12: 1 sc, dec 1 st, 2 sc, dec 1 st, 5 sc, dec 1 st, 2 sc, dec 1 st, 4 sc. (18 sts)
Rnd 13: Dec 1 st, 2 sc, dec 1 st, 3 sc, dec 1 st, 2 sc, dec 1 st, 3 sc. (14 sts)
Rnd 14: Dec 1 st each twice, 3 sc, dec 1 st each twice, 3 sc. (10 sts)
Rnd 15: * Skip 1 st, 1 sl-st *, rep from * to * 4 times more. (5 sts)

Break the working yarn, and secure the end.

Don't stuff. Press Rnds 10–15 into the bulge of Rnds 1–9, which creates the lip of the ladle along Rnd 9.

FINISHING

Insert the wooden dowel at the 20th stitch of Rnd 9 into the lip of the bowl, up to the Magic Ring. Now sew the last rnd of the handle to Rnd 9 of the bowl.

Between the 3rd and 5th stitch of Rnd 10, sew a small stitch in Silver to shape the pour spout of the ladle.

KITCHEN KNIFE

MATERIALS

- crochet hook, 2.5 mm (US B-1 or C-2)
- tapestry needle
- Schachenmayr Catania (100% cotton): 1 skein (1.75 oz/50 g) each in Silver (Silber) and Black (Schwarz)
- polyester fiberfill
- flat wooden handle or dowel

INSTRUCTIONS

HANDLE

Work in rounds. Begin every rnd with ch1, and end every rnd with 1 sl-st into the 1st st of the rnd. Do not turn work.

Rnd 1: In Black, work 6 sc into an adjustable magic ring. (6 sts)
Rnd 2: Inc 1 st, 2 sc, inc 1 st, 2 sc. (8 sts)
Rnd 3: 1 sc in every st of the prev rnd. (8 sts)
Rnd 4: 3 sc, dec 1 st, 3 sc. (7 sts)
Rnds 5 and 6: 1 sc in every st of the prev rnd. (7 sts)
Rnd 7: 3 sc, inc 1 st, 3 sc. (8 sts)
Rnds 8–10: 1 sc in every st of the prev rnd. (8 sts)

Stuff with fiberfill up to Rnd 7.

Rnd 11: 4 sc, inc 1 st, 3 sc. (9 sts)
Rnds 12–14: 1 sc in every st of the prev rnd. (9 sts)

Rnd 15: 4 sc, dec 1 st, 3 sc. (8 sts)
Rnd 16: 3 sc, dec 1 st, 3 sc. (7 sts)
Rnd 17: 1 sc in every st of the prev rnd. (7 sts)

Break the working yarn, and secure the end.

BLADE

Work in rows. At the end of the row, work 1 sl-st into the 1st st of the row, chain 1, and turn work.

In Silver, crochet a chain of 14. Join the chain into the round with 1 sl-st into the 1st ch of the chain.

Row 1: 1 sc into every ch. (14 sts)
Rows 2–8: 1 sc in every st of the prev row. (14 sts)
Row 9: Dec 1 st, 10 sc, dec 1 st. (12 sts)
Rows 10–12: 1 sc in every st of the prev row. (12 sts)
Row 13: Dec 1 st, 8 sc, dec 1 st. (10 sts)
Row 14: 1 sc in every st of the prev row. (10 sts)
Row 15: Dec 1 st, 1 sc, dec 1 st each twice, 1 sc, dec 1 st. (6 sts)
Row 16: 1 sc in every st of the prev row. (6 sts)
Row 17: Dec 1 st, 2 sc, dec 1 st. (4 sts)
Row 18: * Skip 1 st, 1 sl-st *, rep from * to * once more. (2 sts)

Break the working yarn, and secure the end.

FINISHING

Using Silver, embroider 3 rivets each on both sides of the handle in French knots. Insert one end of the flat wooden handle or dowel into the crocheted handle, and the other end into the crocheted blade. Using Silver, going only through the back loop of the last black rnd, sew the handle in whipstitch to the blade.

ROLLING PIN

MATERIALS

- crochet hook, 2.5 mm (US B-1 or C-2)
- tapestry needle
- Schachenmayr Catania (100% cotton): 1 skein (1.75 oz/50 g) in Gold
- polyester fiberfill
- toilet paper core

Work in rounds. Begin every round with 1 chain, and end every round with 1 sl-st into the first stitch of the round. Do not turn work.

INSTRUCTIONS

HANDLE (MAKE 2)

Rnd 1: In Gold, work 6 sc into an adjustable magic ring. (6 sts)
Rnd 2: Inc 1 st each, 6 times in all. (12 sts)
Rnds 3–5: 1 sc in every st of the prev rnd. (12 sts)
Rnd 6: * 2 sc, dec 1 st *, rep from * to * 2 times more. (9 sts)

Stuff this half-sphere with polyester fiberfill.

Rnd 7: * 1 sc, dec 1 st *, rep from * to * 2 times more. (6 sts)
Rnds 8–10: 1 sc in every st of the prev rnd. (6 sts)
Rnd 11: * 1 sc, inc 1 st *, rep from * to * 2 times more. (9 sts)
Rnd 12: 1 sc in every st of the prev rnd. (9 sts)

Break the working yarn, and secure the end.

Now stuff the remainder of the handle with polyester fiberfill.

BODY

Work in rows. At the end of the row, work 1 sl-st into the 1st st of the row, chain 1, and turn work.

Row 1: Work 6 sc into an adjustable magic ring. (6 sts)
Row 2: Inc 1 st each, 6 times in all. (12 sts)
Row 3: * 1 sc, inc 1 st *, rep from * to * 5 times more. (18 sts)
Row 4: * 2 sc, inc 1 st *, rep from * to * 5 times more. (24 sts)
Row 5: 1 sc, inc 1 st, * 3 sc, inc 1 st *, rep from * to * 4 times more, 2 sc. (30 sts)

From here on, work in rounds. Do not turn work any more at the end of the rnd.

Rnd 6: 1 bpsc in every st of the prev rnd. (30 sts)
Rnds 7–30: 1 sc in every st of the prev rnd. (30 sts)

Now insert the toilet paper core into the body, and stuff it with polyester fiberfill. If the body is still shorter than the toilet paper core, work additional rounds. Should the body be longer than the core, unravel a corresponding number of rnds.

Rnd 31: Working through the back loop of the st only: * 3 sc, dec 1 st *, rep from * to * 5 times more. (24 sts)

From here on, work in rows again, and resume turning work at the end of every row.

Row 32: * 2 sc, dec 1 st *, rep from * to * 5 times more. (18 sts)
Row 33: * 1 sc, dec 1 st *, rep from * to * 5 times more. (12 sts)
Row 34: Dec 1 st each, 6 times in all. (6 sts)
Row 35: * Skip 1 st, 1 sl-st *, rep from * to * 2 times more. (3 sts)

Break the working yarn, and secure the end.

FINISHING

Sew the handles centered to the ends of the body in mattress stitch.

COOKING SPOON

MATERIALS

- crochet hook, 2.5 mm (US B-1 or C-2)
- tapestry needle
- Schachenmayr Catania (100% cotton): 1 skein (1.75 oz/50 g) in Tan (Taupe)
- wooden dowel

INSTRUCTIONS

Work in rounds. Begin every round with 1 chain, and end every round with 1 sl-st into the first stitch of the round. Do not turn work.

Rnd 1: In Tan, work 6 sc into an adjustable magic ring. (6 sts)
Rnds 2–21: 1 sc in every st of the prev rnd. (6 sts)
Rnd 22: Inc 1 st each, 6 times in all. (12 sts)

Insert the wooden dowel into the crocheted handle.

Rnd 23: * 1 sc, inc 1 st *, rep from * to * 5 times more. (18 sts)
Rnd 24: Inc 1 st, 8 sc, inc 1 st, 8 sc. (20 sts)
Rnd 25: 1 sc, inc 1 st, 9 sc, inc 1 st, 8 sc. (22 sts)
Rnds 26–29: 1 sc in every st of the prev rnd. (22 sts)
Rnd 30: 1 sc, dec 1 st, 9 sc, dec 1 st, 8 sc. (20 sts)
Rnd 31: Dec 1 st, 8 sc, dec 1 st, 8 sc. (18 sts)
Rnd 32: * 1 sc, dec 1 st *, rep from * to * 5 times more. (12 sts)
Rnd 33: Dec 1 st each, 6 times in all. (6 sts)
Rnd 34: * Skip 1 st, 1 sl-st *, rep from * to * 2 times more. (3 sts)

Break the working yarn, and secure the end.

PEPPER MILL

MATERIALS

- crochet hook, 2.5 mm (US B-1 or C-2)
- tapestry needle
- Wolle Rödel Mille Fili (100% cotton): 1 skein (1.75 oz/50 g) in Red (Rot)
- polyester fiberfill
- toilet paper core

INSTRUCTIONS

First, cut off a 1.6 in (4 cm) long piece from the toilet paper core.

Crochet a circle from Basic pattern (Rnds 1–5, see page 23).

Rnds 6–8: 1 sc in every st of the prev rnd. (30 sts)

Rnd 9: * 3 sc, dec 1 st *, rep from * to * 5 times more. (24 sts)

Rnd 10: * 2 sc, dec 1 st *, rep from * to * 5 times more. (18 sts)

Rnd 11: 1 bpsc in every st of the prev rnd. (18 sts)

Rnd 12: 1 hdc in every st of the prev rnd. (18 sts)

Rnd 13: 1 bpsc in every st of the prev rnd. (18 sts)

Rnd 14: * 2 sc, inc 1 st *, rep from * to * 5 times more. (24 sts)

Rnd 15: 1 sc, inc 1 st, * 3 sc, inc 1 st *, rep from * to * 4 times more, 2 sc. (30 sts)

Rnd 16: 1 bpsc in every st of the prev rnd. (30 sts)

Rnd 17: * 3 sc, dec 1 st *, rep from * to * 5 times more. (24 sts)

Rnd 18: * 2 sc, dec 1 st *, rep from * to * 5 times more. (18 sts)

Rnd 19: 1 sc in every st of the prev rnd. (18 sts)

Rnd 20: * 4 sc, dec 1 st *, rep from * to * 2 times more. (15 sts)

Rnds 21 and 22: 1 sc in every st of the prev rnd. (15 sts)

Rnd 23: * 4 sc, inc 1 st *, rep from * to * 2 times more. (18 sts)

Rnd 24: * 2 sc, inc 1 st *, rep from * to * 5 times more. (24 sts)

Rnd 25: 1 sc in every st of the prev rnd. (24 sts)

Rnd 26: 1 bpsc in every st of the prev rnd. (24 sts)

Rnd 27: 1 hdc in every st of the prev rnd. (24 sts)

Rnd 28: 1 bpsc in every st of the prev rnd. (24 sts)

Rnd 29: 1 sc in every st of the prev rnd. (24 sts)

Rnd 30: 1 bpsc in every st of the prev rnd. (24 sts)

Rnd 31: * 3 sc, inc 1 st *, rep from * to * 5 times more. (30 sts)

Stuff the pepper mill with polyester fiberfill.

Rnd 32: Working through the back loop of the st only: 1 sc in every st of the prev rnd. (30 sts)

Rnds 33–40: 1 sc in every st of the prev rnd. (30 sts)

Insert the 1.6 in (4 cm) long piece from the toilet paper core up to Rnd 33.

Stuff the toilet paper core with polyester fiberfill.

Rnd 41: Working through the back loop of the st only: * 3 sc, dec 1 st *, rep from * to * 5 times more. (24 sts)

Rnd 42: * 2 sc, dec 1 st *, rep from * to * 5 times more. (18 sts)

Rnd 43: * 1 sc, dec 1 st *, rep from * to * 5 times more. (12 sts)

Rnd 44: Dec 1 st each, 6 times in all. (6 sts)

Rnd 45: * Skip 1 st, 1 sl-st *, rep from * to * 2 times more. (3 sts)

Break the working yarn, and secure the end.

MEASURING CUPS IN THREE SIZES

MATERIALS

- crochet hook, 2.5 mm (US B-1 or C-2)
- tapestry needle
- Schachenmayr Catania (100% cotton): 1 skein (1.75 oz/50 g) each in Tangerine (Mandarine), Sun (Sonne), and Apple (Apfel)

INSTRUCTIONS

LARGE MEASURING CUP

In Tangerine, crochet a circle from Basic pattern (Rnds 1–7, see page 23).

Rnd 8: 1 bpsc in every st of the prev rnd. (42 sts)
Rnds 9–15: 1 sc in every st of the prev rnd. (42 sts)
Rnd 16: 1 bpsc in every st of the prev rnd. (42 sts)

Work the handle in rows. At the end of every row, chain 1, and turn work.

Row 17: 6 sc. (6 sts) The remaining sts stay unworked.
Rows 18–22: 1 sc in every st of the prev row. (6 sts)
Row 23: 2 sc, ch2, skip 2 sts, 2 sc. (6 sts)
Row 24: 2 sc, 2 sc in ch-sp, 2 sc. (6 sts)
Row 25: 1 sc in every st of the prev row. (6 sts)
Row 26: Working through the back loop of the st only: 1 sc in every st of the prev row. (6 sts)
Row 27: 1 sc in every st of the prev row. (6 sts)
Row 28: 2 sc, ch2, skip 2 sts, 2 sc. (6 sts)

Row 29: 2 sc, 2 sc in ch-sp, 2 sc. (6 sts)
Rows 30–34: 1 sc in every st of the prev row. (6 sts)

Break the working yarn, and secure the end.

SMALL (AND MEDIUM) MEASURING CUP

Numbers and colors for the medium size measuring cup are listed in parentheses after the numbers for the smaller cup.

In Apple (Sun), work Rnds 1–5 (1–6) from instructions for large measuring cup. [30 sts (36 sts)]

Rnd 6 (7): 1 bpsc in every st of the prev rnd. [30 sts (36 sts)]
Rnds 7–11 (8–13): 1 sc in every st of the prev rnd. [30 sts (36 sts)]

Rnd 12 (14): 1 bpsc in every st of the prev rnd. [30 sts (36 sts)]

For the handle, now continue in rows. At the end of every row, chain 1, and turn work.

Row 13 (15): 4 sc. (4 sts) The remaining sts stay unworked.
Rows 14–18 (16–20): 1 sc in every st of the prev row. (4 sts)
Row 19 (21): 1 sc, ch2, skip 2 sts, 1 sc. (4 sts)
Row 20 (22): 1 sc, 2 sc in ch-sp, 1 sc. (4 sts)
Row 21 (23): 1 sc in every st of the prev row. (4 sts)
Row 22 (24): Working through the back loop of the st only: 1 sc in every st of the prev row. (4 sts)
Row 23 (25): 1 sc in every st of the prev row. (4 sts)
Row 24 (26): 1 sc, ch2, skip 2 sts, 1 sc. (4 sts)

Row 25 (27): 1 sc, 2 sc in ch-sp, 1 sc. (4 sts)
Rows 26–30 (28–32): 1 sc in every st of the prev row. (4 sts)

Break the working yarn, and secure the end.

FINISHING

Numbers for medium and small measuring cup are listed in parentheses after numbers for large cup.

Fold the tab of crocheted rows down along Row 26 (24, 22), and, using the long tail, sew Row 34 (32, 30) to Rnd 16 (14, 12) of the cup in whipstitch, and then sew the side edges of the handle together in backstitch.

KITCHEN SCALES

MATERIALS

- crochet hook, 2.5 mm (US B-1 or C-2)
- tapestry needle
- Schachenmayr Catania (100% cotton): 1 skein (1.75 oz/50 g) each in Reseda Green (Reseda Grün), Soft Apricot, and Silver (Silber), and approx. 0.5 oz (15 g) in Black (Schwarz)
- polyester fiberfill
- cardboard
- 1 toilet paper core

INSTRUCTIONS

Work in rounds, beginning every round with ch1, and ending every round with 1 sl-st into the first stitch of the rnd. Do not turn work.

DIAL

In Soft Apricot, crochet a circle from Basic pattern (Rnds 1–9, see page 23).

Rnd 10: 1 bpsc in every st of the prev rnd. (54 sts)

Change color to Reseda Green.

Rnd 11: * 8 sc, inc 1 st *, rep from * to * 5 times more. (60 sts)
Rnd 12: 1 bpsc in every st of the prev rnd. (60 sts)
Rnds 13–22: 1 sc in every st of the prev rnd. (60 sts)
Rnd 23: Working through the back loop of the st only: * 8 sc, dec 1 st *, rep from * to * 5 times more. (54 sts)
Rnd 24: 3 sc, dec 1 st, * 7 sc, dec 1 st *, rep from * to * 4 times more, 4 sc. (48 sts)

Rnd 25: * 6 sc, dec 1 st *, rep from * to * 5 times more. (42 sts)
Rnd 26: 2 sc, dec 1 st, * 5 sc, dec 1 st *, rep from * to * 4 times more, 3 sc. (36 sts)

Stuff the dial with polyester fiberfill.

Rnd 27: * 4 sc, dec 1 st *, rep from * to * 5 times more. (30 sts)
Rnd 28: * 3 sc, dec 1 st *, rep from * to * 5 times more. (24 sts)
Rnd 29: * 2 sc, dec 1 st *, rep from * to * 5 times more. (18 sts)
Rnd 30: * 1 sc, dec 1 st *, rep from * to * 5 times more. (12 sts)
Rnd 31: Dec 1 st each, 6 times in all. (6 sts)
Rnd 32: * Skip 1 st, 1 sl-st *, rep from * to * 2 times more. (3 sts)

Break the working yarn, and secure the end.

BACK OF BASE

First, work in rows. At the end of every row, chain 1, and turn work.

Row 1: In Reseda Green, crochet a chain of 37, 1 sc into the 2nd chain from the hook, 1 sc in every following ch. (36 sts)
Rows 2–4: 1 sc in every st of the prev row. (36 sts)
Row 5: Dec 1 st, 32 sc, dec 1 st. (34 sts)
Row 6: Dec 1 st, 30 sc, dec 1 st. (32 sts)
Row 7: Dec 1 st, 28 sc, dec 1 st. (30 sts)
Row 8: Dec 1 st, 7 sc, crochet 3 sts together. Leave the remaining sts unworked for now. (9 sts)
Row 9: Dec 1 st, 5 sc, dec 1 st. (7 sts)
Row 10: Dec 1 st, 3 sc, dec 1 st. (5 sts)
Row 11: Dec 1 st, 1 sc, dec 1 st. (3 sts)
Row 12: 1 sc, dec 1 st. (2 sts)
Row 13: 1 sc in every st of the prev row. (2 sts)

Break the working yarn, and secure the end.

Now continue in Row 8:

Row 8: Skip 6 sts, and then join new working yarn in Reseda Green to the next stitch. Crochet 3 sts together, 7 sc, dec 1 st. (9 sts)
Row 9: Dec 1 st, 5 sc, dec 1 st. (7 sts)
Row 10: Dec 1 st, 3 sc, dec 1 st. (5 sts)
Row 11: Dec 1 st, 1 sc, dec 1 st. (3 sts)
Row 12: Dec 1 st, 1 sc. (2 sts)
Row 13: 1 sc in every st of the prev row. (2 sts)

Crochet 1 rnd of sc edging around the piece, working 3 sc each in the two bottom corner sts (first and last st of Row 1). At the end, join into the round with 1 sl-st into the 1st st of the rnd.

Break the working yarn, and secure the end.

For the front of the base, repeat instructions for the back of the base, but do not break the working yarn; continue in the round for the middle part. Begin every rnd with ch1, and end every rnd with 1 sl-st into the 1st st of the rnd. Do not turn work.

MIDDLE PART

Rnd 1: 1 bpsc in every st of the prev rnd.
Rnds 2–17: 1 sc in every st of the prev rnd.

Break the working yarn, and secure the end.

Now sew the back of the base in mattress stitch to the remaining opening of the middle part, inserting stuffing as you go.

WEIGHING PAN

Rnd 1: In Silver, crochet a chain of 52. Join the crocheted chain into the round with 1 sl-st into the first chain. Work 1 sc into every ch. (52 sts)
Rnds 2–29: 1 sc in every st of the prev rnd. (52 sts)

Break the working yarn, and secure the end.

Turn the piece inside out, and pat it flat. Then cut a piece of cardboard to the size of the weighing pan, and slide it into the crocheted tube. In Silver, close both openings by sewing together the pairs of sts from both layers in whipstitch.

CONNECTOR

Rnd 1: In Silver, crochet a chain of 30, and join the crocheted chain into the round with 1 sl-st into the first chain. Chain 1, 1 sc into every chain.
Rnds 2–6: 1 sc in every st of the prev rnd. (30 sts)

Cut a piece of toilet paper core to the length of the connector, and insert the core. Additionally, stuff the piece with polyester fiberfill.

FINISHING

Sew the dial to the middle of the base. Sew the connector centered to the edge of the dial, and the weighing pan on top of the connector. In Black, embroider hands and scales onto the front face of the dial with simple satin stitch (individual running sts).

HAND-HELD BLENDER

MATERIALS

- crochet hook, 2.5 mm (US B-1 or C-2)
- tapestry needle
- Schachenmayr Catania (100% cotton): 1 skein (1.75 oz/50 g) each in Pastel Blue (Hellblau) and Silver (Silber), and 0.5 oz (15 g) each in Cyclam and Peacock (Pfau)
- polyester fiberfill
- wooden dowel

INSTRUCTIONS

Work in rounds. Begin every rnd with ch1, and end every rnd with 1 sl-st into the 1st st of the rnd. Do not turn work.

Rnd 1: In Pastel Blue, work 6 sc into an adjustable magic ring. (6 sts)
Rnd 2: 3 sc into the same st, 2 sc, 3 sc into the same st, 2 sc. (10 sts)

Rnd 3: Inc 1 st, 1 sc, inc 1 st, 2 sc, inc 1 st, 1 sc, inc 1 st, 2 sc. (14 sts)
Rnd 4: Inc 1 st each twice, 1 sc, inc 1 st each twice, 2 sc, inc 1 st each twice, 1 sc, inc 1 st each twice, 2 sc. (22 sts)
Rnd 5: 1 sc, inc 1 st each twice, 3 sc, inc 1 st each twice, 4 sc, inc 1 st each twice, 3 sc, inc 1 st each twice, 3 sc. (30 sts)
Rnd 6: 2 sc, inc 1 st each twice, 5 sc, inc 1 st each twice, 6 sc, inc 1 st each twice, 5 sc, inc 1 st each twice, 4 sc. (38 sts)
Rnd 7: Working through the back loop of the st only: 2 sc, dec 1 st each twice, 5 sc, dec 1 st each twice, 23 sc. (34 sts)

Rnd 8: 1 sc, dec 1 st each twice, 3 sc, dec 1 st each twice, 22 sc. (30 sts)
Rnd 9: Dec 1 st each twice, 1 sc, dec 1 st each twice, 21 sc. (26 sts)
Rnd 10: Dec 1 st, 1 sc, dec 1 st, 21 sc. (24 sts)
Rnds 11–15: 24 sc. (24 sts)
Rnd 16: * 3 sc, inc 1 st *, rep from * to * 5 times more. (30 sts)
Rnds 17–23: 1 sc each in every st of the prev rnd. (30 sts)
Rnd 24: * 3 sc, dec 1 st *, rep from * to * 5 times more. (24 sts)
Rnds 25–28: 1 sc each in every st of the prev rnd. (24 sts)
Rnd 29: * 6 sc, dec 1 st *, rep from * to * 2 times more. (21 sts)

Rnds 30–32: 1 sc each in every st of the prev rnd. (21 sts)

Rnd 33: * 6 sc, inc 1 st *, rep from * to * 2 times more. (24 sts)

Rnd 34: * 3 sc, inc 1 st *, rep from * to * 5 times more. (30 sts)

Rnd 35: 1 sc each in every st of the prev rnd. (30 sts)

Insert the wooden dowel into the handle up to the upper end, and then stuff the handheld blender with polyester fiberfill.

Rnd 36: Working through the back loop of the st only: * 3 sc, dec 1 st *, rep from * to * 5 times more. (24 sts)

Rnd 37: * 2 sc, dec 1 st *, rep from * to * 5 times more. (18 sts)

Rnd 38: * 1 sc, dec 1 st *, rep from * to * 5 times more. (12 sts)

Change color to Silver.

Rnd 39: Working through the back loop of the st only: * 1 sc, dec 1 st *, rep from * to * 3 times more. (8 sts)

Rnds 40–71: 1 sc each in every st of the prev rnd. (8 sts)

Should your work have turned out shorter than the wooden dowel, work a few additional rounds. If the crocheted piece is too long, work fewer rounds than stated, so that the top end of the dowel matches the height of the last crochet row.

Rnd 72: Inc 1 st each, 8 times in all. (16 sts)

Rnd 73: * 1 sc, inc 1 st *, rep from * to * 7 times more. (24 sts)

Rnd 74: 1 sc in every st of the prev rnd. (24 sts)

Rnd 75: * 3 sc, inc 1 st *, rep from * to * 5 times more. (30 sts)

Rnd 76: 1 bpsc in every st of the prev rnd. (30 sts)

Rnds 77–79: 1 sc in every st of the prev rnd. (30 sts)

Rnd 80: 1 bpsc in every st of the prev rnd. (30 sts)

Rnd 81: * 3 sc, dec 1 st *, rep from * to * 5 times more. (24 sts)

Rnds 82 and 83: 1 sc in every st of the prev rnd. (24 sts)

Rnd 84: * 2 sc, dec 1 st *, rep from * to * 5 times more. (18 sts)

Rnd 85: * 1 sc, dec 1 st *, rep from * to * 5 times more. (12 sts)

Rnd 86: Dec 1 st each, 6 times in all. (6 sts)

Rnd 87: * Skip 1 st, 1 sl-st *, rep from * to * 2 times more. (3 sts)

Break the working yarn, and secure the end.

Don't stuff the last round, but instead press the piece from Rnd 81 on into the previous rounds so that Rnd 80 creates the rim of the blender attachment.

BUTTON

Work in rounds. Begin every round with 1 chain, and end every round with 1 sl-st into the first stitch of the round. Do not turn work.

Rnd 1: In Cyclam, crochet a chain of 8. 1 sc into the 2nd chain from the hook, 1 sc each into the next 5 chains, 5 sc into the last chain. Now continue in the round, working in the ch-sp, around the chain, do not turn work. 5 sc, 4 sc into the same stitch, into which the 1st sc of the rnd had been worked earlier. (20 sts)

Rnd 2: 7 sc, inc 1 st, 1 sc, inc 1 st, 7 sc, inc 1 st, 1 sc, inc 1 st. (24 sts)

Break the working yarn, and secure the end.

In Peacock, work 6 sc into an adjustable magic ring.

Break the working yarn, and secure the end.

Sew the Cyclam-colored part of the button to the front between Rnds 15 and 25 of the handheld blender. Then sew the Peacock-colored part onto the Cyclam-colored one.

HAND MIXER

MATERIALS

- crochet hook, 2.5 mm (US B-1 or C-2)
- tapestry needle
- Schachenmayr Catania (100% cotton): 1 skein (1.75 oz/50 g) each in Anise (Anis) and Silver (Silber), and 0.5 oz (15 g) each in Violet (Violett) and Peacock (Pfau)
- polyester fiberfill
- 2 cake pop sticks

BOTTOM OF BODY

Work in rows. At the end of every row, chain 1, and turn work.

Row 1: In Anise, crochet a chain of 17, 1 sc into the 2nd chain from the hook, 1 sc in every following ch. (16 sts)

Rows 2–13: 1 sc in every st of the prev row. (16 sts)

Row 14: Dec 1 st, 12 sc, dec 1 st. (14 sts)

Row 15: 1 sc in every st of the prev row. (14 sts)

Row 16: Dec 1 st, 10 sc, dec 1 st. (12 sts)

Row 17: 1 sc in every st of the prev row. (12 sts)

Row 18: Dec 1 st, 8 sc, dec 1 st. (10 sts)

Rows 19–27: 1 sc in every st of the prev row. (10 sts)

Row 28: Dec 1 st, 6 sc, dec 1 st. (8 sts)

Row 29: Dec 1 st, 4 sc, dec 1 st. (6 sts)

Row 30: Dec 1 st, 2 sc, dec 1 st. (4 sts) Chain 1, but do not turn work.

BODY

From here on, continue in rounds. Begin every round with 1 chain, and end every round with 1 sl-st into the first stitch of the round. Do not turn work.

Rnd 1: Work crocheted bpsc edging around the piece as follows:

Work 1 bpsc in every end of the row (30 sts), 16 bpsc into Row 1 of the bottom of the body, 1 bpsc in every end of the row (30 sts), 2 sc into Row 30 of the bottom of the body. (78 sts)

Rnds 2–4: 1 sc in every st of the prev row. (78 sts)

Rnd 5: 29 sc, dec 1 st, 12 sc, dec 1 st, 33 sc. (76 sts)

Rnd 6: 28 sc, dec 1 st each twice, 8 sc, dec 1 st each twice, 32 sc. (72 sts)

Rnd 7: 27 sc, dec 1 st each twice, 6 sc, dec 1 st each twice, 31 sc. (68 sts)

Rnd 8: Dec 1 st, 24 sc, dec 1 st each twice, 4 sc, dec 1 st each twice, 24 sc, dec 1 st, 4 sc. (62 sts)

Break the working yarn, and secure the end.

MIDDLE PART

Skip the first 6 sts of Rnd 8, and join new working yarn in Anise to the 7th stitch of Rnd 8. Continue in rows. At the end of every row, chain 1, and turn work.

Row 1: 13 sc, ch1, turn work. The remaining sts stay unworked for now. (13 sts)

Row 2: Dec 1 st, 9 sc, dec 1 st. (11 sts)

Row 3: Dec 1 st, 7 sc, dec 1 st. (9 sts)

Row 4: Dec 1 st, 5 sc, dec 1 st. (7 sts)

Row 5: 1 sc in every st of the prev row. (7 sts)

Row 6: Inc 1 st, 5 sc, inc 1 st. (9 sts)

Rnds 39–48: 1 sc in every st of the prev rnd. (24 sts)

Break the working yarn, and secure the end. Stuff the handle with polyester fiberfill, taking care not to overstuff it to prevent the sts from unsightly stretching. At the level of Rnds 38–40 of the handle, use only a very small amount of stuffing so it will bend more easily in this spot.

Sew Row 48 of the handle to the remaining opening of the body in whipstitch.

DOUGH HOOK ATTACHMENTS

Work in spiral rounds. Omit the chain at the beginning of the round, and do not join the round with a sl-st into the 1st st of the rnd. Do not turn work.

Rnd 1: In Silver, work 6 sc into an adjustable magic ring. (6 sts)

Continue in spiral rounds, until you have created a tube of about 6.1 in (15.5 cm) length.

Break the working yarn, and secure the end.

Make a second tube of the same length the same way, and 2 more of 5.9 in (15 cm) length. Bring the respective first and last round of a short tube together, and sew these ends together with the first and last round of a long tube with a few stitches. The longer tube should be positioned at a 90-degree angle around the outside of the short tube. Sew the other two tubes together the same way.

DOUGH HOOK RODS (MAKE 2)

Work in rounds. Begin every round with 1 chain, and end every round with 1 sl-st into the first stitch of the round. Do not turn work.

Row 7: Inc 1 st, 7 sc, inc 1 st. (11 sts)
Row 8: Inc 1 st, 9 sc, inc 1 st. (13 sts)
Row 9: 1 sc in every st of the prev row. (13 sts)

Break the working yarn, and secure the end.

Using the long tail, sew the 13 sts of the last row to the 40th–52nd st of Rnd 8 of the body. Stuff the body with polyester fiberfill.

HANDLE

Join new working yarn in Anise to the 20th st of Rnd 8 of the body, and continue along the edge of the remaining opening in rounds. Begin every round with 1 chain, and end every round with 1 sl-st into the first stitch of the round. Do not turn work.

Rnd 1: 20 sc, 1 sc into the 40th st of Rnd 8 of the body, 9 sc into the end-of-the-row sts of the middle part, 1 sc into the 19th st of Rnd 8 of the body. (31 sts)
Rnd 2: 20 sc, dec 1 st, 7 sc, dec 1 st. (29 sts)
Rnds 3–5: 1 sc in every st of the prev rnd. (29 sts)
Rnd 6: 9 sc, dec 1 st each twice, 11 sc, inc 1 st each twice, 3 sc. (29 sts)
Rnd 7: 7 sc, dec 1 st, 2 sc, dec 1 st, 16 sc. (27 sts)
Rnds 8 and 9: 1 sc in every st of the prev rnd. (27 sts)
Rnd 10: 9 sc, dec 1 st, 16 sc. (26 sts)

Rnd 11: 8 sc, dec 1 st, 11 sc, inc 1 st, 4 sc. (26 sts)
Rnd 12: 9 sc, dec 1 st, 10 sc, inc 1 st, 4 sc. (26 sts)
Rnds 13–26: 1 sc in every st of the prev rnd. (26 sts)
Rnd 27: 10 sc, dec 1 st, 10 sc, inc 1 st, 3 sc. (26 sts)
Rnd 28: 1 sc in every st of the prev rnd. (26 sts)
Rnd 29: 10 sc, dec 1 st, 11 sc, inc 1 st, 2 sc. (26 sts)
Rnds 30–35: 1 sc in every st of the prev rnd. (26 sts)
Rnd 36: 11 sc, sc4tog, 9 sc, inc 1 st, 1 sc. (24 sts)
Rnd 37: 1 sc in every st of the prev rnd. (24 sts)
Rnd 38: 11 sc, dec 1 st, 9 sc, inc 1 st, 1 sc. (24 sts)

Rnd 1: In Silver, crochet a chain of 8, join into the round with 1 sl-st in into the first chain. Work 1 sc into every ch. (8 sts)
Rnds 2–11: 1 sc in every st of the prev rnd. (8 sts)

Break the working yarn, and secure the end.

Sew one of the openings of the hook rod to the seam of the dough hook attachment in whipstitch. Insert one of the cake pop sticks, and stuff with a small amount of additional filling. Sew the other dough hook rod the same way to the other dough hook attachment.

Sew the remaining openings of the two dough hook rods on parallel to one another in whipstitch at the level of Rnd 4 of the bottom of the body. In the spot where to be sewn on, push the part of the cake pop stick that juts out of the crocheted hook rod through the respective crochet stitch of the bottom of the body.

BLUE BUTTON

Rnd 1: In Peacock, crochet a chain of 7, work 1 sc into the 2nd chain from the hook, 4 sc, 3 sc into the last chain. Do not turn work, but, now working in the ch-sp, around the chain, work: 5 sc, 2 sc into the chain, into which the first stitch had been worked earlier. Join into the round with 1 sl-st into the first stitch. (15 sts)

Rnd 2: 1 sc in every st of the prev rnd. (15 sts)

Break the working yarn, and secure the end.

Lightly stuff the button with polyester fiberfill, and sew it on in mattress stitch at the level of Rnds 24/25 of the handle.

KNOB

Work in rounds. Begin every round with 1 chain, and end every round with 1 sl-st into the first stitch of the round. Do not turn work.

Rnd 1: In Violet, work 6 sc into an adjustable magic ring. (6 sts)
Rnd 2: Working through the back loop of the st only: 1 sc in every st of the prev rnd. (6 sts)

Break the working yarn, and secure the end.

Lightly stuff the knob with polyester fiberfill, and sew it to the side of the mixer housing in mattress stitch at the level of Rnds 5–7 of the body.

MUFFIN PAN

MATERIALS

- crochet hook, 3 mm (US C-2 or D-3)
- tapestry needle
- Schachenmayr Catania (100% cotton): 2 skeins (3.5 oz/100 g) in Capri, and approx. 0.5 oz (15 g) in Raspberry (Himbeer)

SINGLE MOLD (MAKE 6)

In Capri, crochet a circle from Basic pattern (Rnds 1–6, see page 23).

Rnd 7: 1 bpsc in every st of the prev rnd. (36 sts)
Rnds 8–12: 1 sc in every st of the prev rnd. (36 sts) Ch1, turn.
Rnd 13: 1 bpsc in every st of the prev rnd. (36 sts) Do not turn any more.
Rnd 14: 2 sc, 1 hdc, 1 dc, 3 dc into the same st, 1 dc, 1 hdc, 2 sc *, rep from * to * 3 times more. (44 sts)
Rnd 15: Work 1 sc in every st of the prev rnd, except for the middle st of the group of 3 dc's of the previous rnd (corner st): There, work 6 sc into the same st. (64 sts)

Break the working yarn, and secure the end.

FINISHING

Arrange the molds in two strips of 3 to join them together, attaching the 2nd and 3rd mold of the same strip while crocheting the last rnd by crocheting it onto one side of the previous mold. To do this, first work the sc only into the st of the not-yet-finished mold, and then draw the working yarn through the sts of both molds to be joined. Finally, sew both strips of 3 together along the long sides in whipstitch.

Now join new working yarn in Raspberry to any stitch at the edge of the muffin pan, and crochet 1 rnd of sc edging around the whole piece. In every one of the 4 corners, additionally ch3 between the 3rd and 4th st of the group of 6 sts (sc) of the previous rnd. Finish by working 1 sl-st into the 1st st of the rnd.

Break the working yarn, and secure the end.

EGG CUP

MATERIALS

- crochet hook, 2.5 mm (US B-1 or C-2)
- tapestry needle
- Schachenmayr Catania (100% cotton): 1 skein (1.75 oz/50 g) each in Apple (Apfel), Orchid (Orchidee), and Sun (Sonne)
- polyester fiberfill
- cardboard
- pink craft felt
- glue
- compass

INSTRUCTIONS

In Apple, crochet a circle from Basic pattern (Rnds 1–5, see page 23).

Now adjust the width of the compass arms to the radius of the circle crocheted so far by inserting the needle of the compass into the center of the magic ring.

Using this radius, now draw a circle on the cardboard, and cut it out.

Rnd 6: Working through the back loop of the st only: * 3 sc, dec 1 st *, rep from * to * 5 times more. (24 sts)

Now place the cardboard circle into the egg cup base, and continue:

Rnd 7: * 2 sc, dec 1 st *, rep from * to * 5 times more. (18 sts)
Rnd 8: 1 sc in every st of the prev rnd. (18 sts)
Rnd 9: * 1 sc, dec 1 st *, rep from * to * 5 times more. (12 sts)
Rnds 10–12: 1 sc in every st of the prev rnd. (12 sts)

Change color to Orchid.

Rnds 13–15: 1 sc in every st of the prev rnd. (12 sts)

Stuff the egg cup base with polyester fiberfill up to this level. The remainder will stay unstuffed.

Rnd 16: * 1 sc, inc 1 st *, rep from * to * 5 times more. (18 sts)
Rnd 17: * 2 sc, inc 1 st *, rep from * to * 5 times more. (24 sts)
Rnd 18: 1 sc in every st of the prev rnd. (24 sts)
Rnd 19: 1 sc, inc 1 st, * 3 sc, inc 1 st *, rep from * to * 4 times more, 2 sc. (30 sts)
Rnd 20: * 4 sc, inc 1 st *, rep from * to * 5 times more. (36 sts)

Rnds 21–23: 1 sc in every st of the prev rnd. (36 sts)
Rnd 24: Working through the back loop of the st only: * 4 sc, dec 1 st *, rep from * to * 5 times more. (30 sts)

Change color to Sun.

Rnds 25–27: 1 sc in every st of the prev rnd. (30 sts)
Rnd 28: * 3 sc, dec 1 st *, rep from * to * 5 times more. (24 sts)
Rnd 29: 1 sc in every st of the prev rnd. (24 sts)
Rnd 30: * 2 sc, dec 1 st *, rep from * to * 5 times more. (18 sts)
Rnd 31: * 1 sc, dec 1 st *, rep from * to * 5 times more. (12 sts)

Rnd 32: Dec 1 st each, 6 times in all. (6 sts)
Rnd 33: * Skip 1 st, 1 sl-st *, rep from * to * 2 times more. (3 sts)

Break the working yarn, and secure the end.

Press the Sun-colored rnd inward into the Orchid-colored part of the piece, so that Rnd 24 forms the rim of the egg cup.

Using the template from page 128, cut out a tulip shape from craft felt, and glue it onto the Orchid-colored part of the egg cup.

Note: Instructions for individual eggs to place in the Egg Cup begin on page 54 (Sunny-Side-Up Egg).

SPOON

MATERIALS

- crochet hook, 2.5 mm (US B-1 or C-2)
- tapestry needle
- Schachenmayr Catania (100% cotton): 1 skein (1.75 oz/50 g) each in Orchid (Orchidee) and Silver (Silber)
- polyester fiberfill

INSTRUCTIONS

For the spoon handle, work Rnds 1–16 from the instructions for the Bread Knife at right, but begin with Orchid instead of Apple. Stuff the handle up to Rnd 15 lightly with polyester fiberfill. Now continue:

Rnd 17: * 1 sc, dec 1 st *, rep from * to * 2 times more. (6 sts)
Rnd 18: 1 sc in every st of the prev rnd. (6 sts)
Rnd 19: Inc 1 st each, 6 times in all. (12 sts)
Rnd 20: * 1 sc, inc 1 st *, rep from * to * 5 times more. (18 sts)
Rnd 21: 3 sc, inc 1 st, 8 sc, inc 1 st, 5 sc. (20 sts)
Rnd 22: 4 sc, inc 1 st, 3 sc, dec 1 st, 4 sc, inc 1 st, 3 sc, dec 1 st. (20 sts)
Rnds 23 and 24: 1 sc in every st of the prev rnd. (20 sts)
Rnd 25: Dec 1 st, 6 sc, dec 1 st, 10 sc. (18 sts)
Rnd 26: 1 sc in every st of the prev rnd. (18 sts)
Rnd 27: * 1 sc, dec 1 st *, rep from * to * 5 times more. (12 sts)
Rnd 28: Dec 1 st each, 6 times in all. (6 sts)

Rnd 29: * Skip 1 st, 1 sl-st *, rep from * to * 2 times more. (3 sts)

Break the working yarn, and secure the end.

PLATE

MATERIALS

- crochet hook, 2.5 mm (US B-1 or C-2)
- tapestry needle
- Schachenmayr Catania (100% cotton): 1 skein (1.75 oz/50 g) each in Soft Apricot and Cyclam

INSTRUCTIONS

In Soft Apricot, crochet a circle from Basic pattern (Rnds 1–11, see page 23).

Break the working yarn, and secure the end.

Work a second circle, repeating Rnds 1–11. Then place both circles together, wrong sides facing each other, and crochet them together in Cyclam in rounds as follows:

Rnd 1: In the circle nearer to you, work through the back loop of the stitch only, in the circle underneath it, work through both loops of the stitch: 1 sc in every st of the prev rnd. (66 sts)
Rnd 2: 1 hdc in every st of the prev rnd. (66 sts) Turn work.
Rnd 3: 1 bpsc in every st of the prev rnd. (66 sts)

Break the working yarn, and secure the end.

Attach new working yarn in Cyclam between Rnds 6 and 7 of the bottom part of the plate (circle underneath). Hold the piece so that you look into the magic ring from above, and work 1 rnd of hdc. Join into the round with 1 sl-st into the 1st st of the rnd.

Break the working yarn, and secure the end.

BREAD KNIFE

MATERIALS

- crochet hook, 2.5 mm (US B-1 or C-2)
- tapestry needle
- Schachenmayr Catania (100% cotton): 1 skein (1.75 oz/50 g) each in Apple (Apfel) and Silver (Silber)
- popsicle stick (ice cream stick)

INSTRUCTIONS

Work in rounds. Begin every rnd with ch1, and end every rnd with 1 sl-st into the 1st st of the rnd. Do not turn work.

Rnd 1: In Apple, work 6 sc into an adjustable magic ring. (6 sts)
Rnd 2: * 1 sc, inc 1 st *, rep from * to * 2 times more. (9 sts)
Rnds 3–15: 1 sc in every st of the prev rnd. (9 sts)

Change color to Silver.

Rnd 16: Working through the back loop of the st only: 1 sc in every st of the prev rnd. (9 sts)

Rnd 17: 6 sc, inc 1 st each twice, 1 sc. (11 sts)
Rnds 18 and 19: 1 sc in every st of the prev rnd. (11 sts)
Rnd 20: 7 sc, inc 1 st each twice, 2 sc. (13 sts)
Rnds 21–24: 1 sc in every st of the prev rnd. (13 sts)
Rnd 25: 8 sc, dec 1 st each twice, 1 sc. (11 sts)
Rnds 26 and 27: 1 sc in every st of the prev rnd. (11 sts)
Rnd 28: 7 sc, dec 1 st each twice. (9 sts)

Insert the wooden stick into the crocheted knife.

Rnd 29: 1 sc in every st of the prev rnd. (9 sts)
Rnd 30: * 1 sc, dec 1 st *, rep from * to * 2 times more. (6 sts)
Rnd 31: * Skip 1 st, 1 sl-st *, rep from * to * 2 times more. (3 sts)

Break the working yarn, and secure the end.

FORK

MATERIALS

- crochet hook, 2.5 mm (US B-1 or C-2)
- tapestry needle
- Schachenmayr Catania (100% cotton): 1 skein (1.75 oz/50 g) each in Capri and Silver (Silber)
- polyester fiberfill

INSTRUCTIONS

For the handle, work Rnds 1–15 from the instructions for the Bread Knife (see page 47). Begin with Capri instead of Apple. Stuff the handle up to Rnd 15 lightly with polyester fiberfill.

Change color to Silver.

Rnd 16: Working through the back loop of the st only: * 1 sc, dec 1 st *, rep from * to * 2 times more. (6 sts)

Rnds 17 and 18: 1 sc in every st of the prev rnd. (6 sts)

Rnd 19: Inc 1 st each, 6 times in all. (12 sts)

Rnd 20: 1 sc in every st of the prev rnd. (12 sts)

Rnd 21: * Inc 1 st, 5 sc *, rep from * to * once more. (14 sts)

Rnds 22 and 23: 1 sc in every st of the prev rnd. (14 sts)

Rnd 24: 2 sc, ch1, skip 10 sts, 2 sc. (5 sts)

Rnd 25: 2 sc, 1 sc into the chain of the previous rnd, 2 sc. (5 sts)

Rnd 26: 1 sc in every st of the prev rnd. (5 sts)

Rnd 27: * Skip 1 st, 1 sl-st *, rep from * to * once more, skip 1 st. (2 sts)

Break the working yarn, and secure the end.

Attach new working yarn in Silver to the 3rd stitch of Rnd 23, and work:

Rnd 24: 1 sc, dec 1 st, ch1, skip 4 sts, 1 sc, dec 1 st, 1 sl-st into the 1st st. (5 sts)

Rnd 25: 2 sc, 1 st into the chain of the previous rnd, 2 sc. (5 sts)

Rnd 26: 1 sc in every st of the prev rnd. (5 sts)

Rnd 27: * Skip 1 st, 1 sl-st *, rep from * to * once more, skip 1 st. (2 sts)

Break the working yarn, and secure the end.

Attach new working yarn in Silver to the 6th stitch of Rnd 23, and:

Rnd 24: 4 sc, ch1, 1 sl-st into the 1st st. (5 sts)

Rnd 25: 4 sc, 1 sc into the chain of the previous rnd. (5 sts)

Rnd 26: 1 sc in every st of the prev rnd. (5 sts)

Rnd 27: * Skip 1 st, 1 sl-st *, rep from * to * once more, skip 1 st. (2 sts)

Break the working yarn, and secure the end.

The Silver-colored part of the fork stays unstuffed.

CHEF'S HAT

MATERIALS

- crochet hook, 6.0 mm (US J-10)
- tapestry needle
- ONline Linie 305 Maxi Corso (35% cotton, 30% viscose, 35% acrylic): 2 skeins (1.75 oz/50 g per skein) in 01 White (Weiß)

GAUGE

- 4 x 4 in (10 x 10 cm) = 11 sc and 13 rows, or
- 3.5 x 3.15 in (9 x 8 cm) = 10 sc and 10 rows

INSTRUCTIONS

MAIN PART

First, work in rows. At the end of every row, chain 1, and turn work.

Row 1: In White, crochet a chain of 8, work 1 sc into the 2nd chain from the hook, 1 sc in every following ch. (7 sts)

Rows 2–40: Working through the back loop of the st only: 1 sc in every st of the prev row. (7 sts)

Break the working yarn, and secure the end.

Sew the sts of the first and the last row together in whipstitch.

HAT BRIM

From here on, continue in rounds. Begin every round with 1 chain, and end every round with 1 sl-st into the first stitch of the round. Do not turn work.

Rnd 1: Attach new working yarn in White to the end of one row of the brim, and now work 1 sc in every end of the row. (40 sts)

Rnds 2–9: 1 sc in every st of the prev rnd. (40 sts)

Rnd 10: Inc 1 st, 39 sc. (41 sts)

Rnd 11: 16 sc, inc 1 st, 24 sc. (42 sts)

Rnd 12: 1 sc in every st of the prev rnd. (42 sts)

Rnd 13: Inc 1 st, 41 sc. (43 sts)

Rnd 14: 1 sc in every st of the prev rnd. (43 sts)

Break the working yarn, and secure the end.

CROWN

Continue to work in the round. Begin every round with 1 chain, and end every round with 1 sl-st into the first stitch of the round. Do not turn work.

Rnd 1: In White, work 5 sc into an adjustable magic ring. (5 sts)

Rnd 2: Inc 1 st each, 5 times in all. (10 sts)

Rnd 3: * 1 sc, inc 1 st *, rep from * to * 4 times more. (15 sts)

Rnd 4: * 2 sc, inc 1 st *, rep from * to * 4 times more. (20 sts)

Rnd 5: 1 sc, inc 1 st, * 3 sc, inc 1 st *, rep from * to * 3 times more, 2 sc. (25 sts)

Rnd 6: * 4 sc, inc 1 st *, rep from * to * 4 times more. (30 sts)

Rnd 7: 2 sc, inc 1 st, * 5 sc, inc 1 st *, rep from * to * 3 times more, 3 sc. (35 sts)

Rnd 8: * 6 sc, inc 1 st *, rep from * to * 4 times more. (40 sts)

Break the working yarn, leaving a long tail, and sew the crown to the main part in whipstitch, using this long end.

OVEN MITT

MATERIALS

- crochet hook, 6.0 mm (US J-10)
- tapestry needle
- ONline Linie 305 Maxi Corso (35% cotton, 30% viscose, 35% acrylic): 1 skein (1.75 oz/50 g) in 04 Blue (Blau)
- ONline Linie 305 Maxi Corso Color (35% cotton, 30% viscose, 35% acrylic): 1 skein (1.75 oz/ 50 g) in 103 Pastel Blue (Hellblau)

GAUGE

- 4 x 4 in (10 x 10 cm) = 11 sc and 13 rows, or
- 3.5 x 3.15 in (9 x 8 cm) = 10 sc and 10 rows

INSTRUCTIONS

Work in rows. End every row with 1 sl-st into the first stitch of the row, chain 1, and turn work.

Row 1: In Pastel Blue, crochet a chain of 24, and join the crocheted chain into the round with 1 sl-st into the first stitch of the chain. Chain 1, turn, work 1 sc into every chain. (24 sts)

Rows 2 and 3: 1 sc in every st of the prev row. (24 sts)

Change color to Blue.

Rows 4–11: 1 sc in every st of the prev row. (24 sts)

Row 12: 1 sc, ch4, skip 4 sts, 19 sc. (24 sts)

Rows 13–16: 1 sc in every st of the prev row. (24 sts)

Row 17: Dec 1 st, 8 sc, dec 1 st each twice, 8 sc, dec 1 st. (20 sts)

Row 18: Dec 1 st, 6 sc, dec 1 st each twice, 6 sc, dec 1 st. (16 sts)

Row 19: Dec 1 st, 4 sc, dec 1 st each twice, 4 sc, dec 1 st. (12 sts)

Row 20: Dec 1 st, 2 sc, dec 1 st each twice, 2 sc, dec 1 st. (8 sts)

Row 21: * Skip 1 st, 1 sl-st *, rep from * to * 3 times more. (4 sts)

Break the working yarn, and secure the end.

THUMB

Attach new working yarn in Blue to the first one of the skipped sts of Row 12, and continue in the round:

1 sl-st into the 1st st of the rnd, ch1, but do not turn here.

Rnd 1: 1 sc in every one of the skipped sts of Row 12 (4 sc), 1 sc into the same stitch, into which the 1st sc after the skipped sts had been worked earlier. Now rotate work slightly as you go, and crochet around the opening in a circle: 4 sc, crochet 2 sts together. (10 sts)

Rnd 2: 3 sc, dec 1 st, 3 sc, dec 1 st. (8 sts)

Rnds 3 and 4: 1 sc in every st of the prev rnd. (8 sts)

Rnd 5: Dec 1 st each 4 times in all. (4 sts)

To close the small opening, from the back, work 1 sl-st into the 3rd st of the prev rnd.

Break the working yarn, and secure the end.

HANGING LOOP

Attach new working yarn in Pastel Blue to the 14th st of Row 3 of the oven mitt, and crochet a chain of 16. Join the crocheted chain into the round with 1 sl-st into the same stitch, into which the new working yarn had just been joined.

HALF APRON

MATERIALS

- crochet hook, 6.0 mm (US J-10)
- tapestry needle
- ONline Linie 305 Maxi Corso Color (35% cotton, 30% viscose, 35% acrylic): 2 skeins (1.75 oz/ 50 g per skein) in 103 Blue (Blau)
- ONline Linie 305 Maxi Corso (35% cotton, 30% viscose, 35% acrylic): 1 skein (1.75 oz/50 g) in 01 White (Weiß)

GAUGE

- 4 x 4 in (10 x 10 cm) = 11 sc and 13 rows, or
- 3.5 x 3.15 in (9 x 8 cm) = 10 sc and 10 rows

INSTRUCTIONS

APRON

Work in rows. At the end of every row, chain 1, and turn work.

Row 1: In Blue, crochet a chain of 29, work 1 sc into the 2nd chain from the hook, 1 sc in every following chain. (28 sts)
Rows 2–22: 1 sc in every st of the prev row. (28 sts)
Row 23: Dec 1 st, 24 sc, dec 1 st. (26 sts)
Row 24: Dec 1 st, 22 sc, dec 1 st. (24 sts)
Row 25: Dec 1 st, 20 sc, dec 1 st. (22 sts)
Row 26: Dec 1 st, 18 sc, dec 1 st. (20 sts)

Break the working yarn, and secure the end.

WHITE BORDER:

Work in rows. At the end of every row, chain 1, and turn work. Attach new working yarn in White to the first stitch of Row 1 of the apron, and continue as follows (every end of the row counts as 1 st):

Row 1 (RS): 1 sc in every st (26 end-of-the-row sts + 20 sts of the last row + 26 end-of-the-row sts = 72 sts), chain 1, and turn work.
Row 2: * [1 sc + 1 dc] into the same st, 1 sl-st *, rep from * to * 35 times more. (108 sts)

Break the working yarn, and secure the end.

WAIST TIES

Turn the apron right side up, with the edges with unused sts at the top. In White, crochet a chain of 56. Do not break yarn.

Row 1: Work 1 sl-st into the last st of Row 1 of the white border, 1 sc in every st of Row 1 of the apron, 1 sc into the 1st st of Row 1 of the white border, ch57.
Row 2: 1 sc into the 2nd chain from the hook, 1 sc in every following ch (56 sts), through the back loop of the stitch only: 1 sc into every sl-st of the prev row (30 sts), 1 sc into every one of the 56 chains of the beginning chain (56 sts).

POCKET

Work in rows. At the end of every row, chain 1, and turn work.

Row 1: In Blue, crochet a chain of 15. 1 sc into the 2nd chain from the hook, 1 sc in every following ch. (14 sts)
Rows 2–9: 1 sc in every st of the prev row. (14 sts)

Row 10: Dec 1 st, 10 sc, dec 1 st. (12 sts)
Row 11: Dec 1 st, 8 sc, dec 1 st. (10 sts)
Row 12: Dec 1 st, 6 sc, dec 1 st. (8 sts)

Break the working yarn and secure the end.

Sew the pocket to the center of the apron front.

FULL APRON

MATERIALS

- crochet hook, 6.0 mm (US J-10)
- tapestry needle
- ONline Linie 305 Maxi Corso Color (35% cotton, 30% viscose, 35% acrylic): 2 skeins (1.75 oz/ 50 g per skein) in 104 Pink
- ONline Linie 305 Maxi Corso (35% cotton, 30% viscose, 35% acrylic): 1 skein (1.75 oz/50 g) in 01 White (Weiß)

GAUGE

- 4 x 4 in (10 x 10 cm) = 11 sc and 13 rows, or
- 3.5 x 3.15 in (9 x 8 cm) = 10 sc and 10 rows

INSTRUCTIONS

Work in rows. At the end of every row, chain 1, and turn work.

Row 1 (RS): In Pink, crochet a chain of 23, work 1 sc into the 2nd chain from the hook, 1 sc in every following ch. (22 sts)

Rows 2–24: 1 sc in every st of the prev row. (22 sts)

Row 25: Inc 1 st, 20 sc, inc 1 st. (24 sts)

Row 26: 1 sc in every st of the prev row. (24 sts)

Row 27: Inc 1 st, 22 sc, inc 1 st. (26 sts)

Row 28: 1 sc in every st of the prev row. (26 sts)

Row 29: Inc 1 st, 24 sc, inc 1 st. (28 sts)

Rows 30–50: 1 sc in every st of the prev row. (28 sts)

Row 51: Dec 1 st, 24 sc, dec 1 st. (26 sts)

Row 52: Dec 1 st, 22 sc, dec 1 st. (24 sts)

Row 53: Dec 1 st, 20 sc, dec 1 st. (22 sts)

Row 54: Dec 1 st, 18 sc, dec 1 st. (20 sts)

Break the working yarn, and secure the end.

WHITE BOTTOM EDGING (RUFFLE)

Place the apron RS up and look at the apron from the top, with Row 1 of the apron located to the right of you. Attach new working yarn in White to the first stitch of Row 29. Now work edging around the apron as follows (the end of the row is considered 1 stitch):

Row 1: [1 sc, 1 hdc, 1 dc] into the 1st st, * 3 dc in 1 st *, rep from * to * 67 times more, [1 dc, 1 hdc, 1 sc, 1 sl-st] into the next st (which should be the last stitch of Row 29 of the apron).

Break the working yarn, and secure the end.

WAIST TIES AND WHITE TOP EDGING

RS row: In White, crochet a chain of 55. Work 1 sl-st into the same stitch into which the last 4 sts of the white bottom edging had been worked earlier (last stitch of Row 29 of the apron). Work an edging along the top part of the apron up to and including the first stitch of the bottom edging (ruffle), by working 1 sl-st into every st widthwise and every row heightwise, and then crochet a chain of 56.

WS row: Turn the apron WS up, with the top part of the apron to your left. Work 1 sc into the 2nd chain from the hook, and 1 sc in every following ch. Continue at the top part of the apron: 1 sc through the front loop of the stitch only in every stitch of the prev row. Work an additional 1 sc into every ch of the beginning chain of 55 from the RS row.

Break the working yarn, and secure the end.

NECK TIES

Place the apron RS up and look at the apron from the top. Attach new working yarn in White to the corner st of the corner located to your right at the top part of the apron. Crochet a chain of 50. Work 1 sc into the 2nd chain from the hook. 1 sc in every following ch. (49 sts) Skip the stitch after the stitch into which you have just joined the working yarn, and work 1 sl-st into the next st.

Break the working yarn, and secure the end.

Attach new working yarn in White to the other corner of the top part of the apron, and work the same as for the first neck tie.

POCKET

Work in rows. At the end of every row, chain 1, and turn work.

Row 1: In White, crochet a chain of 15. Work 1 sc into the 2nd chain from the hook. 1 sc in every following ch. (14 sts)

Rows 2–10: 1 sc in every st of the prev row. (14 sts)

Row 11: Dec 1 st, 10 sc, dec 1 st. (12 sts)

Row 12: Dec 1 st, 8 sc, dec 1 st. (10 sts)

Row 13: Dec 1 st, 6 sc, dec 1 st. (8 sts)

Row 14: Dec 1 st, 4 sc, dec 1 st. (6 sts)

Break the working yarn, and secure the end.

Sew the pocket to the middle of the bottom part of the apron front.

ROSE

In Pink, crochet a chain of 10. 3 hdc into the 2nd chain from the hook, * 3 hdc in 1 st *, rep from * to * once more, * 3 dc in 1 st *, rep from * to * 5 times more.

Break the working yarn, and secure the end.

Roll up the strip in a spiral, with the hdc's on the inside. Sew the rose with a few stitches to the pocket of the apron.

DINNER IS SERVED!

Feast on sunny-side up eggs with freshly toasted bread for
breakfast, and French fries and chicken drumsticks for lunch.
For the more refined taste, sushi and lobster are offered, too!
Crochet until you have had enough.

SUNNY-SIDE-UP EGG

MATERIALS

- crochet hook, 2.5 mm (US B-1 or C-2)
- tapestry needle
- Schachenmayr Catania (100% cotton): 1 skein (1.75 oz/50 g) each in Sun (Sonne) and Creme
- polyester fiberfill

INSTRUCTIONS

Work in rounds. Begin every round with 1 chain, and end every round with 1 sl-st into the first stitch of the round. Do not turn work.

EGG YOLK

Rnd 1: In Sun, work 6 sc into an adjustable magic ring. (6 sts)

Rnd 2: Inc 1 st each, 6 times in all. (12 sts)

Rnd 3: * 1 sc, inc 1 st *, rep from * to * 5 times more. (18 sts)

Rnd 4: 1 sc in every st of the prev rnd. (18 sts)

Rnd 5: * 2 sc, inc 1 st *, rep from * to * 5 times more. (24 sts)

Rnd 6: 1 sc in every st of the prev rnd. (24 sts)

Rnd 7: Working through the back loop of the st only: * 2 sc, dec 1 st *, rep from * to * 5 times more. (18 sts)

Stuff the egg yolk with polyester fiberfill.

Rnd 8: * 1 sc, dec 1 st *, rep from * to * 5 times more. (12 sts)

Rnd 9: Dec 1 st each, 6 times in all. (6 sts)

Rnd 10: * Skip 1 st, 1 sl-st *, rep from * to * 2 times more. (3 sts)

Break the working yarn, and secure the end.

EGG WHITE

Join new working yarn in Creme to the front loop of the 1st st of Rnd 6 of the egg yolk, and continue as follows:

Rnd 1: Working through the front loop of the stitch only: 1 sc, inc 1 st, * 3 sc, inc 1 st *, rep from * to * 4 times more, 2 sc. (30 sts)

Rnd 2: * 4 sc, inc 1 st *, rep from * to * 5 times more. (36 sts)

Rnd 3: 2 sc, inc 1 st, * 5 sc, inc 1 st *, rep from * to * 4 times more, 3 sc. (42 sts)

Rnd 4: * 6 sc, inc 1 st *, rep from * to * 5 times more. (48 sts)

Rnd 5: 1 sc, 4 hdc, 1 dc, 3 dc into the same st, 1 hdc, 6 sc, 2 sc into the same st, 1 hdc, 1 dc, 2 dc into the same st, 4 hdc, [1 hdc, 1 dc] into the same st, 2 dc into the same st, 2 dc, 2 dc into the same st, 2 hdc, 6 sc, 2 sc into the same st, 2 sc, 1 hdc, 1 dc, 2 dc into the same st, [1 dc, 1 hdc] into the same st, 6 sc. (58 sts)

Break the working yarn, and secure the end.

BOILED EGG

MATERIALS

- crochet hook, 2.5 mm (US B-1 or C-2)
- tapestry needle
- Schachenmayr Catania (100% cotton): 1 skein (1.75 oz/50 g) in Creme (for darker eggs, Soft Apricot or Raffia [Bast] may be used), and 0.5 oz (15 g) in Sun (Sonne)
- polyester fiberfill

INSTRUCTIONS

WHOLE BOILED EGG

Work in spiral rounds. Omit the chain at the beginning of the round, and do not join the round with a sl-st into the 1st st of the rnd. Do not turn work.

Rnd 1: In Creme, work 6 sc into an adjustable magic ring. (6 sts)
Rnd 2: Inc 1 st each, 6 times in all. (12 sts)
Rnd 3: * 1 sc, inc 1 st *, rep from * to * 5 times more. (18 sts)
Rnd 4: * 2 sc, inc 1 st *, rep from * to * 5 times more. (24 sts)
Rnd 5: 1 sc in every st of the prev rnd. (24 sts)
Rnd 6: * 3 sc, inc 1 st *, rep from * to * 5 times more. (30 sts)
Rnds 7–10: 1 sc in every st of the prev rnd. (30 sts)
Rnd 11: * 3 sc, dec 1 st *, rep from * to * 5 times more. (24 sts)
Rnds 12 and 13: 1 sc in every st of the prev rnd. (24 sts)
Rnd 14: * 2 sc, dec 1 st * rep from * to * 5 times more. (18 sts)
Rnd 15: 1 sc in every st of the prev rnd. (18 sts)

Rnd 16: * 1 sc, dec 1 st * rep from * to * 5 times more. (12 sts)

Stuff the egg with polyester fiberfill.

Rnd 17: Dec 1 st each, 6 times in all. (6 sts)
Rnd 18: * Skip 1 st, 1 sl-st *, rep from * to * 2 times more. (3 sts)

Break the working yarn, and secure the end.

CUT BOILED EGG

BOTTOM PART

Work in rounds. Begin every round with 1 chain, and end every round with 1 sl-st into the first stitch of the round. Do not turn work.

In Soft Apricot, work Rnds 1–9 from instructions for whole egg.

Rnd 10: Working through the back loop of the st only: * 3 sc, dec 1 st *, rep from * to * 5 times more. (24 sts)
Rnd 11: * 2 sc, dec 1 st *, rep from * to * 5 times more. (18 sts) Chain 1, and after this rnd, turn work once (only here)!

Change color to Sun.

Rnd 12: Working through the front loop of the stitch only: 1 sc in every st of the prev rnd. (18 sts)
Rnds 13–15: 1 sc in every st of the prev rnd. (18 sts)

Stuff the bottom part with polyester fiberfill.

Rnd 16: * 1 sc, dec 1 st *, rep from * to * 5 times more. (12 sts)
Rnd 17: Dec 1 st each, 6 times in all. (6 sts)
Rnd 18: * Skip 1 st, 1 sl-st *, rep from * to * 2 times more. (3 sts)

Break the working yarn, and secure the end.

TOP PART

Work in rounds. Begin every rnd with ch1, and end every rnd with 1

sl-st into the 1st st of the rnd. Do not turn work.

Rnd 1: In Soft Apricot, work 6 sc into an adjustable magic ring. (6 sts)
Rnd 2: Inc 1 st each, 6 times in all. (12 sts)
Rnd 3: * 1 sc, inc 1 st *, rep from * to * 5 times more. (18 sts)
Rnd 4: 1 sc in every st of the prev rnd. (18 sts)
Rnd 5: * 2 sc, inc 1 st *, rep from * to * 5 times more. (24 sts)
Rnds 6–8: 1 sc in every st of the prev rnd. (24 sts)
Rnd 9: * 3 sc, inc 1 st *, rep from * to * 5 times more. (30 sts)
Rnd 10: 1 sc in every st of the prev rnd. (30 sts)
Rnd 11: Working through the back loop of the st only: * 3 sc, dec 1 st *, rep from * to * 5 times more. (24 sts)

Rnds 12–14: 1 sc in every st of the prev rnd. (24 sts)
Rnd 15: * 2 sc, dec 1 st *, rep from * to * 5 times more. (18 sts)
Rnd 16: 1 sc in every st of the prev rnd. (18 sts)
Rnd 17: * 1 sc, dec 1 st *, rep from * to * 5 times more. (12 sts)
Rnd 18: Dec 1 st each, 6 times in all. (6 sts)
Rnd 19: * Skip 1 st, 1 sl-st *, rep from * to * 2 times more. (3 sts)

Break the working yarn, and secure the end.

Turn Rnds 12–19 into the first 11 rnds.

SLICE OF TOAST

MATERIALS

- crochet hook, 2.5 mm (US B-1 or C-2)
- tapestry needle
- Schachenmayr Catania (100% cotton): 1 skein (1.75 oz/50 g) each in Soft Apricot and Tan (Taupe)
- polyester fiberfill

INSTRUCTIONS

Work in rows. At the end of every row, chain 1, and turn work.

Row 1 (WS of work): In Soft Apricot, crochet a chain of 17, work 1 sc into the 2nd stitch from the hook, 1 sc in every following ch. (16 sts)
Rows 2–18: 1 sc in every st of the prev row. (16 sts)
Row 19: Inc 1 st, 14 sc, inc 1 st. (18 sts)

Rows 20 and 21: 1 sc in every st of the prev row. (18 sts)
Row 22: [1 hdc, 1 dc] into the same st, 6 dc, 1 hdc, 2 sc, 1 hdc, 6 dc, [1 dc, 1 hdc] into the same st. (20 sts)

Break the working yarn, and secure the end.

Work edging in Tan around the crocheted piece: 1 rnd of sc.

Make a second piece the same way (repeating Rnds 1–22). Continue as follows in rnds:

Rnd 1: 1 bpsc in every st of the prev rnd.
Rnd 2: 1 sc in every st of the prev rnd.

Now place both crocheted pieces together, wrong sides facing each other, and hold it so you look at the second piece from above. Crochet the two pieces together with 1 rnd of sl-st. After having worked ¾ of the rnd, stuff the slice of toast with polyester fiberfill.

SALAMI

MATERIALS

- crochet hook, 2.5 mm (US B-1 or C-2)
- tapestry needle
- Schachenmayr Catania (100% cotton): 1 skein (1.75 oz/50 g) each in Strawberry (Erdbeere), Freesia (Fresie), Soft Apricot, and Creme, and approx. 0.5 oz (15 g) in Silver (Silber)
- polyester fiberfill

INSTRUCTIONS

Work in rounds. Begin every rnd with ch1, and end every rnd with 1 sl-st into the 1st st of the rnd. Do not turn work.

Rnd 1: Holding 2 strands of yarn together (1 strand Strawberry + 1 strand Freesia), work 6 sc into an adjustable magic ring. (6 sts)
Rnd 2: Inc 1 st each, 6 times in all. (12 sts)
Rnd 3: * 1 sc, inc 1 st *, rep from * to * 5 times more. (18 sts)

Change color to 1 strand Creme held together with 1 strand Soft Apricot.

Rnd 4: Work with 2 strands held together through the back loop of the stitch only: 1 sc in every st of the prev rnd. (18 sts)
Rnds 5–14: 1 sc in every st of the prev rnd. (18 sts)

Stuff the Salami with polyester fiberfill.

Rnd 15: * 1 sc, dec 1 st *, rep from * to * 5 times more. (12 sts)
Rnd 16: 1 sc in every st of the prev rnd. (12 sts)
Rnd 17: Dec 1 st each, 6 times in all (6 sts), chain 1, and turn work once (here only).
Rnd 18: 1 hdc in every st of the prev rnd. (6 sts)

Break the working yarn, and secure the end.

FINISHING

In Creme, embroider a few French knots onto the first 3 rounds.

Wrap a piece of Silver yarn around the last round of the Salami 4 times, and knot the ends.

FARFALLE AND ROTINI

MATERIALS

- crochet hook, 2.5 mm (US B-1 or C-2)
- tapestry needle
- Schachenmayr Catania (100% cotton): 1 skein (1.75 oz/50 g) in Sun (Sonne)

INSTRUCTIONS

FARFALLE

Work in rows. At the end of every row, chain 1, and turn work.

Row 1: In Sun, crochet a chain of 16, work 1 sc into the 2nd chain from the hook, 3 sc into the same st, 1 sc, sc3tog, 1 sc, 3 sc into the same st, 1 sc, sc3tog, 1 sc, 3 sc into the same st, 1 sc. (17 sts)

Row 2: 2 sc, 3 sc into the same st, 1 sc, sc3tog, 1 sc, 3 sc into the same st, 1 sc, sc3tog, 1 sc, 3 sc into the same st, 2 sc. (19 sts)

Row 3: 3 sc, 3 sc into the same st, 1 sc, sc3tog, 1 sc, 3 sc into the same st, 1 sc, sc3tog, 1 sc, 3 sc into the same st, 3 sc. (21 sts)

Row 4: 4 sc, 3 sc into the same st, 1 sc, sc3tog, 1 sc, 3 sc into the same st, 1 sc, sc3tog, 1 sc, 3 sc into the same st, 4 sc. (23 sts)

Break the working yarn, and secure the end.

Make a second piece following the instructions above, and sew the respective last rows of both pieces together in Sun in whipstitch. Make a stitch in the center of the pasta, and pull the piece together from one end of the row to the other. This creates the curly shape.

ROTINI

In Sun, crochet a chain of 20, work 2 sc into the 2nd chain from the hook, 2 sc in every following ch. (38 sts)

Break the working yarn, and secure the end.

PIZZA

MATERIALS

- crochet hook, 2.5 mm (US B-1 or C-2)
- tapestry needle
- Pizza: Schachenmayr Catania (100% cotton), 1 skein (1.75 oz/50 g) each in Soft Apricot and Signal Red (Signalrot)
- Olive: Schachenmayr Catania (100% cotton), 0.5 oz (15 g) each in Signal Red (Signalrot), Kiwi, and Apple (Apfel)
- Mushroom: Schachenmayr Catania (100% cotton), 0.5 oz (15 g) each in Soft Apricot and Black (Schwarz)
- Salami: Schachenmayr Catania (100% cotton), 0.5 oz (15 g) each in Freesia (Fresie), and Strawberry (Erdbeere)
- polyester fiberfill

INSTRUCTIONS

Work in rows. At the end of every row, chain 1, and turn work.

Row 1 (WS): In Soft Apricot, crochet a chain of 2, work 1 sc into the 2nd chain from the hook. (1 st)
Row 2 (RS): Inc 1 st. (2 sts)
Row 3: Inc 1 st each twice. (4 sts)
Rows 4–6: 1 sc in every st of the prev row. (4 sts)
Row 7: Inc 1 st, 2 sc, inc 1 st. (6 sts)
Rows 8–10: 1 sc in every st of the prev row. (6 sts)
Row 11: Inc 1 st, 4 sc, inc 1 st. (8 sts)
Rows 12–14: 1 sc in every st of the prev row. (8 sts)

Row 15: Inc 1 st, 6 sc, inc 1 st. (10 sts)
Rows 16–18: 1 sc in every st of the prev row. (10 sts)
Row 19: Inc 1 st, 8 sc, inc 1 st. (12 sts)
Rows 20–22: 1 sc in every st of the prev row. (12 sts)
Row 23: Inc 1 st, 10 sc, inc 1 st. (14 sts)
Rows 24–26: 1 sc in every st of the prev row. (14 sts)
Row 27: Inc 1 st, 12 sc, inc 1 st. (16 sts)
Rows 28–33: 1 sc in every st of the prev row. (16 sts)

Change color to Signal Red.

Row 34: Dec 1 st, 12 sc, dec 1 st. (14 sts)
Rows 35–37: 1 sc in every st of the prev row. (14 sts)
Row 38: Dec 1 st, 10 sc, dec 1 st. (12 sts)
Rows 39–41: 1 sc in every st of the prev row. (12 sts)
Row 42: Dec 1 st, 8 sc, dec 1 st. (10 sts)
Rows 43–45: 1 sc in every st of the prev row. (10 sts)
Row 46: Dec 1 st, 6 sc, dec 1 st. (8 sts)
Rows 47–49: 1 sc in every st of the prev row. (8 sts)
Row 50: Dec 1 st, 4 sc, dec 1 st. (6 sts)
Rows 51–53: 1 sc in every st of the prev row. (6 sts)
Row 54: Dec 1 st, 2 sc, dec 1 st. (4 sts)
Rows 55–57: 1 sc in every st of the prev row. (4 sts)
Row 58: Dec 1 st each twice. (2 sts)
Row 59: Dec 1 st. (1 st)
Row 60: 1 sc. (1 st)

Break the working yarn, and secure the end.

Fold the piece with wrong sides facing each other, so that the two triangles are stacked exactly on top of each other. Hold work so that you look onto the red triangle from above, and the tip of the slice of pizza points to the left. Join new working yarn in Soft Apricot to the end of Row 33 of the pizza, insert the hook through the sts of both layers (Red and Apricot-colored edge stitch), and work 1 sc in every edge stitch, 3 sc into the stitch at the tip, and then work the other side, again 1 sc in every edge stitch, up to the first Apricot-colored row.

Break the working yarn, and secure the end.

Sew Row 33 to the bottom of the pizza in running stitch.

Stuff the rim of the pizza with a small amount of polyester fiberfill, and close the 2 remaining openings as follows:

Rnd 1: Join new working yarn in Soft Apricot to the end of one row of the opening, and work 6 sc along the edge of the opening. 1 sl-st into the 1st st of the rnd. Chain 1.
Rnd 2: * Skip 1 st, 1 sl-st *, rep from * to * 2 times more. (3 sts)

Break the working yarn, and secure the end.

PIZZA TOPPINGS

OLIVE

Work in rounds. Begin every round with 1 chain, and end every round with 1 sl-st into the first stitch of the round. Do not turn work.

Rnd 1: In Signal Red, work 6 sc into an adjustable magic ring. (6 sts)
Change color to Kiwi.

Rnd 2: Working through the back loop of the st only: inc 1 st each, 6 times in all. (12 sts)

Change color to Apple.

Rnd 3: Working through the back loop of the st only: 1 sc in every st of the prev rnd. (12 sts)

Break the working yarn, and secure the end.

SLICE OF SALAMI

Work Rounds 1–3 from the instructions for the Salami (see page 56).

TIP: For a slice of mozzarella, use 2 strands of yarn (1 White + 1 Creme) held together, and follow instructions for Slice of Salami.

HALF MUSHROOM

Work in rows in sc. At the end of every row, chain 1, and turn work.

Row 1: In Soft Apricot, crochet a chain of 9, crochet the 2nd and 3rd chain from the hook together, 4 sc, sc2tog. (6 sts)
Row 2: 1 sc in every st of the prev row. (6 sts)
Row 3: 1 sc in Soft Apricot, change color to Black: 1 sc, change color to Soft Apricot: 2 sc, change color to Black: 1 sc, change color to Soft Apricot: 1 sc. (6 sts)

When changing colors, don't break the yarn, but carry up the unused color within the current stitch.

Break the working yarn, and secure the end.

Turn work.

Row 4: Join new working yarn in Soft Apricot to the 3rd stitch of Row 3 (counted from the right edge), and work [2 sc into the same st] twice. (4 sts)
Row 5: Dec 1 st each twice. (2 sts)
Rows 6 and 7: 1 sc in every st of the prev row. (2 sts)

Break the working yarn, and secure the end.

Now decorate the pizza to your taste! Grated cheese can be made from a long chain in Yellow.

FRENCH FRIES

MATERIALS

- crochet hook, 2.5 mm (US B-1 or C-2)
- tapestry needle
- Schachenmayr Catania (100% cotton): 1 skein (1.75 oz/50 g) in Sun (Sonne)

INSTRUCTIONS

Work in rows. At the end of every row, chain 1, and turn work.

Row 1 (RS): In Sun, crochet a chain of 14, work 1 sc into the 2nd chain from the hook, 1 sc in every following ch. (13 sts)

Row 2: Working through the front loop of the stitch only: 1 sc in every st of the prev row. (13 sts)

Row 3: Working through the back loop of the st only: 1 sc in every st of the prev row. (13 sts)

Row 4: Working through the front loop of the stitch only: 1 sc in every st of the prev row. (13 sts)

Now place Rows 1 and 4 atop each other, and crochet the pieces together with sl-st. Stuff the piece very lightly with polyester fiberfill, and weave in the yarn tails with a few stitches. When working the beginning chain with a different stitch count, French fries of other lengths can be made.

CHICKEN DRUMSTICK

MATERIALS

- crochet hook, 2.5 mm (US B-1 or C-2)
- tapestry needle
- Schachenmayr Catania (100% cotton): 1 skein (1.75 oz/50 g) each in Creme and Cinnamon (Zimt)

INSTRUCTIONS

Work in rounds. Begin every rnd with ch1, and end every rnd with 1 sl-st into the 1st st of the rnd. Do not turn work.

Rnd 1: In Creme, work 6 sc into an adjustable magic ring. (6 sts)
Rnd 2: * 1 sc, inc 1 st *, rep from * to * 2 times more. (9 sts)
Rnd 3: 1 sc in every st of the prev rnd. (9 sts)

Break the working yarn, and secure the end.

Repeat Rounds 1–3. Now work:

Rnd 4: 1 sc in every st of the prev rnd. Continue working in the 1st st of Round 3 of the first piece: 1 sc in every st of the prev rnd. (18 sts)
Rnd 5: * 4 sc, dec 1 st *, rep from * to * 2 times more. (15 sts)
Rnd 6: 2 sc, dec 1 st, * 3 sc, dec 1 st *, rep from * to * once more, 1 sc. (12 sts)
Rnd 7: 1 sc in every st of the prev rnd. (12 sts)
Rnd 8: * 2 sc, dec 1 st *, rep from * to * 2 times more. (9 sts)
Rnd 9: 1 sc in every st of the prev rnd. (9 sts)

Change color to Cinnamon.

Rnds 10 and 11: 1 sc in every st of the prev rnd. (9 sts)
Rnd 12: * 2 sc, inc 1 st *, rep from * to * 2 times more. (12 sts)
Rnds 13–16: 1 sc in every st of the prev rnd. (12 sts)
Rnd 17: * Inc 1 st, 3 sc *, rep from * to * 2 times more. (15 sts)
Rnd 18: 1 sc, inc 1 st, 11 sc, inc 1 st, 1 sc. (17 sts)
Rnd 19: 1 sc, inc 1 st, 12 sc, inc 1 st, 2 sc. (19 sts)
Rnd 20: 1 sc in every st of the prev rnd. (19 sts)
Rnd 21: 4 sc, inc 1 st, 8 sc, inc 1 st, 4 sc, inc 1 st. (22 sts)
Rnd 22: 1 sc, inc 1 st, 6 sc, inc 1 st, 6 sc, inc 1 st, 6 sc. (25 sts)
Rnd 23: 5 sc, inc 1 st, * 4 sc, inc 1 st *, rep from * to * 2 times more, 3 sc, inc 1 st. (30 sts)
Rnds 24–27: 1 sc in every st of the prev rnd. (30 sts)
Rnd 28: * 3 sc, dec 1 st *, rep from * to * 5 times more. (24 sts)
Rnd 29: 1 sc in every st of the prev rnd. (24 sts)

Stuff the drumstick with polyester fiberfill.

Rnd 30: * 2 sc, dec 1 st *, rep from * to * 5 times more. (18 sts)
Rnd 31: * 1 sc, dec 1 st *, rep from * to * 5 times more. (12 sts)
Rnd 32: Dec 1 st each, 6 times in all. (6 sts)
Rnd 33: * Skip 1 st, 1 sl-st *, rep from * to * 2 times more. (3 sts)

Break the working yarn, and secure the end.

CHEESEBURGER

MATERIALS

- crochet hook, 2.5 mm (US B-1 or C-2)
- tapestry needle
- Schachenmayr Catania (100% cotton): 1 skein (1.75 oz/50 g) each in Tangerine (Mandarine), Soft Apricot, Sun (Sonne), and Coffee (Kaffee)
- polyester fiberfill

INSTRUCTIONS

The cheeseburger goes well with a salad leaf and tomato; for instructions, see page 62.

TOP BUN

In Soft Apricot, crochet a circle from Basic pattern (Rnds 1–8, see page 23).

Rnd 9: 1 bpsc in every st of the prev rnd. (48 sts)

The next rnd is worked alternatingly in Soft Apricot (SA) and Tangerine (T). Carry the unused color inside the current stitch.

Rnd 10: 4 sc in SA, 3 sc in T, 2 sc in SA, 5 sc in T, 3 sc in SA, 6 sc in T, 4 sc in SA, 4 sc in T, 3 sc in SA, 5 sc in T, 2 sc in SA, 4 sc in T, 3 sc in SA. (48 sts)

Change color to Tangerine.

Rnds 11 and 12: 1 sc in every st of the prev rnd. (48 sts)
Rnd 13: * 6 sc, skip 1 st *, rep from * to * 5 times more, 6 sc. (42 sts)
Rnd 14: * 5 sc, skip 1 st *, rep from * to * 6 times more. (35 sts)
Rnd 15: * 4 sc, skip 1 st *, rep from * to * 6 times more. (28 sts)

Stuff the top bun with polyester fiberfill.

Rnd 16: * 3 sc, skip 1 st *, rep from * to * 6 times more. (21 sts)
Rnd 17: * 2 sc, skip 1 st *, rep from * to * 6 times more. (14 sts)
Rnd 18: * 1 sc, skip 1 st *, rep from * to * 6 times more. (7 sts)
Rnd 19: * Skip 1 st, 1 sl-st *, rep from * to * 2 times more, skip 1 st. (3 sts)

Break the working yarn, and secure the end.

In Soft Apricot, embroider the Tangerine-colored top with French knots for sesame seeds.

TIP: To turn the top bun into a cookie with sugar icing and choco-

late sprinkles, instead of Tangerine, use color of choice (such as Pink or Blue) for icing, and embroider French knots in Coffee.

BOTTOM BUN

Work Rnds 1–9 as for the top bun. The next rnd is worked alternatingly in Soft Apricot (SA) and Tangerine (T). Carry the unused color inside the current stitch.

Rnd 10: 2 sc in SA, 3 sc in T, 3 sc in SA, 6 sc in T, 3 sc in SA, 6 sc in T, 2 sc in SA, 5 sc in T, 2 sc in SA, 6 sc in T, 2 sc in SA, 8 sc in T. (48 sts)

Change color to Tangerine.

Then continue from Round 13 of instructions for top bun.

BURGER PATTY

In Coffee, work Rnds 1–8 as for the bottom bun. Here, however, the WS of work will stay as the outside of the patty.

Rnd 9: 1 fpsc in every st of the prev rnd. (48 sts)
Rnd 10: * 6 sc, dec 1 st *, rep from * to * 5 times more. (42 sts)
Rnd 11: * 5 sc, dec 1 st *, rep from * to * 5 times more. (36 sts)

Stuff the burger patty lightly with polyester fiberfill.

Rnd 12: * 4 sc, dec 1 st *, rep from * to * 5 times more. (30 sts)
Rnd 13: * 3 sc, dec 1 st *, rep from * to * 5 times more. (24 sts)
Rnd 13: * 2 sc, dec 1 st *, rep from * to * 5 times more. (18 sts)
Rnd 14: * 1 sc, dec 1 st *, rep from * to * 5 times more. (12 sts)
Rnd 15: Dec 1 st each, 6 times in all. (6 sts)
Rnd 16: * Skip 1 st, 1 sl-st *, rep from * to * 2 times more. (3 sts)

Break the working yarn, and secure the end.

SLICE OF CHEESE

Work in rows. At the end of every row, chain 1, and turn work.

Row 1: In Sun, crochet a chain of 11, work 1 sc into the 2nd chain from the hook, 1 sc in every following ch. (10 sts)
Row 2: 2 sc, ch1, skip 1 st, 7 sc. (10 sts)
Row 3: 2 sc, ch1, skip 1 st, 2 sc, dec 1 st, 3 sc in ch-sp, dec 1 st. (10 sts)
Row 4: 5 sc, dec 1 st, 3 sc in ch-sp, dec 1 st. (10 sts)
Row 5: 4 sc, ch1, skip 1 st, 5 sc. (10 sts)
Row 6: 3 sc, dec 1 st, 3 sc in ch-sp, dec 1 st, 2 sc. (10 sts)
Row 7: 1 sc in every st of the prev row. (10 sts)
Row 8: 2 sc, ch1, skip 1 st, 4 sc, ch1, skip 1 st, 2 sc. (10 sts)
Row 9: Dec 1 st, 3 sc in ch-sp, dec 1 st each twice, 3 sc in ch-sp, dec 1 st. (10 sts)
Row 10: 3 sc, ch1, skip 1 st, 6 sc. (10 sts)

Now work 1 rnd around the whole square:

Rnd 1: 4 sc, dec 1 st, 3 sc in ch-sp, dec 1 st, 3 sc into the last stitch; continue into the end-of-the-row sts: 8 sc, 3 sc into the corner st, 8 sc, 3 sc into the corner st, 8 sc, 2 sc into the corner st. (44 sts) Join into the round with 1 sl-st into the first stitch.

MATERIALS

- crochet hook, 2.5 mm (US B-1 or C-2)
- tapestry needle
- Schachenmayr Catania (100% cotton): 0.5 oz (15 g) each in Golf Green (Golfgrün), Apple (Apfel), Kiwi, Soft Apricot, Signal Red (Signalrot), Burgundy (Weinrot), Strawberry (Erdbeer), Pink (Rosa), Sun (Sonne), and Agave

INSTRUCTIONS

SALAD LEAF

Work in rows. At the end of every row, chain 1, and turn work.

Row 1: In Soft Apricot, crochet a chain of 15, work 1 sc into the 2nd chain from the hook, 2 sc (= branch), ch4, 1 sc into the 2nd chain from the hook, 2 sc (= 2nd branch) 1 sl-st into the next still unused chain, 6 hdc, 4 sc. (17 sts)

Change color to Kiwi.

Row 2: 4 sc, 2 sc into the same st, 4 sc, inc 1 st, 3 sc, 3 sc into the same st, work around the sts of the small branch: 2 sc, continue into the other branch: 2 sc, 3 sc into the same st, here, too, crochet around the branch again: 3 sc, and then resume crocheting into the sts of the longer branch: 2 sc, 2 sc into the same st, 4 sc, 2 sc into the same st, 1 sc. (39 sts)

Change color to Apple.

Row 3: 5 sc, 2 sc into the same st, 5 sc, 1 hdc, 1 dc, 3 dc into the same st, 3 dc into the same st, 2 dc into the same st, 1 dc, 1 hdc, 1 sc, 1 hdc, 3 dc into the same st, 2 dc into the same st, 1 dc, 3 dc into the same st, 2 dc, 1 hdc, 3 sc, 2 sc into the same st, 1 sc, 2 sc into the same st, 6 sc. (52 sts)

Row 4: 10 sc, ch4, 1 sc into the 2nd chain from the hook, 2 hdc, 1 sl-st into the next st of the prev row, 1 sc, 2 dc into the same st, 1 dc, 2 dc into the same st, 1 dc, 2 dc into the same st, 1 sl-st, ch4, 1 sc into the 2nd chain from the hook, 2 hdc, 1 sl-st into the next st of the prev row, 1 sc, 3 dc into the same st, 1 sl-st, ch4, 1 sc into the 2nd chain from the hook, 2 hdc, 1 sl-st into the next st of the prev row, 1 sc, 3 dc into the same st, 1 hdc, 3 sc, [2 sc into the same st] 3 times, 3 dc into the same st, [2 dc into the same st] 3 times, 1 hdc, [2 sc into the same st] twice, 2 sc, 3 dc into the same st, 1 dc, 1 hdc, 2 sc into the same st, 1 sc, [2 sc into the same st] 4 times, 2 sc. (85 sts)

Break the working yarn, and secure the end.

TOMATO SLICE

Work in rounds. Begin every round with 1 chain, and end every round with 1 sl-st into the first stitch of the round. Do not turn work.

Rnd 1: In Pink, work 7 sc into an adjustable magic ring. (7 sts)
Rnd 2: 3 sc into the same st, 1 hdc, [2 dc, 1 hdc] into the same st, 1 sl-st, [1 hdc, 2 dc] into the same st, 1 hdc, 3 sc into the same st. (15 sts)

Change color to Burgundy.

Rnd 3: 1 sc, 2 hdc, [2 dc into the same st] twice, [2 dc, 1 hdc] into the same st, 1 sc, 1 sl-st, 1 sc, [1hdc, 2 dc] into the same st, [2 dc into the same st] twice, 2 hdc, 1 sc. (23 sts)

Change color to Strawberry.

Rnd 4: 3 sc, 2 sc into the same st, 2 hdc into the same st, 1 hdc, 2 hdc into the same st, [1 hdc, 1 sc] into the same st, 1 sc, 5 sl-st, 1 sc, [1 sc, 1 hdc] into the same st, 2 hdc into the same st, 1 hdc, 2 hdc into the same st, 2 sc into the same st, 3 sc. (31 sts)

Change color to Signal Red.

Rnd 5: This rnd is worked in sc only: 3 sc, inc 1 st, 4 sc, inc 1 st, 2 sc, inc 1 st, 7 sc, inc 1 st, 2 sc, inc 1 st, 4 sc, inc 1 st, 3 sc. (37 sts)

Break the working yarn, and secure the end.

In Sun, embroider the burgundy surface with 2 stitches for flesh to the left and right as well as French knots for seeds. In Pink, embroider 3 small stitches between the first and last st of Rnds 2 and 3. At the opposite side, embroider 3 stitches in Pink between Rnds 2 and 3, too.

CUCUMBER SLICE

Work in rounds. Begin every round with 1 chain, and end every round with 1 sl-st into the first stitch of the round. Do not turn work.

Rnd 1: In Golf Green, work 6 sc into an adjustable magic ring. (6 sts)
Rnd 2: Inc 1 st each, 6 times in all. (12 sts)

Change color to Kiwi.

Rnd 3: * 1 spike stitch sc worked into the center of the magic ring, inc 1 st *, rep from * to * 5 times more. (18 sts)
Rnd 4: * 2 sc, inc 1 st *, rep from * to * 5 times more. (24 sts)

Change color to Apple.

Rnd 5: 1 sc, inc 1 st, * 3 sc, inc 1 st *, rep from * to * 4 times more, 2 sc. (30 sts)

Change color to Agave.

Rnd 6: 1 sc in every st of the prev rnd. (30 sts)

Break the working yarn, and secure the end.

PEPPER SLICE

Work sc in the round. Begin every round with chain 1, and end every round with 1 sl-st into the first stitch of the round.

Do not turn work.

Rnd 1: In Kiwi, crochet a chain of 24, and join the chain into the round with 1 sl-st into the first chain, ch1, * dec 1 st, inc 1 st each twice, dec 1 st *, rep from * to * 3 times more. (24 sts)

Change color to Golf Green.

Rnd 2: Dec 1 st, [6 sc inthe same stitch] twice, dec 1 st *, rep from * to * 3 times more. (56 sts)

Break the working yarn, and secure the end.

FISH

MATERIALS

- crochet hook, 2.5 mm (US B-1 or C-2)
- tapestry needle
- Schachenmayr Catania (100% cotton): 1 skein (1.75 oz/50 g) in Silver (Silber), and approx. 0.5 oz (15 g) in Regatta
- polyester fiberfill

INSTRUCTIONS

Work in rounds. Begin every round with 1 chain, and end every round with 1 sl-st into the first stitch of the round. Do not turn work.

Rnd 1: In Silver, work 6 sc into an adjustable magic ring. (6 sts)
Rnd 2: * Inc 1 st, 2 sc *, rep from * to * once more. (8 sts)
Rnd 3: * Inc 1 st each twice, 2 sc *, rep from * to * once more. (12 sts)
Rnd 4: 1 sc, inc 1 st each twice, 4 sc, inc 1 st each twice, 3 sc. (16 sts)
Rnd 5: 1 bpsc in every st of the prev rnd. (16 sts)

Rnd 6: 1 sc in every st of the prev rnd. (16 sts)
Rnds 7–10: Working through the back loop of the st only: 1 sc in every st of the prev rnd. (16 sts)
Rnd 11: Working through the back loop of the st only: 2 sc, dec 1 st each twice, 4 sc, dec 1 st each twice, 2 sc. (12 sts)
Rnd 12: Working through the back loop of the st only: 1 sc in every st of the prev rnd. (12 sts)
Rnd 13: Working through the back loop of the st only: 1 sc, dec 1 st each twice, 2 sc, dec 1 st each twice, 1 sc. (8 sts)
Rnd 14: Working through the back loop of the st only: 1 sc in every st of the prev rnd. (8 sts)
Rnd 15: Working through the back loop of the st only: * dec 1 st, 2 sc *, rep from * to * once more. (6 sts)
Rnd 16: * Skip 1 st, 1 sl-st *, rep from * to * 2 times more. (3 sts)

Chain 3, 5 dc in 1 st of the last rnd, ch3, 1 sl-st into the same stitch, into which the 5 dc had just been worked.

Break the working yarn, and secure the end.

In Regatta, embroider French knots for eyes.

MAKI SUSHI ROLL

MATERIALS

- crochet hook, 2.5 mm (US B-1 or C-2)
- tapestry needle
- Schachenmayr Catania (100% cotton): 0.5 oz (15 g) each in Agave, White (Weiß), Pink (Rosa), Tangerine (Mandarine), and Kiwi
- polyester fiberfill

INSTRUCTIONS

Work in rounds. Begin every rnd with ch1, and end every rnd with 1 sl-st into the 1st st of the rnd. Do not turn work. In this pattern, the tulip sts are worked with only 2 instead of 3 unfinished hdc's.

Rnd 1: Work 2 sc each in Tangerine, Pink, and Kiwi into an adjustable magic ring. (6 sts)
Rnd 2: Tangerine: inc 1 st each twice, Pink: inc 1 st each twice, Kiwi: inc 1 st each twice. (12 sts)

Change color to White.

Rnd 3: * 1 tulip-st, 2 tulip-sts into the same st *, rep from * to * 5 times more. (18 sts)

Change color to Agave.

Rnd 4: Working through the back loop of the st only: * 2 sc, inc 1 st *, rep from * to * 5 times more. (24 sts)
Rnd 5: 1 bpsc in every st of the prev rnd. (24 sts)
Rnds 6–9: 1 sc in every st of the prev rnd. (24 sts)

Change color to White.

Rnd 10: Working through the back loop of the st only: * 2 sc, dec 1 st *, rep from * to * 5 times more. (18 sts)

Stuff with polyester fiberfill.

Rnd 11: * 1 tulip-st, hdc2tog *, rep from * to * 5 times more. (12 sts)
Rnd 12: Tangerine: dec 1 st each twice, Pink: dec 1 st each twice, Kiwi: dec 1 st each twice. (6 sts) Do not break the working yarns.
Rnd 13: Skip 1 st, 1 sl-st in Tangerine, skip 1 st, 1 sl-st in Pink, skip 1 st, 1 sl-st in Kiwi. (3 sts)

Break the working yarn, and secure the end.

CALIFORNIA SUSHI ROLL

MATERIALS

- crochet hook, 2.5 mm (US B-1 or C-2)
- embroidery needle and sewing needle
- Schachenmayr Catania (100% cotton): 1 skein (1.75 oz/50 g) in White (Weiß), and 0.5 oz (15 g) each in Soft Apricot, Tangerine (Mandarine), Kiwi, Apple (Apfel), Mimosa (Mimose), and Agave
- polyester fiberfill
- salmon-colored seed beads (Rocailles)
- sewing thread in a matching color

INSTRUCTIONS

First, work in the round. Begin every round with 1 chain, and end every round with 1 sl-st into the first stitch of the round. Do not turn work.

CRAB MEAT

Rnd 1 (RS of work): In Soft Apricot, work 6 sc into an adjustable magic ring. (6 sts)
Rnd 2: Inc 1 st each, 6 times in all. (12 sts)

AVOCADO PIECES

Change color to Apple. From here on, work in rows; at the end of every row, ch1, and turn work.

Row 1: 1 sc, inc 1 st, 1 hdc, 1 dc. (5 sts) Change color to Kiwi. The remaining sts will stay unworked for the time being.
Row 2: 1 sc in every st of the prev row. (5 sts)

Change color to Mimosa.

Row 3: Dec 1 st, 1 sc, dec 1 st. (3 sts)

Break the working yarn, and secure the end.

CUCUMBER

Hold the California Roll RS up and look onto it from above. Join new working yarn in Kiwi to the left end of Row 2.

Row 1: 1 sc into the st at the end of Row 2, 1 sc into the st at the end of Row 1, through the back loop of the stitch only: 1 sc into the 4th st of Rnd 4 of the crab meat part, 1 sc each into the next 3 sts of the crab meat part. (6 sts)
Row 2: 1 sc in every st of the prev row. (6 sts)

Break the working yarn, and secure the end.

Now work sc edging around the piece as follows:

Rnd 1: Join new working yarn in White to the 8th st of Rnd 2 of the crab meat part, and, working through the back loop of the st only: inc 1 st, 1 sc, inc 1 st, 1 sc, inc 1 st, 1 sc into the st at the end of Row 1 of the avocado, 1 sc into the st at the end of Row 2, 1 sc into the st at the end of Row 3, through the back loop of the stitch only: 2 sc into the 1st st of Row 3 of the avocado, 1 sc, 2 sc into the last st of Row 3 of the avocado, 1 sc each into the 2 end-of-the-row sts of the cucumber, 2 sc into the same st, 4 sc, 2 sc into the same st, 1 sc into the st at the end of Row 1 of the cucumber. Join into the round with 1 sl-st into the first stitch. (27 sts)
Rnd 2: 4 sc, 2 sc into the same st, 3 sc, 2 hdc, 2 sc, 2 sc into the same st, 3 sc, 2 dc, 1 sc, 2 sc into the same st, 7 sc. (30 sts)
Rnd 3: 1 bpsc in every st of the prev rnd. (30 sts)
Rnds 4–7: 1 sc in every st of the prev rnd. (30 sts)
Rnd 8: Working through the back loop of the st only, * 3 sc, dec 1 st *, rep from * to * 5 times more. (24 sts)
Rnd 9: * 2 sc, dec 1 st *, rep from * to * 5 times more. (18 sts)

Stuff the California Sushi Roll with polyester fiberfill.

Rnd 10: * 1 sc, dec 1 st *, rep from * to * 5 times more. (12 sts)
Rnd 11: Dec 1 st each, 6 times in all. (6 sts)
Rnd 12: * Skip 1 st, 1 sl-st *, rep from * to * 2 times more. (3 sts)

Break the working yarn, and secure the end.

Sew seed beads onto the sides of the California roll. In Tangerine and working in backstitch, embroider first the traced outlines of the crab meat part and then, also in backstitch but in Agave, the outlines of the whole filling.

LOBSTER

MATERIALS

- crochet hook, 2.5 mm (US B-1 or C-2)
- tapestry needle
- Schachenmayr Catania (100% cotton): 1 skein (1.75 oz/50 g) in Signal Red (Signalrot), and 0.5 oz (15 g) in Black (Schwarz)
- polyester fiberfill
- pipe cleaners or craft wire

INSTRUCTIONS

Work in rounds. Begin every rnd with ch1, and end every rnd with 1 sl-st into the 1st st of the rnd. Do not turn work.

BODY

Rnd 1: In Signal Red, work 6 sc into an adjustable magic ring. (6 sts)
Rnd 2: Inc 1 st each, 6 times in all. (12 sts)
Rnds 3 and 4: 1 sc in every st of the prev rnd. (12 sts)
Rnd 5: Working through the front loop of the stitch only: 1 sc in every st of the prev rnd. (12 sts)
Rnd 6: Working through the back loop of the sts of Rnd 4, 1 sc in every st of Rnd 4. (12 sts)
Rnd 7: * 3 sc, inc 1 st *, rep from * to * 2 times more. (15 sts)
Rnd 8: Working through the front loop of the stitch only, 1 sc in every st of the prev rnd. (15 sts)
Rnd 9: Working through the back loop of the sts of Rnd 7, 1 sc in every st of Rnd 7. (15 sts)
Rnd 10: 3 sc, inc 1 st, * 4 sc, inc 1 st *, rep from * to * once more, 1 sc. (18 sts)

Rnd 11: Working through the front loop of the stitch only: * 5 sc, inc 1 st *, rep from * to * 2 times more. (21 sts)
Rnd 12: Working through the back loop of the sts of Rnd 10, 1 sc in every st of Rnd 10. (18 sts)
Rnd 13: * 5 sc, inc 1 st *, rep from * to * 2 times more. (21 sts)
Rnd 14: Working through the front loop of the stitch only, 2 sc, inc 1 st, * 6 sc, inc 1 st *, rep from * to * once more, 4 sc. (24 sts)
Rnd 15: Working through the back loop of the sts of Rnd 13, 1 sc in every st of Rnd 13. (21 sts)
Rnds 16 and 17: 1 sc in every st of the prev rnd. (21 sts)
Rnd 18: * 6 sc, inc 1 st *, rep from * to * 2 times more. (24 sts)
Rnd 19: 1 sc in every st of the prev rnd. (24 sts)
Rnd 20: Inc 1 st, 10 sc, inc 1 st each twice, 10 sc, inc 1 st. (28 sts)
Rnd 21: 1 sc in every st of the prev rnd. (28 sts)
Rnd 22: Inc 1 st, 12 sc, inc 1 st each twice, 12 sc, inc 1 st. (32 sts)
Rnd 23: 1 sc in every st of the prev rnd. (32 sts)
Rnd 24: Dec 1 st, 12 sc, dec 1 st each twice, 12 sc, dec 1 st. (28 sts)
Rnd 25: 1 sc in every st of the prev rnd. (28 sts)
Rnd 26: Dec 1 st, 10 sc, dec 1 st each twice, 10 sc, dec 1 st. (24 sts)
Rnd 27: 1 sc in every st of the prev rnd. (24 sts)
Rnd 28: Dec 1 st, 8 sc, dec 1 st each twice, 8 sc, dec 1 st. (20 sts)
Rnd 29: 1 sc in every st of the prev rnd. (20 sts)
Rnd 30: Dec 1 st, 6 sc, dec 1 st each twice, 6 sc, dec 1 st. (16 sts)

Stuff the Lobster with polyester fiberfill.

Rnd 31: 1 sc in every st of the prev rnd. (16 sts)

Rnd 32: Dec 1 st, 4 sc, dec 1 st each twice, 4 sc, dec 1 st. (12 sts)
Rnd 33: 1 sc in every st of the prev rnd. (12 sts)

Stuff the head of the Lobster with polyester fiberfill.

Rnd 34: Dec 1 st each, 6 times in all. (6 sts)
Rnd 35: * Skip 1 st, 1 sl-st *, rep from * to * 2 times more. (3 sts)

Do not break the working yarn, continue with Antennae.

ANTENNAE

Crochet a chain of 12.

Break the working yarn, and secure the end.

Join new working yarn in Signal Red to the last rnd and again, crochet a chain of 12.

Break the working yarn, and secure the end.

Repeat this step 2 times more for the two longer antennae, chaining 20 for each long antenna.

EYES

Embroider two eyes in Black with French knots at the level of Rnd 33 of the head.

TAIL

Place the Lobster right side up, with the head facing you. Join new working yarn in Signal Red at right to the outermost stitch between Rnds 1 and 2 of the body, and continue as follows: * ch4, 3 tr into the same st, ch4, 1 sl-st into the same stitch into which the 3 tr had been worked earlier, 1 sl-st into the next st *, rep from * to * 3 times more, but on the 3rd repeat omit the last sl-st.

CLAWS

BIG CLAWS (MAKE 2)

Work in rounds. Begin every round with 1 chain, and end every round with 1 sl-st into the first stitch of the round. Do not turn work.

Rnd 1: In Signal Red, work 3 sc into an adjustable magic ring. (3 sts)
Rnd 2: 1 sc in every st of the prev rnd. (3 sts)
Rnd 3: Inc 1 st each 3 times in all. (6 sts)
Rnd 4: 1 sc in every st of the prev rnd. (6 sts)
Rnd 5: 1 sc, inc 1 st, 4 sc. (7 sts)
Rnd 6: 2 sc, inc 1 st, 4 sc. (8 sts)
Rnd 7: 3 sc, inc 1 st, 4 sc. (9 sts)
Rnd 8: 4 sc, inc 1 st, 4 sc. (10 sts)
Rnd 9: * 1 sc, inc 1 st *, rep from * to * 4 times more. (15 sts)
Rnd 10: 8 sc, inc 1 st, 6 sc. (16 sts)
Rnd 11: 8 sc, inc 1 st, 1 sc, inc 1 st, 5 sc. (18 sts)
Rnd 12: 1 sc in every st of the prev rnd. (18 sts)

Break the working yarn, and secure the end.

SMALL CLAWS (MAKE 2)

Work in rounds. Begin every round with 1 chain, and end every round with 1 sl-st into the first stitch of the round. Do not turn work.

Rnd 1: In Signal Red, work 3 sc into an adjustable magic ring. (3 sts)
Rnd 2: 1 sc in every st of the prev rnd. (3 sts)
Rnd 3: Inc 1 st each 3 times in all. (6 sts)
Rnd 4: 2 sc, inc 1 st, 3 sc. (7 sts)
Rnd 5: 3 sc, inc 1 st, 3 sc. (8 sts)
Rnd 6: 4 sc, inc 1 st, 3 sc. (9 sts)

In the following rnd, the last rnd of the big claws will be joined with the last rnd of the small claws:

Rnd 7: 5 sc (small claws), 1 sc into the 11th st of Rnd 12 of the big claws, 17 sc into the remaining sts of Rnd 12, 1 sc into the 6th st of Rnd 6 of the small claws, 3 sc. (27 sts)

Rnd 8: 1 sc in every st of the prev rnd. (27 sts)

Rnd 9: * 7 sc, dec 1 st *, rep from * to * 2 times more. (24 sts)

Rnd 10: 11 sc, dec 1 st, 11 sc. (23 sts)

Rnd 11: Dec 1 st, 10 sc, dec 1 st, 9 sc. (21 sts)

Rnd 12: 1 sc in every st of the prev rnd. (21 sts)

Stuff the claws with polyester fiberfill.

Rnd 13: 10 sc, dec 1 st, 9 sc. (20 sts)

Rnd 14: Dec 1 st, 16 sc, dec 1 st. (18 sts)

Rnd 15: 1 sc in every st of the prev rnd. (18 sts)

Rnd 16: 9 sc, dec 1 st, 7 sc. (17 sts)

Rnd 17: Dec 1 st, 15 sc. (16 sts)

Stuff the remainder of the claws with polyester fiberfill.

Rnd 18: 7 sc, dec 1 st each twice, 5 sc. (14 sts)

Rnd 19: Dec 1 st each 7 times in all. (7 sts)

Rnd 20: * 1 sl-st, skip 1 st *, rep from * to * 2 times more, 1 sl-st. (4 sts)

Break the working yarn, and secure the end.

Close the small remaining opening between the two claws in whip-stitch.

CONNECTORS (MAKE 2)

Work in rounds. Begin every round with 1 chain, and end every round with 1 sl-st into the first stitch of the round. Do not turn work.

Rnd 1: In Signal Red, work 6 sc into an adjustable magic ring. (6 sts)

Rnd 2: * 1 sc, inc 1 st *, rep from * to * 2 times more. (9 sts)

Rnds 3–5: 1 sc in every st of the prev rnd. (9 sts)

Rnd 6: Inc 1 st, 8 sc. (10 sts)

Rnd 7: 1 sc, inc 1 st, 8 sc. (11 sts)

Rnd 8: Inc 1 st, 1 sc, inc 1 st, 8 sc. (13 sts)

Rnd 9: 1 sc in every st of the prev rnd. (13 sts)

Break the working yarn, and secure the end.

LEGS (MAKE 8)

Work in rounds. Begin every rnd with ch1, and end every rnd with 1 sl-st into the 1st st of the rnd. Do not turn work. Hold work WS facing out.

Rnd 1: In Signal Red, work 3 sc into an adjustable magic ring. (3 sts)

Rnd 2: 1 sc in every st of the prev rnd. (3 sts)

Rnd 3: Inc 1 st each 3 times in all. (6 sts)

Rnds 4–10: 1 sc in every st of the prev rnd. (6 sts)

Break the working yarn, and secure the end.

FINISHING

Stuff the connector with polyester fiberfill, and sew the opening on the bias to the last 4 rnds of the claws in mattress stitch, so that the connector ends up on the same side as the small scissors.

Now sew the magic ring of the connector to the side of the body at the level of Rnd 25 of the body. Repeat the steps for the second claw.

Cut 8 pieces of pipe cleaner or craft wire to a length slightly longer than the legs of the lobster. Slide the pipe cleaner into the leg, and sew the last rnd to the side of the body in mattress stitch. Push the protruding piece of the pipe cleaner through the appropriate stitch of the body.

COFFEE BREAK AND FOUR-O'CLOCK TEA

It's teatime! Or would you prefer coffee? Either way, in the following chapter, you will find what your heart desires! Combine your Earl Grey or your favorite roast with a piece of yummy layer cake, cupcakes, or French macarons, all served on your very own crocheted étagère. What an eye candy (pun intended)! For a trendy in-between snack, try Kawaii-style cake pops, too.

DESSERT STAND

MATERIALS

- crochet hook, 2.5 mm (US B-1 or C-2)
- tapestry needle
- Schachenmayr Catania (100% cotton): 1 skein (1.75 oz/50 g) each in Lilac (Flieder) and White (Weiß)
- Schewe Baumwolle-Classic (100% cotton): 1 skein (1.75 oz/ 50 g) in 0025 Dark Pink (Dunkel-rosa)
- polyester fiberfill
- 2 toilet paper cores
- thin wooden dowel
- cardboard
- compass

INSTRUCTIONS

FOOT

Work the foot in Dark Pink from the instructions for the foot for the ice cream bowl (see page 93) and cut the piece of toilet paper core the same way. Stuff the foot with polyester fiberfill.

LOWER PLATE

In Dark Pink, crochet a circle from Basic pattern (Rnds 1–20, see page 23).

Break the working yarn, and secure the end.

Make a second circle in Lilac from the instructions for the lower plate. Adjust the compass to the radius of the lower plate by inserting the compass needle centered into the magic ring and then extending the compass leg to the outer edge of the crocheted circle. Using this radius, draw a circle onto a piece of cardboard. Cut out the circle, and insert it between the two crocheted circles, which should be placed on the cardboard with their RS outward, the Lilac-colored circle on top. In Dark Pink, crochet both circles together with 1 rnd of sl-sts, on the Lilac-colored circle working through the back loop of the stitch only.

UPPER PLATE

Crochet 2 circles (Basic circle pattern, Rnds 1–15, see page 23), 1 in Dark Pink, and 1 in White. For this plate, too, prepare a cardboard circle (the same way as for the lower plate), and place it between the crocheted circles. Here, the White circle should be on top. Crochet both together in White as described above.

CONNECTOR

Work in rounds. Begin every round with 1 chain, and end every round with 1 sl-st into the first stitch of the round. Do not turn work.

Rnd 1: In Dark Pink, crochet a chain of 24, and join the crocheted chain into the round with 1 sl-st into the first stitch of the chain. Chain 1, 1 sc into every chain.
Rnds 2–21: 1 sc in every st of the prev rnd. (24 sts)

Break the working yarn, and secure the end.

Cut a piece of toilet paper core to the length of the connector, and insert the core. Additionally, stuff the piece with polyester fiberfill.

HANDLE

Work in spiral rounds. At the end of the round, do not join with 1 sl-st into the 1st st of the rnd. Do not turn work.

Rnd 1: In Dark Pink, work 6 sc into an adjustable magic ring. (6 sts)
Rnds 2–14: 1 sc in every st of the prev rnd. (6 sts)

Break the working yarn, and secure the end.

FINISHING

Sew the foot to the center of the pink side of the lower plate in mattress stitch. Then sew one opening of the connector to the center of the Lilac-colored side of the lower plate in mattress stitch, the other opening to the center of the Dark Pink side of the upper plate. Insert the wooden dowel into the crocheted handle, and slide the protruding portion of the dowel on the White side of the upper plate through the magic ring. Sew the handle to the upper plate in mattress stitch.

MATERIALS

FOR THE CHEESECAKE:

- Schachenmayr Catania (100% cotton): 1 skein (1.75 oz/50 g) each in Tan (Taupe), Creme, and Mimosa (Mimose), and about 0.5 oz (15 g) in White (Weiß)

FOR THE CHERRY-CHOCOLATE LAYER CAKE:

- Schachenmayr Catania (100% cotton): 1 skein (1.75 oz/50 g) each in Coffee (Kaffee), Freesia (Fresie), and White (Weiß)
- 1 cherry-red colored wooden bead

FOR BOTH:

- crochet hook, 2.5 mm (US B-1 or C-2)
- tapestry needle
- sewing needle and thread
- polyester fiberfill
- cardboard

INSTRUCTIONS

Work in rows. At the end of the row, chain 1, and turn work. Colors listed first are for the cheesecake, colors in parentheses for the cherry-chocolate layer cake.

BOTTOM

Row 1: In Tan (Coffee), crochet a chain of 15, 1 sc into the 2nd chain from the hook, 1 sc in every following ch. (14 sts)
Row 2: Dec 1 st, 10 sc, dec 1 st. (12 sts)
Row 3: 1 sc in every st of the prev row. (12 sts)

Row 4: Dec 1 st, 8 sc, dec 1 st. (10 sts)
Row 5: 1 sc in every st of the prev row. (10 sts)
Row 6: Dec 1 st, 6 sc, dec 1 st. (8 sts)
Row 7: 1 sc in every st of the prev row. (8 sts)
Row 8: Dec 1 st, 4 sc, dec 1 st. (6 sts)
Row 9: 1 sc in every st of the prev row. (6 sts)
Row 10: Dec 1 st, 2 sc, dec 1 st. (4 sts)
Row 11: 1 sc in every st of the prev row. (4 sts)
Row 12: Dec 1 st each twice. (2 sts)
Row 13: Dec 1 st. (1 st) Chain 1, and turn work.

Do not break the working yarn, but use it to continue working in rounds around the triangle. Begin every round with 1 chain, and end every round with 1 sl-st into the first stitch of the round. Do not turn work.

Rnd 1: Work bpsc edging around the triangle: 13 bpsc at the sides where the row ends are, and 12 sc along Row 1 of the bottom. (38 sts)
Rnd 2: 1 sc in every st of the prev rnd. (38 sts)

Change color to Creme (Freesia).

Rnds 3–6 (cheesecake): 1 sc in every st of the prev rnd. (38 sts)
Rnd 3 (layer cake): Working through the back loop of the st only: 1 sc in every st of the prev rnd. (38 sts)

Change color to White.

Rnd 4: Working through the back loop of the st only: 1 sc in every st of the prev rnd. (38 sts)
Rnds 5–6: 1 sc in every st of the prev rnd. (38 sts)

Break the working yarn, and secure the end.

TOP OF THE CAKE

For the cheesecake (layer cake), work Rows 1–13 from the instructions for the bottom in Mimosa (Freesia).

FINISHING

Cut two cardboard triangles to the size of the top of the cake, and place one cardboard triangle into the cake bottom. Stuff the slice of cake with polyester fiberfill. Now crochet the top of the cake together with the last rnd of the cake bottom.

CHEESECAKE

With the top of the cake facing away from you, sl-st the two pieces together in Mimosa.

Break the working yarn, and secure the end.

CREAM PIPING

In White, crochet a chain of 17, work 5 dc into the 4th chain from the hook. Now work 1 pop-dc, by inserting the hook into the 17th chain instead of into the first one of the 5 dc, 1 sl-st, * 1 pop-dc, 1 sl-st *, rep from * to * 5 times more. This has yielded 7 pop-dc with accompanying 1 sl-st in-between. Now sew the cream piping to the top of the cheesecake.

Break the working yarn, and secure the end.

LAYER CAKE

Looking from above onto the top of the cake, now crochet the top of the cake together with the bottom in White in sc.

Break the working yarn, and secure the end.

DOLLOP OF CREAM

Work in rounds. Begin every round with 1 chain, and end every round with 1 sl-st into the first stitch of the round. Do not turn work.

Rnd 1: In White, work 6 sc into an adjustable magic ring. (6 sts)
Rnd 2: 1 pop-dc (here only consisting of 3 dc) in every st of the prev rnd. (6 sts)

Break the working yarn, and secure the end.

Using sewing thread in a matching color, sew the cherry-red wooden bead to the dollop of cream. Sew the dollop of cream to the narrow end of the slice of cake.

CREAM PIPING

With the narrow end of the slice of cake facing you, join new working yarn to the right corner st of the outside edge of the slice of cake, and work [3 sc in 1 st] up to next corner st.

Break the working yarn, and secure the end.

MINI TARTLET

MATERIALS

- crochet hook, 2.5 mm (US B-1 or C-2)
- tapestry needle
- sewing needle and thread
- Schachenmayr Catania (100% cotton): 1 skein (1.75 oz/50 g) each in Orchid (Orchidee) and Freesia (Fresie), 0.5 oz (15 g) each in Coffee (Kaffee) and Creme
- polyester fiberfill
- toilet paper core
- cherry-red seed beads (Rocailles)

INSTRUCTIONS

In Orchid, crochet a circle from Basic pattern (Rnds 1–5, see page 23).

Rnd 6: 1 bpsc in every st of the prev rnd. (30 sts)

Rnds 7–9: 1 sc in every st of the prev rnd. (30 sts)

Rnd 10: 1 bpsc in every st of the prev rnd. (30 sts)

Change color to Freesia.

Rnds 11 and 12: 1 sc in every st of the prev rnd. (30 sts)

Rnd 13: 1 bpsc in every st of the prev rnd. (30 sts)

Change color to Coffee.

Rnd 14: 1 sc in every st of the prev rnd. (30 sts)

Rnd 15: Working through the back loop of the st only, 1 sc in every st of the prev rnd. (30 sts)

Cut a piece of toilet paper core to the length of the crocheted tube, and place it inside. Stuff the piece with polyester fiberfill.

Rnd 16: Working through the back loop of the st only, * 3 sc, dec 1 st *, rep from * to * 5 times more. (24 sts)

Rnd 17: * 2 sc, dec 1 st *, rep from * to * 5 times more. (18 sts)

Rnd 18: * 1 sc, dec 1 st *, rep from * to * 5 times more. (12 sts)

Rnd 19: Dec 1 st each, 6 times in all. (6 sts)

Rnd 20: * Skip 1 st, 1 sl-st *, rep from * to * 2 times more. (3 sts)

Break the working yarn, and secure the end.

PIPED CREAM RING

In Creme, crochet a chain of 20, and join the chain into the round with 1 sl-st into the first chain.

Rnd 1: * 1 pop-dc, 1 sl-st *, rep from * to * 9 times more.

Break the yarn, leaving a long tail, and secure the end.

Place the piped cream ring in the center of the top of the tartlet, and sew it on. Additionally decorate the piped cream ring by sewing on seed beads.

BLUEBERRY PIE

MATERIALS

- crochet hook, 2.5 mm (US B-1 or C-2)
- tapestry needle
- Schachenmayr Catania (100% cotton): 1 skein (1.75 oz/50 g) each in Raffia (Bast) and Regatta, and about 0.5 oz (15 g) in Marine
- polyester fiberfill

INSTRUCTIONS

CRUST

In Raffia, crochet a circle from Basic pattern (Rnds 1–12, see page 23).

Rnd 13: 1 bpsc in every st of the prev rnd. (72 sts)
Rnds 14 and 15: 1 sc in every st of the prev rnd. (72 sts)

Break the working yarn, and secure the end.

BLUEBERRY FILLING

In Regatta, work Rnds 1–11 from the instructions for the crust.

Change color to Raffia.

Rnd 12: Working through the back loop of the st only: * 10 sc, inc 1 st *, rep from * to * 5 times more. (72 sts)

Do not break the working yarn.

CRIMPED EDGE

Place the filling RS up onto the last rnd of the bottom, and crochet both circles together in sc. Shortly before completing the round, stuff the pie with polyester fiberfill.

Rnd 1: Ch3 to replace the first dc, 2 dc into the 1st st, and from here on, work [3 dc in 1 st] to the end of the rnd.

Break the working yarn, and secure the end.

LATTICE TOP

Work in rows. At the end of every row, chain 1, and turn work.

Row 1: In Raffia, crochet a chain of 23, work 1 sc into the 2nd chain from the hook, 1 sc in every following ch. (22 sts)
Row 2: 1 sc in every st of the prev row. (22 sts)

Break the working yarn, and secure the end.

Work 3 more strips the same way, as well as 2 longer strips with a stitch count of 25 sts (starting with a beginning chain of 26).

BLUEBERRIES (MAKE 2)

Work in rounds. Begin every round with 1 chain, and end every round with 1 sl-st into the first stitch of the round. Do not turn work.

Rnd 1: In Marine, work 6 sc into an adjustable magic ring. (6 sts)
Rnds 2 and 3: 1 sc in every st of the prev rnd. (6 sts)

Stuff the blueberry with a very small amount of polyester fiberfill.

Rnd 4: * Skip 1 st, 1 sl-st *, rep from * to * 2 times more. (3 sts)

Break the working yarn, and secure the end.

FINISHING

Place one of the longer (25 sts) strips sideways over the blueberry filling so that it goes right over the magic ring, and sew the two narrow ends of the strip to the sts of Rnd 12. Now place the second long strip onto the filling at a 90-degree angle to the first one, and likewise sew it to the sts of Rnd 12. Parallel and to the left and right of the first middle strip, sew on 2 of the shorter (22 sts) strips (side strips). Thread the two remaining strips always over an already sewn-on side strip, under the middle strip, and over the other side strip, and sew the ends to Rnd 12, too.

Sew on the two blueberries in the center.

MATERIALS

- crochet hook, 2.5 mm (US B-1 or C-2)
- tapestry needle
- sewing needle and thread
- Schachenmayr Catania (100% cotton): 1 skein (1.75 oz/50 g) each in Soft Apricot, Orchid (Orchidee), Coffee (Kaffee), Fuchsia, Cyclam, White (Weiß), Lilac (Flieder), 0.5 oz (15 g) each in Kiwi, Freesia (Fresie), Pastel Blue (Hellblau), Sun (Sonne), Tangerine (Mandarine)
- polyester fiberfill
- 4 cake pop sticks
- 8 wooden beads in different colors
- cardboard
- adhesive tape
- compass

INSTRUCTIONS

UNDERSIDE OF THE BOTTOM TIER

In Soft Apricot, crochet a circle from Basic pattern (Rnds 1–14, see page 23).

Adjust the compass to the radius of the crocheted circle by inserting the compass needle into the magic ring and then extending the compass leg to the outer edge of the crocheted circle. Using this radius, draw a circle on the cardboard, and cut it out.

Rnd 15: 1 bpsc in every st of the prev rnd. (84 sts)

Rnd 16: Working through the front loop of the stitch only: * 1 sl-st, 1 hdc, 2 dc, 1 hdc, 1 sl-st *, rep from * to * 13 times more. (84 sts)

Change color to Orchid.

Rnd 17: Working through the back loop of the sts of Rnd 15 only: 1 sc in every st of the prev rnd (84 sts), chain 1, and turn work once (here only).

Now place the cardboard circle inside the crocheted piece.

Rnds 18–23: 1 sc in every st of the prev rnd. (84 sts)

Break the working yarn, and secure the end.

Cut a strip, about 1.2 in (3 cm) wide and 16.1 in (41 cm) long, from cardboard. Place the cardboard strip at the inside edge of the cake with ends overlapping. Tape the ends together with a piece of adhesive tape.

TOPSIDE OF THE BOTTOM TIER

In Coffee, work Rnds 1–14 from Basic pattern for the circle. Now sl-st the last rnd of the topside together with the last rnd of the underside sl-st. Make sure to insert the hook on the topside piece only through the back loop, and on the underside piece, only through the front loop of the sts. A few sts before the end of the rnd, stuff the bottom tier of the cake with polyester fiberfill.

MIDDLE TIER OF CAKE

Now, in Soft Apricot, work Rnds 1–10 from Basic pattern for the circle. Change color to Fuchsia.

Rnd 11: 1 bpsc in every st of the prev rnd. (60 sts) Chain 1, and turn work.

From here on, continue in rows. End every row with ch1 and 1 sl-st into the 1st st of the row, and turn work.

Rows 12–19: 1 sc in every st of the prev row. (60 sts)

Break the working yarn, and secure the end.

Cut a strip, about 1.6 in (4 cm) wide and 12.2 in (31 cm) long, from cardboard. Place the cardboard strip around the inside edge of the middle tier of the cake with ends overlapping. Tape the ends together with a piece of adhesive tape, stuff the middle tier of the cake with polyester fiberfill, and sew the last row centered onto the coffee-colored topside of the bottom tier of the cake in mattress stitch.

TOP TIER OF CAKE

In Coffee, work Rnds 1–6 from Basic pattern for the circle (see page 23).

Change color to Cyclam.

Rnds 7–15: 1 bpsc in every st of the prev rnd. (36 sts)

Break the working yarn, and secure the end.

Cut a strip, about 1.6 in (4 cm) wide and 6.7 in (17 cm) long, from cardboard. Place the cardboard strip around the inside edge with ends overlapping. Tape the ends together with a piece of adhesive tape. Stuff the top tier of the cake with polyester fiberfill, and sew the last rnd centered onto the topside of the middle tier of the cake (Soft Apricot) in mattress stitch.

CANDLE (MAKE 4)

Work 1 candle each in Lilac, Freesia, Kiwi, and Pastel Blue:

Work in rounds. Begin every round with 1 chain, and end every round with 1 sl-st into the first stitch of the round. Do not turn work.

Rnd 1: In Lilac (or Freesia, Kiwi, or Pastel Blue, respectively), work 6 sc into an adjustable magic ring. (6 sts)
Rnd 2: Working through the back loop of the st only: 1 sc in every st of the prev rnd. (6 sts)
Rnds 3–10: 1 sc in every st of the prev rnd. (6 sts)

Break the working yarn, and secure the end.

FLAME (MAKE 4)
Rnd 1: In Tangerine, work 6 sc into an adjustable magic ring (6 sts), 1 sl-st into the 1st st, chain 1. Do not turn work.

Change color to Sun.

Rnd 2: 1 sc, 2 hdc into the same st, 3 dc into the same st, 2 hdc into the same st, 2 sc. (10 sts)

Break the working yarn, and secure the end.

Sew each flame onto the magic ring of a candle.

FINISHING
Sew the 8 wooden beads onto the topside of the middle tier of the cake.

WIGGLY CREAM PIPING ON BOTTOM TIER OF CAKE
Join new working yarn in White to the next-to-last rnd on the Coffee-colored topside of the layer, and work 1 rnd wiggly lines, working from the outside in (toward the center of the cake): * [3 dc in 1 st] (replacing the very first dc with ch3). Then work 1 dc into 1st of this rnd, before again working [3 dc in 1 st] in a rnd closer to the center. Again, work 1 dc in 1 st *, and rep

from * to * to the beginning of the rnd. Work 1 sl-st into the 3rd ch of the ch3 replacing the first dc.

Break the working yarn, and secure the end.

Embroider wavy lines on the side of the middle tier of the cake in chain stitch, staggering lines in Lilac and Kiwi.

EDGES
Join new working yarn in Lilac (or Violet) to the back loop of a st of the last rnd of the topside of the top tier of the cake (or the topside of the middle tier of the cake, respectively), and work 1 rnd as follows: ch2, 1 sc into the 1st st, 2 sl-sts, * ch2, 1 sc into the same st as the last sl-st had been worked, 2 sl-st *, rep from * to * to the 1st st of the rnd, and then join into the round with 1 sl-st into the 1st st.

Finish by inserting a cake pop stick into each candle. Push the still protruding part of the stick into a stitch of the topside of the top tier of the cake, and sew on the last rnd of the candle in mattress stitch.

"KAWAII" CAKE POPS

MATERIALS

- crochet hook, 2.5 mm (US B-1 or C-2)
- tapestry needle
- sewing needle and black thread
- Schachenmayr Catania (100% cotton): 0.5 oz (15 g) in color of choice (here, shown in Anise [Anis], Cyclam, and Lilac [Flieder]), and about 0.5 oz (15 g) in Black (Schwarz)
- polyester fiberfill
- cake pop sticks
- pink craft felt
- craft glue

INSTRUCTIONS

Work in spiral rounds. At the end of the round, do not join with 1 sl-st into the 1st st of the rnd. Do not turn work.

BOTTOM

Rnd 1: In color of your choice, work 6 sc into an adjustable magic ring. (6 sts)

Rnd 2: Inc 1 st each 6 times in all. (12 sts)

Rnd 3: * 1 sc, inc 1 st *, rep from * to * 5 times more. (18 sts)

Rnd 4: * 2 sc, inc 1 st *, rep from * to * 5 times more. (24 sts)

Rnds 5–7: 1 sc in every st of the prev rnd. (24 sts)

Stuff the cake pop with polyester fiberfill.

Rnd 8: * 2 sc, dec 1 st *, rep from * to * 5 times more. (18 sts)

Rnd 9: * 1 sc, dec 1 st *, rep from * to * 5 times more. (12 sts)

Rnd 10: Dec 1 st each, 6 times in all. (6 sts)

Rnd 11: * Skip 1 st, 1 sl-st *, rep from * to * 2 times more. (3 sts)

Break the working yarn, and secure the end.

Using crochet yarn in Black, embroider 2 dots for eyes with French knots, and after this, a mouth in black sewing thread.

Cut two small ovals from pink craft felt, and glue them onto the cake pop at the sides below the eyes. Insert the cake pop stick through the opening of the last rnd.

MATERIALS

- crochet hook, 2.5 mm (US B-1 or C-2)
- tapestry needle
- sewing needle and thread
- Schachenmayr Catania (100% cotton): 1 skein (1.75 oz/50 g) each in Violet (Violett) and Soft Apricot, and 0.5 oz (15 g) in Cyclam (for chocolate version, 1 skein each in Coffee and Cyclam)
- polyester fiberfill
- pink seed beads (Rocailles)
- craft felt
- glue

INSTRUCTIONS

Work in rounds. Begin every round with 1 chain, and end every round with 1 sl-st into the first stitch of the round. Do not turn work.

In Soft Apricot, crochet a chain of 24, and join into the round with 1 sl-st into the first chain.

Rnd 1: 1 sc into every ch. (24 sts)
Rnd 2: 1 sc in every st of the prev rnd. (24 sts)

Change color to Violet.

Rnds 3 and 4: 1 sc in every st of the prev rnd. (24 sts)
Rnd 5: 1 sc, inc 1 st, * 3 sc, inc 1 st *, rep from * to * 4 times more, 2 sc. (30 sts)
Rnd 6: * 4 sc, inc 1 st *, rep from * to * 5 times more. (36 sts)
Rnd 7: 2 sc, inc 1 st, * 5 sc, inc 1 st *, rep from * to * 4 times more, 3 sc. (42 sts)

Rnd 8: * 6 sc, inc 1 st *, rep from * to * 5 times more. (48 sts)
Rnds 9–11: 1 sc in every st of the prev rnd. (48 sts)

Change color to Soft Apricot.

Rnd 12: 1 sc in every st of the prev rnd. (48 sts)
Rnd 13: * 6 sc, dec 1 st *, rep from * to * 5 times more. (42 sts)
Rnd 14: 3 sc, dec 1 st, * 5 sc, dec 1 st *, rep from * to * 4 times more, 2 sc. (36 sts)
Rnd 15: * 4 sc, dec 1 st *, rep from * to * 5 times more. (30 sts)
Rnd 16: 1 sc, dec 1 st, * 3 sc, dec 1 st * rep from * to * 4 times more, 2 sc. (24 sts)

Break the yarn, leaving a long tail, and secure the end.

Place the first and last rnd of the donut on top of each other, and, using the long tail, sew both together in whipstitch. Stuff the ring with polyester fiberfill as you go.

In Cyclam, embroider a wavy stripe in chain stitch, and then sew beads to the top in a staggered fashion.

CHOCOLOATE DONUT WITH PINK FROSTING

In Coffee, work Rnds 1–3 of the donut.

Change color to Cyclam.

Work Rnds 4–9 of the donut.

Rnd 10: Working alternatingly in Cyclam and Coffee, * 3 sc in Cyclam, 3 sc in Coffee *, rep from * to * 7 times more. (48 sts)

Change color to Coffee.

Work Rnds 11–16 as described above.

Cut two small hearts from pink craft felt, glue them onto the donut, and sew a bead to each one of them. If desired, sew on additional beads.

MACARONS

MATERIALS

- crochet hook, 2.5 mm (US B-1 or C-2)
- tapestry needle
- Schachenmayr Catania (100% cotton): 1 skein (1.75 oz/50 g) in a bright color A (for instance, Cyclam or Capri), and about 0.5 oz (15 g) in a pastel-colored shade B (for instance, Pink or Pastel Blue)
- polyester fiberfill

INSTRUCTIONS

In color A, crochet a circle from Basic pattern (Rnds 1–4, see page 23).

Rnd 5: 1 sc in every st of the prev rnd. (24 sts)

Rnd 6: * 1 hdc through the front loop of the stitch only, 1 hdc through the back loop of the stitch only *, rep from * to * 11 times more. (24 sts)

Rnd 7: 1 bpsc in every st of the prev rnd. (24 sts)

Change color to B.

Rnds 8 and 9: 1 sc in every st of the prev rnd. (24 sts)

Change color to A.

Rnd 10: 1 fpsc in every st of the prev rnd. (24 sts)

Rnd 11: Now work 1 hdc in every st of Rnd 9. (24 sts)

Rnd 12: * 1 sc through the back loop of the stitch only, 1 sc through the front loop of the stitch only *, rep from * to * 11 times more. (24 sts)

Stuff the macaron with polyester fiberfill.

Rnd 13: * 2 sc, dec 1 st *, rep from * to * 5 times more. (18 sts)

Rnd 14: * 1 sc, dec 1 st *, rep from * to * 5 times more. (12 sts)

Rnd 15: Dec 1 st each, 6 times in all. (6 sts)

Rnd 16: * Skip 1 st, 1 sl-st *, rep from * to * 2 times more. (3 sts)

Break the working yarn, and secure the end.

CUPCAKES FOR EVERY TASTE

MATERIALS

- crochet hook, 2.5 mm (US B-1 or C-2)
- tapestry needle
- polyester fiberfill

BUTTERCREAM CUPCAKE (C1)

- Schachenmayr Catania (100% cotton): 1 skein (1.75 oz/50 g) each in Kiwi, Sun (Sonne), and Orchid (Orchidee)

BUTTERCREAM CUPCAKE WITH CANDIED CHERRY (C2)

- Schachenmayr Catania (100% cotton): 1 skein (1.75 oz/50 g) each in Pastel Blue (Hellblau), Soft Apricot, and Orchid (Orchidee), and 0.5 oz (15 g) each in Burgundy (Weinrot) and Raspberry (Himbeer)
- ONline Linie 165 Sandy (100% cotton): 0.5 oz (15 g) in 17 Pink (Rosa)

LEMON CUPCAKE (C3)

- Schachenmayr Catania (100% cotton): 1 skein (1.75 oz/50 g) each in Coffee (Kaffee) and Mimosa (Mimose), and about 0.5 oz (15 g) each in Sun (Sonne), Creme, White (Weiß), and Tangerine (Mandarine)

RASPBERRY CUPCAKE (C4)

- Schachenmayr Catania (100% cotton): 1 skein (1.75 oz/50 g) each in Coffee (Kaffee) and Orchid (Orchidee), and about 0.5 oz (15 g) each in Creme and Cyclam

CUPCAKE WITH BLUE ICING (C5)

- Schachenmayr Catania (100% cotton): 1 skein (1.75 oz/50 g) each in Lilac (Flieder), Soft Apricot, Peacock (Pfau), and about 0.5 oz (15 g) in Freesia (Fresie)

INSTRUCTIONS

BOTTOM (ALL CUPCAKE VARIETIES)

In Kiwi (Pastel Blue, Coffee, or Lilac), work 1 circle from Basic pattern (Rnds 1–6, see page 23).

Rnd 7: 1 bpsc in every st of the prev rnd. (36 sts)

Rnd 8: 1 sc in every st of the prev rnd. (36 sts)

Rnds 9–12: Ch3 (replaces the first dc), 1 fpdc,* 1 hdc, 1 fpdc *, rep from * to * 17 times more. (36 sts)

Break the working yarn, and secure the end.

UPPER PART OF THE CUPCAKE (ALL VARIETIES EXCEPT C3 AND C4)

Join new working yarn in Soft Apricot (or in Sun for C1) to the first stitch of Rnd 12 of the bottom, and work as follows:

Rnd 1: Working through the back loop of the st only, 1 sc in every st of the prev rnd. (36 sts)

Rnds 2 and 3: 1 sc in every st of the prev rnd. (36 sts)

(For C1: Change color to Orchid.)

Rnd 4: * 4 sc, dec 1 st *, rep from * to * 5 times more. (30 sts)

Rnd 5: 1 sc in every st of the prev rnd. (30 sts)

Rnd 6: * 3 sc, dec 1 st *, rep from * to * 5 times more. (24 sts)

Rnd 7: 1 sc in every st of the prev rnd. (24 sts)

Stuff the cupcake with polyester fiberfill.

Rnd 8: * 2 sc, dec 1 st *, rep from * to * 5 times more. (18 sts)

Rnd 9: * 1 sc, dec 1 st *, rep from * to * 5 times more. (12 sts)

Rnd 10: Dec 1 st each, 6 times in all. (6 sts)

Rnd 11: * Skip 1 st, 1 sl-st *, rep from * to * 2 times more. (3 sts)

Break the working yarn, and secure the end.

For C3, work icing in Mimosa. Work decreases not by crocheting sts together, but instead by skipping 1 st each. Additionally, work all dec rnds directly one after another, meaning skip Rnds 5 and 7 of the instructions for the upper part.

For C4, work all rnds in Orchid and through the back loop of the stitch only.

CUPCAKE EDGING

PAPER BAKING CUPS (C1, C2, C5)

With the top part of the cupcake facing you, join new working yarn in bottom color to Rnd 12 of the bottom, and work through the back loop of the sts of Rnd 12: * ch2, 1 sl-st into the next st *, rep from * to * 17 times. 1 sl-st into the 1st st of the rnd.

Break the working yarn, and secure the end.

ICING (C3 AND C4)

Still with the top part of the cupcake facing you, join new working yarn in appropriate color for top part of cupcake to Rnd 1 of top part, and work as follows:

Chain 3 (counts as first dc), 4 dc into the 1st st, skip 1 st, 1 sl-st, * 5 dc into the same st, skip 1 st, 1 sl-st *, rep from * to * 10 times more. 1 sl-st into the 1st st of the rnd.

Break the working yarn, and secure the end.

BUTTERCREAM TOPPINGS

C1: Now with the top part of the cupcake facing away from you, join new working yarn in Orchid to the first stitch of the first Orchid-colored rnd. Work in spiral rnds: 1 sc in every st. At the end of the rnd, proceed to the next rnd without sl-st and without ch. Instead, work 1 sc between rnds.

C2: Looking from above onto the last rnd of the cupcake, join new working yarn in Raspberry between Rnds 9 and 10 of the top part of the cupcake. Work 1 rnd wavy lines by working between the two rnds (Rnds 9 and 10) * 3 dc in 1 st (replacing the very first dc with ch3), and then 1 dc in 1st of Rnd 10, before again working 3 dc in 1 st from the top down toward Rnd 9. Work 1 dc in 1st of this rnd *, and rep from * to * to the beginning of the rnd. Work 1 sl-st into the 3rd ch of the ch3 replacing the first dc.

Break the working yarn, and secure the end.

Repeat these steps in Orchid between Rnds 7 and 8, and in Pink between Rnds 4 and 6 (here, always work 3 dc in 2 sts when you crochet between rnds).

These wavy lines are not wavy enough for you? No problem—depending on your preferences, work 4 or more dc in the st between rnds, and, if needed, also 3 dc into the st worked within a rnd.

CANDIED CHERRY (C2 AND C5)

Rnd 1: In Burgundy (or in Freesia for C5), work 6 sc into an adjustable magic ring. (6 sts)

Rnd 2: Inc 1 st each 6 times in all. (12 sts)

Rnds 3 and 4: 1 sc in every st of the prev rnd. (12 sts)

Stuff the cherry with polyester fiberfill.

Rnd 5: Dec 1 st each, 6 times in all. (6 sts)

Rnd 6: * Skip 1 st, 1 sl-st *, rep from * to * 2 times more. (3 sts)

Break the working yarn, and secure the end.

Sew the cherry onto the cupcake (C2).

BLUE ICING FOR C5

Work in rounds. Begin every rnd with ch1, and end every rnd with 1 sl-st into the 1st st of the rnd. Do not turn work.

Rnd 1: In Peacock, work 6 sc into an adjustable magic ring. (6 sts)

Rnd 2: Inc 1 st each 6 times in all. (12 sts)

Rnd 3: * 1 sc, inc 1 st *, rep from * to * 5 times more. (18 sts)

Rnd 4: * 2 sc, inc 1 st *, rep from * to * 5 times more. (24 sts)

Rnd 5: 1 sc, inc 1 st, * 3 sc, inc 1 st *, rep from * to * 4 times more, 2 sc. (30 sts)

Rnd 6: Ch4, 1 sl-st into the 2nd chain from the hook, 2 sc, skip 1 st, 1 sl-st into the 2nd stitch of the previous rnd, 1 sc, ch6, 1 sc into the 2nd chain from the hook, 2 sc, 2 hdc, 1 sl-st into the next st of the previous rnd, 2 sc, ch3, 1 sl-st into the 2nd chain from the hook, 1 sc, 1 sl-st into the next st of the previous rnd, 1 sc, ch6, 1 sl-st into the 2nd chain from the hook, 1 sc, 3 hdc, 1 sl-st into the next st of the previous rnd, 2 sc, ch3, 1 sc into the 2nd chain from the hook, 1 sc, 1 sl-st into the next st of the previous rnd, 2 sc, ch5, 1 sc into the 2nd chain from the hook, 3 sc, 1 sl-st into the next st of the previous rnd, 1 sc, ch3, 1 sl-st into the 2nd chain from the hook, 1 sc, 1 sl-st into the next st of the previous rnd, 2 sc, ch4, 1 sl-st into the 2nd chain from the hook, 2 sc, 1 sl-st into the next st of the previous rnd, 2 sc, ch3, 1 sl-st

into the 2nd chain from the hook, 1 sc, 1 sl-st into the next st of the previous rnd, 3 sc, ch5, 1 sl-st into the 2nd chain from the hook, 3 sc, 1 sl-st into the next st of the previous rnd, 2 sc, ch3, 1 sl-st into the 2nd chain from the hook, 1 sc, 1 sl-st into the next st of the previous rnd. (63 sts)

Break the working yarn, and secure the end.

Sew the icing to the center of the topside of the cupcake, and then sew the candied cherry centered onto the magic ring of the icing.

DOLLOP OF CREAM (C3 AND C4)

In Creme, crochet a circle from Basic pattern (Rnds 1–3, see page 23).

Rnd 4: * 1 sc, 1 pop-dc *, rep from * to * 8 times more. (18 sts)

Break the working yarn, and secure the end.

Sew the dollop of cream centered onto the topside of the cupcake. For C4, sew 1 raspberry (for instructions, refer to page 115) centered to the dollop of cream. For C3, sew on a small lemon slice at the end, crocheted as follows:

Work in rounds. Begin every round with 1 chain, and end every round with 1 sl-st into the first stitch of the round. Do not turn work.

Rnd 1: In Mimosa, work 6 sc into an adjustable magic ring. (6 sts)

Change color to White.

Rnd 2: Inc 1 st each, 6 times in all. (12 sts)

Change color to Sun.

Rnd 3: * 1 sc, inc 1 st *, rep from * to * 5 times more. (18 sts)

Break the working yarn, and secure the end.

In Tangerine, embroider a few evenly spaced satin stitches, starting at the magic ring, toward the sts of Rnd 2.

Finally, embroider a few French knots in Sun (C3) and Cyclam (C4).

TEACUP

MATERIALS

- crochet hook, 2.5 mm (US B-1 or C-2)
- tapestry needle
- Schachenmayr Catania (100% cotton): 1 skein (1.75 oz/50 g) each in Peacock (Pfau), Creme, and Freesia (Fresie)
- polyester fiberfill

INSTRUCTIONS

In Peacock, crochet a circle from Basic pattern (Rnds 1–8, see page 23).

Rnds 9–15: In this section, work 1 sc in every st of the prev rnd. (48 sts)

Rnd 16: Working through the back loop of the st only: * 6 sc, dec 1 st *, rep from * to * 5 times more. (42 sts)

Change color to Creme.

Rnd 17: Working through the back loop of the st only: 1 sc in every st of the prev rnd. (42 sts)

Rnds 18–23: 1 sc in every st of the prev rnd. (42 sts)

Rnd 24: 2 sc, dec 1 st, * 5 sc, dec 1 st *, rep from * to * 4 times more, 3 sc. (36 sts)

Rnd 25: * 4 sc, dec 1 st *, rep from * to * 5 times more. (30 sts)

Rnd 26: 1 sc, dec 1 st, * 3 sc, dec 1 st *, rep from * to * 4 times more, 2 sc. (24 sts)

Rnd 27: * 2 sc, dec 1 st *, rep from * to * 5 times more. (18 sts)

Rnd 28: * 1 sc, dec 1 st *, rep from * to * 5 times more. (12 sts)

Rnd 29: Dec 1 st each, 6 times in all. (6 sts)

Rnd 30: * Skip 1 st, 1 sl-st *, rep from * to * 2 times more. (3 sts)

Break the working yarn, and secure the end.

Turn the Creme-colored part into the Peacock-colored part of the teacup, so that Rnd 16 forms the rim of the teacup.

Hold the teacup with the magic ring facing you, and join new working yarn in Freesia between Rnds 3 and 4. Work 1 rnd of hdc, ending the rnd with 1 sl-st into the first stitch of the round.

Break the working yarn, and secure the end.

HANDLE

Work in rounds. Begin every round with 1 chain, and end every round with 1 sl-st into the first stitch of the round. Do not turn work.

Rnd 1: In Freesia, work 6 sc into an adjustable magic ring. (6 sts)

Rnds 2–14: 1 sc in every st of the prev rnd. (6 sts)

Rnd 15: 2 sc, inc 1 st each twice, 2 sc. (8 sts)

Rnd 16: 3 sc, inc 1 st each twice, 3 sc. (10 sts)

Break the working yarn, and secure the end.

Stuff only the last 2 rnds of the handle with polyester fiberfill.

Sew Rnd 16 of the handle to the teacup in mattress stitch at the level of Rnds 11–14, so that the increases of the last rnd of the handle point downward. Sew the other end of the handle to the teacup at the level of Rnd 9.

MATERIALS

- crochet hook, 2.5 mm (US B-1 or C-2)
- tapestry needle
- Schachenmayr Catania (100% cotton): 1 skein (1.75 oz/50 g) each in Tan (Taupe) and Creme (tea bag in Tan and Creme shown on page 82), and about 0.5 oz (15 g) in Orchid (Orchidee)
- polyester fiberfill
- 1 short length of sewing thread in off-white, or a genuine tea bag string
- turquoise craft felt
- glue

INSTRUCTIONS

Work in rows. At the end of every row, join with 1 sl-st into the 1st st of the row (to form a round), chain 1, and turn work.

Row 1 (WS): In Tan, crochet a chain of 16. Join into the round with 1 sl-st into the 1st chain. Chain 1, 1 sc into every ch. (16 sts) Turn work.
Rows 2–5: 1 sc in every st of the prev row. (16 sts)

Pat the piece flat, and sew the bottom together through the sts of the crochet chain ring.

Fill the tea bag up to this point with very little polyester fiberfill.

Change color to Creme.

Rows 6–10: 1 sc in every st of the prev row. (16 sts)

Row 11: 6 sc, dec 1 st, 6 sc, dec 1 st. (14 sts)
Row 12: 5 sc, dec 1 st, 5 sc, dec 1 st. (12 sts)
Row 13: 4 sc, dec 1 st, 4 sc, dec 1 st. (10 sts)
Row 14: 3 sc, dec 1 st, 3 sc, dec 1 st. (8 sts) Chain 1, but do not turn work.
Row 15: Place the edges of the tea bag opening atop each other, and crochet them together in sc. (4 sts) Chain 1, and resume turning.
Row 16: Working through the front loop of the stitch only, 2 sc, dec 1 st. (3 sts)
Row 17: 1 sc, dec 1 st. (2 sts)
Row 18: Dec 1 st. (1 st)

Break the working yarn, and secure the end.

LABEL
Work in rows. At the end of every row, chain 1, and turn work.

Row 1: In Orchid, crochet a chain of 4. 1 sc into the 2nd chain from the hook. 1 sc in every following ch. (3 sts)
Rows 2 and 3: 1 sc in every st of the prev row. (3 sts)

Now work sc edging around the small rectangular piece, working 2 sc into 2 adjoining corners, and 1 sc into the two other corners. End the rnd with 1 sl-st into the 1st st of the rnd.

FINISHING
Cut a small heart from craft felt, and glue it onto the label. Attach the label to the tea bag with a piece of sewing thread or use an authentic tea bag string.

MATERIALS

- crochet hook, 2.5 mm (US B-1 or C-2)
- tapestry needle
- Schachenmayr Catania (100% cotton): 1 skein (1.75 oz/50 g) each in Peacock (Pfau) and Pastel Blue (Hellblau), and about 0.5 oz (15 g) in Cyclam

INSTRUCTIONS

In Pastel Blue, crochet a circle from Basic pattern (Rnds 1–4, see page 23).

Change color to Peacock.

Rnd 5: Working through the back loop of the st only, 1 sc in every st of the prev rnd. (24 sts)

Rnd 6: 1 sc, inc 1 st, * 3 sc, inc 1 st *, rep from * to * 4 times more, 2 sc. (30 sts)
Rnd 7: * 4 sc, inc 1 st *, rep from * to * 5 times more. (36 sts)
Rnd 8: 2 sc, inc 1 st, * 5 sc, inc 1 st *, rep from * to * 4 times more, 3 sc. (42 sts)
Rnd 9: * 6 sc, inc 1 st *, rep from * to * 5 times more. (48 sts)
Rnd 10: 3 sc, inc 1 st, * 7 sc, inc 1 st *, rep from * to * 4 times more, 4 sc. (54 sts)
Rnd 11: * 8 sc, inc 1 st *, rep from * to * 5 times more. (60 sts)
Rnd 12: 4 sc, inc 1 st, * 9 sc, inc 1 st *, rep from * to * 4 times more, 5 sc. (66 sts)
Rnd 13: 1 fpsc in every st of the prev rnd. (66 sts)

Break the working yarn, and secure the end.

With the wrong side of the magic ring facing up, join new working yarn in Cyclam between Rnds 4 and 5, and work 1 rnd of hdc. Join into the round with 1 sl-st into the 1st st of the rnd.

TEAPOT

MATERIALS

- crochet hook, 2.5 mm (US B-1 or C-2)
- tapestry needle
- Schachenmayr Catania (100% cotton): 1 skein (1.75 oz/50 g) each in Peacock (Pfau) and Creme, and 0.5 oz (15 g) each in Cyclam and Anise (Anis)
- polyester fiberfill

INSTRUCTIONS

TEAPOT

In Peacock, crochet a circle from Basic pattern (Rnds 1–9, see page 23).

Rnds 10–16: 1 sc in every st of the prev rnd. (54 sts)
Rnd 17: 22 sc, ch10, skip 10 sts, 22 sc. (54 sts)
Rnd 18: 22 sc, crochet 2 sts together, 6 sc into the next 6 chains, crochet 2 sts together, 22 sc. (52 sts)
Rnd 19: 20 sc, dec 1 st each twice, 4 sc, dec 1 st each twice, 20 sc. (48 sts)
Rnd 20: * 6 sc, dec 1 st *, rep from * to * 5 times more. (42 sts)
Rnd 21: 3 sc, dec 1 st, * 5 sc, dec 1 st *, rep from * to * 4 times more, 2 sc. (36 sts)
Rnds 22–32: 1 sc in every st of the prev rnd. (36 sts)

Stuff the teapot up to Rnd 29 with polyester fiberfill.

Rnd 33: * 5 sc, inc 1 st *, rep from * to * 5 times more. (42 sts)
Rnd 34: 1 sc in every st of the prev rnd. (42 sts)
Rnd 35: 3 sc, inc 1 st, * 6 sc, inc 1 st *, rep from * to * 4 times more, 3 sc. (48 sts)
Rnd 36: Working through the back loop of the stitch only, * 6 sc, dec 1 st *, rep from * to * 5 times more. (42 sts)
Rnd 37: 2 sc, dec 1 st, * 5 sc, dec 1 st *, rep from * to * 4 times more, 3 sc. (36 sts)

Change color to Creme.

Rnd 38: Working through the back loop of the st only, 1 sc in every st of the prev rnd. (36 sts)
Rnds 39–41: 1 sc in every st of the prev rnd. (36 sts)
Rnd 42: * 4 sc, dec 1 st *, rep from * to * 5 times more. (30 sts)
Rnd 43: * 3 sc, dec 1 st *, rep from * to * 5 times more. (24 sts)
Rnd 44: * 2 sc, dec 1 st *, rep from * to * 5 times more. (18 sts)
Rnd 45: * 1 sc, dec 1 st *, rep from * to * 5 times more. (12 sts)
Rnd 46: Dec 1 st each, 6 times in all. (6 sts)
Rnd 47: * Skip 1 st, 1 sl-st *, rep from * to * 2 times more. (3 sts)

Break the working yarn, and secure the end.

Turn the Creme-colored part inward into the teapot, so that Rnds 36 and 37 form the rim of the top opening.

SPOUT

Now crochet the spout onto the remaining opening, working in the round. Begin every round with 1 chain, and end every round with 1 sl-st into the first stitch of the round. Do not turn work.

Join new working yarn in Peacock to the first one of the skipped sts of Rnd 17 (23rd st), and then work:

Rnd 1: 1 sc in every one of the 10 previously skipped sts, 1 sc into the same stitch into which in Rnd 17 the first sc after the 10 chains had been worked, 10 sc into the ch10 of Rnd 17 (now from the other side), 1 sc into the same stitch into which the 22nd sc of Rnd 17 had been worked earlier. (22 sc)
Rnd 2: 10 sc, dec 1 st, 8 sc, dec 1 st. (20 sts)
Rnd 3: 4 sc, dec 1 st, 9 sc, inc 1 st, 4 sc. (20 sts)
Rnd 4: 1 sc in every st of the prev rnd. (20 sts)
Rnd 5: 2 sc, dec 1 st, 1 sc, dec 1 st, 13 sc. (18 sts)
Rnd 6: 1 sc in every st of the prev rnd. (18 sts)
Rnd 7: Dec 1 st, 4 sc, dec 1 st, 5 sc, inc 1 st, 4 sc. (17 sts)

Stuff the spout up to this level with polyester fiberfill.

Rnd 8: 1 sc, dec 1 st each twice, 6 sc, inc 1 st each twice, 4 sc. (17 sts)
Rnd 9: 1 sc in every st of the prev rnd. (17 sts)
Rnd 10: 1 sc, dec 1 st, 14 sc. (16 sts)
Rnd 11: 2 sc, dec 1 st, 6 sc, inc 1 st each twice, 4 sc. (17 sts)
Rnd 12: Dec 1 st, 1 sc, dec 1 st, 12 sc. (15 sts)
Rnd 13: 1 sc in every st of the prev rnd. (15 sts)
Rnd 14: 1 sc, dec 1 st, 12 sc. (14 sts)
Rnd 15: Dec 1 st each twice, 10 sc. (12 sts)
Rnd 16: 1 sc in every st of the prev rnd. (12 sts)
Rnd 17: 1 sc, inc 1 st each twice, 9 sc. (14 sts)

Change color to Creme.

Rnd 18: Working through the back loop of the st only, dec 1 st each 7 times in all. (7 sts)
Rnds 19–21: 1 sc in every st of the prev rnd. (7 sts)
Rnd 22: * Skip 1 st, 1 sl-st *, rep from * to * 2 times more, skip 1 st. (3 sts)

Break the working yarn and secure the end.

Turn the Creme-colored section into the Peacock-colored part of the tip of the spout, so that Rnd 17 of the spout forms the rim of the opening.

HANDLE

Work in rounds. Begin every rnd with ch1, and end every rnd with 1 sl-st into the 1st st of the rnd. Do not turn work.

Rnd 1: Work 7 sc into an adjustable magic ring. (7 sts)
Rnds 2–23: 1 sc in every st of the prev rnd. (7 sts)
Rnd 24: 4 sc, inc 1 st each twice, 1 sc. (9 sts)
Rnd 25: 5 sc, inc 1 st each twice, 2 sc. (11 sts)
Rnd 26: 1 sc in every st of the prev rnd. (11 sts)

Break the working yarn, and secure the end.

Stuff only the last 3 rnds of the handle with polyester fiberfill.

FINISHING

Sew Rnd 26 of the handle to the teapot at the level of Rnds 21–24 of the teapot in mattress stitch, with the increases on the last rnd of the handle pointing downward. Sew Rnd 2 of the handle flat to the teapot at the level of Rnd 11, making sure that the handle ends up exactly opposite the spout.

Hold the teapot with the magic ring facing you, join new working yarn in Cyclam between Rnds 5 and 6 of the teapot. Work 1 rnd of hdc. Join into the round with 1 sl-st into the 1st st of the rnd.

LID

In Peacock, crochet a circle from Basic pattern (Rnds 1–6, see page 23).

Rnd 7: 1 sc in every st of the prev rnd. (36 sts)
Rnd 8: 2 sc, inc 1 st, * 5 sc, inc 1 st *, rep from * to * 4 times more, 3 sc. (42 sts)
Rnd 9: * 6 sc, inc 1 st *, rep from * to * 5 times more. (48 sts)
Rnds 10 and 11: Working through the back loop of the st only, 1 sc in every st of the prev rnd. (48 sts)
Rnd 12: * 6 sc, dec 1 st *, rep from * to * 5 times more. (42 sts)
Rnd 13: 2 sc, dec 1 st, * 5 sc, dec 1 st *, rep from * to * 4 times more, 3 sc. (36 sts)

Change color to Creme.

Rnd 14: * 10 sc, dec 1 st *, rep from * to * 2 times more. (33 sts)
Rnds 15 and 16: 1 sc in every st of the prev rnd. (33 sts)
Rnd 17: * 9 sc, dec 1 st *, rep from * to * 2 times more. (30 sts)
Rnd 18: * 3 sc, dec 1 st *, rep from * to * 5 times more. (24 sts)

Stuff the lid with polyester fiberfill.

Rnd 19: * 2 sc, dec 1 st *, rep from * to * 5 times more. (18 sts)
Rnd 20: * 1 sc, dec 1 st *, rep from * to * 5 times more. (12 sts)
Rnd 21: Dec 1 st each, 6 times in all. (6 sts)
Rnd 22: * Skip 1 st, 1 sl-st *, rep from * to * 2 times more. (3 sts)

Break the working yarn, and secure the end.

Join new working yarn in Cyclam to Rnd 10 of the lid, and work 1 hdc in every st of the prev rnd. (48 sts) Chain 1, and turn work.

Now work 1 sc in every st of the prev row. (48 sts)

Break the working yarn, and secure the end.

KNOB

Work in rounds. Begin every round with 1 chain, and end every round with 1 sl-st into the first stitch of the round. Do not turn work.

Rnd 1: In Anise, work 6 sc into an adjustable magic ring. (6 sts)
Rnd 2: Inc 1 st each 6 times in all. (12 sts)
Rnds 3 and 4: 1 sc in every st of the prev rnd. (12 sts)
Rnd 5: * 1 sc, dec 1 st *, rep from * to * 3 times more. (8 sts)
Rnd 6: 1 sc in every st of the prev rnd. (8 sts)

Break the working yarn, and secure the end.

Stuff the knob with polyester fiberfill, and sew it to the magic ring of the lid in mattress stitch.

SUGAR BOWL

MATERIALS

- crochet hook, 2.5 mm (US B-1 or C-2)
- tapestry needle
- Schachenmayr Catania (100% cotton): 1 skein (1.75 oz/50 g) each in Jade, Freesia (Fresie), and White (Weiß)
- polyester fiberfill

INSTRUCTIONS

SUGAR BOWL

In Jade, crochet a circle from Basic pattern (Rnds 1–7, see page 23).

Rnd 8: 1 bpsc in every st of the prev rnd. (42 sts)
Rnd 9: * 6 sc, inc 1 st *, rep from * to * 5 times more. (48 sts)
Rnd 10: 1 sc in every st of the prev rnd. (48 sts)
Rnd 11: 3 sc, inc 1 st, * 7 sc, inc 1 st *, rep from * to * 4 times more, 4 sc. (54 sts)
Rnds 12–16: 1 sc in every st of the prev rnd. (54 sts)
Rnd 17: * 7 sc, dec 1 st *, rep from * to * 5 times more. (48 sts)

Now stuff the already worked rnds of the sugar bowl with polyester fiberfill.

Rnds 18 and 19: 1 sc in every st of the prev rnd. (48 sts)
Rnd 20: 2 sc, dec 1 st, * 6 sc, dec 1 st *, rep from * to * 4 times more, 4 sc. (42 sts)
Rnd 21: 1 sc in every st of the prev rnd. (42 sts)
Rnd 22: Working through the back loop of the st only: * 5 sc, dec 1 st *, rep from * to * 5 times more. (36 sts)
Rnd 23: 2 sc, dec 1 st *, * 4 sc, dec 1 st *, rep from * to * 4 times more, 2 sc. (30 sts)

Change color to White.

Rnd 24: Working through the back loop of the st only, 1 sc in every st of the prev rnd. (30 sts)
Rnds 25 and 26: 1 sc in every st of the prev rnd. (30 sts)

Add a little more stuffing, but only along the edge.

Rnd 27: * 3 sc, dec 1 st *, rep from * to * 5 times more. (24 sts)
Rnd 28: * 2 sc, dec 1 st *, rep from * to * 5 times more. (18 sts)
Rnd 29: * 1 sc, dec 1 st *, rep from * to * 5 times more. (12 sts)
Rnd 30: Dec 1 st each, 6 times in all. (6 sts)
Rnd 31: * Skip 1 st, 1 sl-st *, rep from * to * 2 times more. (3 sts)

Break the working yarn, and secure the end.

Turn the White part into the sugar bowl, so that Rnds 22 and 23 form the rim of the opening.

HANDLE (MAKE 2)

Work in rounds. Begin every round with 1 chain, and end every round with 1 sl-st into the first stitch of the round. Do not turn work.

In Freesia, crochet a chain of 7, and join into the round with 1 sl-st into the first chain. (7 sts)

Rnds 2–17: 1 sc in every st of the prev rnd. (7 sts)
Rnd 18: 3 sc, inc 1 st, 3 sc. (8 sts)
Rnd 19: 4 sc, inc 1 st, 3 sc. (9 sts)
Rnd 20: 5 sc, inc 1 st, 3 sc. (10 sts)

Break the working yarn, and secure the end.

Stuff only the last 3 rnds of the handle with polyester fiberfill.

FINISHING

Sew Rnd 20 of the handle to the sugar bowl in mattress stitch at the level of Rnds 18–20 of the bowl, with the increases in the last rnd of the handle pointing downward. Press Rnd 1 of the handle flat, sew the sts together, and then sew the handle to the sugar bowl at the level of Rnd 11. Attach the other handle to the sugar bowl exactly opposite the first one.

LID

In Freesia, crochet a circle from Basic pattern (Rnds 1–4, see page 23).

Rnd 5: 1 sc each in every st of the prev rnd. (24 sts)
Rnd 6: 1 sc, inc 1 st, * 3 sc, inc 1 st *, rep from * to * 4 times more, 2 sc. (30 sts)
Rnd 7: 1 sc in every st of the prev rnd. (30 sts)
Rnd 8: * 4 sc, inc 1 st *, rep from * to * 5 times more. (36 sts)
Rnd 9: 1 sc in every st of the prev rnd. (36 sts)
Rnd 10: 2 sc, inc 1 st, * 5 sc, inc 1 st *, rep from * to * 4 times more, 3 sc. (42 sts)
Rnd 11: 1 bpsc in every st of the prev rnd. (42 sts)

Change color to Jade.

Rnd 12: Working through the back loop of the st only, * 1 sc, dec 1 st *, rep from * to * 13 times more. (28 sts)

Change color to White.

Rnds 13–15: 1 sc in every st of the prev rnd. (28 sts)
Rnd 16: * 2 sc, dec 1 st *, rep from * to * 6 times more. (21 sts)

Stuff the lid completely with polyester fiberfill.

Rnd 17: * 1 sc, dec 1 st *, rep from * to * 6 times more. (14 sts)
Rnd 18: Dec 1 st each 7 times in all. (7 sts)
Rnd 19: * Skip 1 st, 1 sl-st *, rep from * to * 2 times more, skip 1 st. (3 sts)

Break the working yarn, and secure the end.

LID RIM

Join new working yarn in Freesia to Rnd 10, attaching it through the protruding part of the bpsc of Rnd 11. First, work 1 rnd sc, and then 1 rnd hdc.

Break the working yarn, and secure the end.

KNOB

In Jade, work the knob for the sugar bowl from the instructions for the teapot lid knob (see page 85), and sew it on in mattress stitch through the magic ring of the lid.

CREAMER

MATERIALS

- crochet hook, 2.5 mm (US B-1 or C-2)
- tapestry needle
- Schachenmayr Catania (100% cotton): 1 skein (1.75 oz/50 g) each in Anise (Anis) and Creme
- polyester fiberfill

INSTRUCTIONS

In Anise, crochet a circle from Basic pattern (Rnds 1–7, see page 23).

Rnd 8: 1 bpsc in every st of the prev rnd. (42 sts)

Rnds 9–12: 1 sc in every st of the prev rnd. (42 sts)

Rnd 13: * 5 sc, dec 1 st *, rep from * to * 5 times more. (36 sts)

Rnds 14–21: 1 sc in every st of the prev rnd. (36 sts)

Stuff the Creamer to about Rnd 16 with polyester fiberfill.

Rnd 22: 15 sc, change color to Creme, and, working through the back loop of the stitch only, 6 sc, change color to Anise, and working again through both loops of the stitch, 15 sc. (36 sts)

Rnd 23: Working through the back loop of the st only, 4 sc, dec 1 st, 4 sc, dec 1 st, 1 sc, dec 1 st, change color to Creme, and working through both loops of the stitch, 6 sc, change color to Anise, and work again through the back loop of the stitch only, dec 1 st, 1 sc, dec 1 st, 4 sc, dec 1 st, 4 sc. (30 sts)

Change color to Creme.

Rnd 24: Working through the back loop of the st only, 12 sc, now work through both loops of the stitch, 6 sc, again through the back loop of the stitch only, 12 sc. (30 sts)

Rnds 25–27: 1 sc in every st of the prev rnd. (30 sts)

Rnd 28: * 3 sc, dec 1 st *, rep from * to * 5 times more. (24 sts)

Rnd 29: * 2 sc, dec 1 st *, rep from * to * 5 times more. (18 sts)

Rnd 30: * 1 sc, dec 1 st *, rep from * to * 5 times more. (12 sts)

Rnd 31: Dec 1 st each, 6 times in all. (6 sts)

Rnd 32: * Skip 1 st, 1 sl-st *, rep from * to * 2 times more. (3 sts)

Break the working yarn, and secure the end.

Turn the Creme-colored part into the creamer, so that Rnd 23 forms the rim of the dish.

Join new working yarn in Anise to the front loop of the 1st st of Rnd 23 of the Creamer.

Rnd 1: Working through the front loop of the stitches of Rnd 23 only: 15 sc, now skip to Rnd 22, and there, work through the remaining front loops as follows: 2 sc, [3 sc into the same st] twice, 2 sc, skip back to Rnd 23, and there, work likewise through the front loop of the stitch only: 15 sc. (40 sts)

Break the working yarn, and secure the end.

HANDLE

In Anise, work 6 sc into an adjustable magic ring and join into the round with 1 sl-st into the 1st st, ch17, 6 sc into the 2nd chain from the hook, 1 sl-st in every following chain, 1 sl-st into the 1st st of the magic ring.

Sew one end of the Handle to Rnd 21 of the Creamer opposite the spout. Sew the other end to the Creamer at the level of Rnd 12.

FOR THE SWEET TOOTH

Dessert lovers alert! If the four-o'clock tea still left room for more, here you can give in to your cravings. Whether you prefer your ice cream on a stick, in a waffle cone, or in a bowl, or would rather snack on hard candy, lollipops, or chocolate pralines—everything is guaranteed calorie-free and completely without sugar!

ICE POP

MATERIALS

- crochet hook, 2.5 mm (US B-1 or C-2)
- tapestry needle
- Schachenmayr Catania (100% cotton): 1 skein (1.75 oz/50 g) in either Mimosa (Mimose) or Coffee (Kaffee), and about 0.5 oz (15 g) in White (Weiß)
- polyester fiberfill
- flat wooden craft stick (ice cream stick)

INSTRUCTIONS

Work in rounds. Begin every round with 1 chain, and end every round with 1 sl-st into the first stitch of the round. Do not turn work.

Rnd 1: Beginning in White, crochet a chain of 13. 1 sc into the 2nd chain from the hook, 1 sc each into the next 10 chains, 5 sc into the last chain. Now continue in the round, working in the ch-sp, around the chain, do not turn work: 4 sc, ch2, skip 2 sts, 4 sc, 4 sc into the same stitch, into which the 1st sc of the rnd had been worked earlier. (30 sts)

Rnd 2: Working through the back loop of the st only, 1 sc in every st of the prev rnd. (30 sts)

Rnd 3: 1 bpsc in every st of the prev rnd. (30 sts)

Rnd 4: 1 sc in every st of the prev rnd. (30 sts)

Change color to Mimosa or, for a chocolate-glazed ice pop, use Coffee instead.

Rnds 5–21: 1 sc in every st of the prev rnd. (30 sts)

Rnd 22: Dec 1 st, 11 sc, dec 1 st each twice, 11 sc, dec 1 st. (26 sts)

Rnd 23: Dec 1 st, 9 sc, dec 1 st each twice, 9 sc, dec 1 st. (22 sts)

Rnd 24: Dec 1 st, 7 sc, dec 1 st each twice, 7 sc, dec 1 st. (18 sts)

Insert the wooden stick through the opening in Rnd 1, and stuff the ice pop with polyester fiberfill, starting at the top.

Rnd 25: * 1 sc, dec 1 st *, rep from * to * 5 times more. (12 sts)

Rnd 26: Dec 1 st each, 6 times in all. (6 sts)

Rnd 27: * Skip 1 st, 1 sl-st *, rep from * to * 2 times more. (3 sts)

Break the working yarn, and secure the end.

FILLED WAFFLE CONE

MATERIALS

- crochet hook, 2.5 mm (US B-1 or C-2)
- tapestry needle
- Schachenmayr Catania (100% cotton): 1 skein (1.75 oz/50 g) in Raffia (Bast), and 0.5 oz (15 g) each in White (Weiß) and Orchid (Orchidee)
- polyester fiberfill

INSTRUCTIONS

In White, crochet a circle from Basic pattern (Rnds 1–4, see page 23).

Rnd 5: 1 bpsc in every st of the prev rnd. (24 sts)

Rnds 6–8: 1 sc in every st of the prev rnd. (24 sts)

Change color to Raffia.

Rnd 9: Working through the back loop of the st only, 1 sc in every st of the prev rnd. (24 sts)

Rnd 10: * 6 sc, dec 1 st *, rep from * to * 2 times more. (21 sts)

Rnds 11 and 12: 1 sc in every st of the prev rnd. (21 sts)

Rnd 13: 2 sc, dec 1 st, * 5 sc, dec 1 st *, rep from * to * once more, 3 sc. (18 sts)

Rnds 14 and 15: 1 sc in every st of the prev rnd. (18 sts)

Rnd 16: * 4 sc, dec 1 st *, rep from * to * 2 times more. (15 sts)

Rnds 17–19: 1 sc in every st of the prev rnd. (15 sts)

Rnd 20: 1 sc, dec 1 st, * 3 sc, dec 1 st *, rep from * to * once more, 2 sc. (12 sts)

Rnds 21 and 22: 1 sc in every st of the prev rnd. (12 sts)

Rnd 23: * 2 sc, dec 1 st *, rep from * to * 2 times more. (9 sts)

Stuff the waffle cone with polyester fiberfill.

Rnds 24 and 25: 1 sc in every st of the prev rnd. (9 sts)

Rnd 26: * 1 sc, dec 1 st *, rep from * to * 2 times more. (6 sts)

Rnd 27: 1 sc in every st of the prev rnd. (6 sts)

If needed, insert more stuffing into the tip of the waffle cone.

Rnd 28: * Skip 1 st, 1 sl-st *, rep from * to * 2 times more. (3 sts)

Break the working yarn, and secure the end.

FINISHING

TOPPING STRIPES

Join new working yarn in Orchid to the front loop of a stitch of Rnd 8 of the waffle cone. The tip should face you. Work sl-st in surface crochet over the white sts toward the magic ring. When you have reached the magic ring, continue on the opposite side of the waffle cone, ending with 1 sl-st through the front loop of the last stitch there.

Break the working yarn, and secure the end.

Join new working yarn in Orchid, 4 sts apart, through the front loop of the appropriate stitch of Rnd 8 of the waffle cone, and work the same as for the first stripe.

Repeat for the third stripe.

With the magic ring of the waffle cone facing up, join new working yarn in Orchid to any Orchid-colored st located next to the magic ring. Now work 1 rnd sc into the adjoining Orchid-colored st, and end the round with 1 sl-st into the 1st st of the rnd.

SOFT SERVE

MATERIALS

- crochet hook, 2.5 mm (US B-1 or C-2)
- tapestry needle
- Schachenmayr Catania (100% cotton): 1 skein (1.75 oz/50 g) in Raffia (Bast)
- Schewe Baumwolle-Classic (100% cotton): 1 skein (1.75 oz/50 g) in 0025 Dark Pink (Dunkelrosa)
- polyester fiberfill

INSTRUCTIONS

Work in rounds. Begin every rnd with ch1, and end every rnd with 1 sl-st into the 1st st of the rnd. Do not turn work.

Rnd 1: In Dark Pink, work 6 sc into an adjustable magic ring. (6 sts)

Rnd 2: Inc 1 st each, 6 times in all. (12 sts)

Rnd 3: * 1 sc, inc 1 st *, rep from * to * 5 times more. (18 sts)

Rnds 4 and 5: 1 sc in every st of the prev rnd. (18 sts)

Rnd 6: * 2 sc, inc 1 st *, rep from * to * 5 times more. (24 sts)

Rnds 7–10: 1 sc in every st of the prev rnd. (24 sts)

Rnd 11: 1 bpsc in every st of the prev rnd. (24 sts)

Change color to Raffia.

Rnd 12: 1 sc in every st of the prev rnd. (24 sts)

Rnds 13 and 14: Working through the back loop of the st only, 1 sc in every st of the prev rnd. (24 sts)

Rnd 15: * 6 sc, dec 1 st *, rep from * to * 2 times more. (21 sts)

Rnd 16: Working through the back loop of the st only, 1 sc in every st of the prev rnd. (21 sts)

Rnd 17: * 5 sc, dec 1 st *, rep from * to * 2 times more. (18 sts)

Rnds 18–19: Working through the back loop of the st only, 1 sc in every st of the prev rnd. (18 sts)

Rnd 20: 1 bpsc in every st of the prev rnd. (18 sts)

Stuff the soft serve cone with polyester fiberfill.

Rnd 21: * 1 sc, dec 1 st *, rep from * to * 5 times more. (12 sts)

Rnd 22: Dec 1 st each, 6 times in all. (6 sts)

Rnd 23: * Skip 1 st, 1 sl-st *, rep from * to * 2 times more. (3 sts)

Break the working yarn, and secure the end.

Hold the Soft Serve with the magic ring facing you, join new working yarn in Dark Pink between the magic ring and Rnd 1 of the soft serve ice cream, and work in spiral rounds. When you've reached 1 st before the end of each rnd, insert the hook into the stitch 1 rnd below.

Rnd 1: [3 hdc in 1 st] 3 times, [3 dc in 1 st] 3 times.

Rnd 2: 3 dc in every st.

Rnds 3–6: 2 dc in every st.

Rnd 7: 2 hdc in every st.

Rnd 8: 2 sc in every st.

Break the working yarn, and secure the end.

WAFFLE RIM

Hold the Soft Serve with the magic ring facing you, and join new working yarn in Raffia between Rnds 12 and 13. Work 1 rnd of hdc around the soft serve. Join into the round with 1 sl-st into the 1st st of the rnd.

EMPTY WAFFLE CONE

MATERIALS

- crochet hook, 2.5 mm (US B-1 or C-2)
- tapestry needle
- Schachenmayr Catania (100% cotton): 1 skein (1.75 oz/50 g) in Raffia (Bast)

INSTRUCTIONS

Work in spiral rounds. Omit the chain at the beginning of the round, and do not join the round with a sl-st into the 1st st of the rnd. Do not turn work.

Rnd 1: In Raffia, work 3 sc into an adjustable magic ring. (3 sts)
Rnd 2: Inc 1 st each 3 times in all. (6 sts)
Rnd 3: 1 sc in every st of the prev rnd. (6 sts)
Rnd 4: * 1 sc, inc 1 st *, rep from * to * 2 times more. (9 sts)
Rnds 5–7: 1 sc in every st of the prev rnd. (9 sts)
Rnd 8: * 2 sc, inc 1 st *, rep from * to * 2 times more. (12 sts)

Rnds 9–11: 1 sc in every st of the prev rnd. (12 sts)
Rnd 12: * 3 sc, inc 1 st *, rep from * to * 2 times more. (15 sts)
Rnds 13–15: 1 sc in every st of the prev rnd. (15 sts)
Rnd 16: * 4 sc, inc 1 st *, rep from * to * 2 times more. (18 sts)
Rnds 17–19: 1 sc in every st of the prev rnd. (18 sts)
Rnd 20: * 5 sc, inc 1 st *, rep from * to * 2 times more. (21 sts)
Rnds 21–23: 1 sc in every st of the prev rnd. (21 sts)
Rnd 24: * 6 sc, inc 1 st *, rep from * to * 2 times more. (24 sts)
Rnds 25–27: 1 sc in every st of the prev rnd. (24 sts)
Rnd 28: * 1 sc, inc 1 st *, rep from * to * 11 times more. (36 sts)
Rnds 29–31: 1 sc in every st of the prev rnd. (36 sts)
Rnd 32: Working through the front loop of the stitch only, * 5 sc, inc 1 st *, rep from * to * 5 times more. (42 sts) Finish by working 1 sl-st into the next st.

Break the working yarn, and secure the end.

SCOOP OF ICE CREAM

MATERIALS

- crochet hook, 2.5 mm (US B-1 or C-2)
- tapestry needle
- Schachenmayr Catania (100% cotton): 1 skein (1.75 oz/50 g) each in Cyclam, Mimosa (Mimose), and Coffee (Kaffee)
- polyester fiberfill

INSTRUCTIONS

Work in spiral rounds. Omit the chain at the beginning of the round, and do not join the round with a sl-st into the 1st st of the rnd. Do not turn work.

Rnd 1: In Cyclam, work 6 sc into an adjustable magic ring. (6 sts)
Rnd 2: Inc 1 st each, 6 times in all. (6 sts)
Rnd 3: * 1 sc, inc 1 st *, rep from * to * 5 times more. (18 sts)
Rnd 4: * 2 sc, inc 1 st *, rep from * to * 5 times more. (24 sts)

Rnd 5: * 3 sc, inc 1 st *, rep from * to * 5 times more. (30 sts)
Rnds 6–10: 1 sc in every st of the prev rnd. (30 sts)
Rnd 11: * 4 sc, skip 1 st *, rep from * to * 5 times more. (24 sts)
Rnd 12: * 3 sc, skip 1 st *, rep from * to * 5 times more. (18 sts)

Now stuff the scoop of ice cream with polyester fiberfill.

Rnd 13: * 2 sc, skip 1 st *, rep from * to * 5 times more. (12 sts)
Rnd 14: * 1 sc, skip 1 st *, rep from * to * 5 times more. (6 sts)
Rnd 15: * Skip 1 st, 1 sl-st *, rep from * to * 2 times more. (3 sts)

Break the working yarn, and secure the end.

TIP: To make a partial scoop of ice cream (to be sewn on top of another scoop), only work up to Rnd 11. Sew the unfinished scoop of ice cream in mattress stitch onto another, complete, scoop of ice cream, and stuff the partial scoop with polyester fiberfill shortly before completely closing it up.

ICE CREAM BOWL

MATERIALS

- crochet hook, 2.5 mm (US B-1 or C-2)
- tapestry needle
- Schachenmayr Catania (100% cotton): 1 skein (1.75 oz/50 g) in White (Weiß)
- ONline Linie 165 Sandy (100% cotton): 1 skein (1.75 oz/50 g) in 17 Pink (Rosa)
- polyester fiberfill
- toilet paper core
- cardboard, pencil
- compass

INSTRUCTIONS

Using a compass, draw a circle with a radius of 1.5 in (3.75 cm) onto a piece of cardboard, and cut it out.

FOOT

In Pink, crochet a circle from Basic pattern (Rnds 1–9, see page 23).

Rnd 10: 1 bpsc in every st of the prev rnd. (54 sts)

Place the cardboard circle into the foot.

Rnd 11: 7 sc, dec 1 st *, rep from * to * 5 times more. (48 sts)
Rnd 12: 2 sc, dec 1 st, * 6 sc, dec 1 st *, rep from * to * 4 times more, 4 sc. (42 sts)
Rnd 13: * 5 sc, dec 1 st *, rep from * to * 5 times more. (36 sts)
Rnd 14: 1 sc in every st of the prev rnd. (36 sts)
Rnd 15: 4 sc, dec 1 st *, rep from * to * 5 times more. (30 sts)

Rnd 16: 3 sc, dec 1 st *, rep from * to * 5 times more. (24 sts)
Rnds 17–27: 1 sc in every st of the prev rnd. (24 sts)

Break the working yarn, and secure the end.

Stuff the the bottom part along the edge with polyester fiberfill, and insert the toilet paper core into the foot. Use a pencil to mark the height of the top edge of the foot on the cardboard core, and cut the core to a matching length. Then stuff it, too, with polyester fiberfill.

BOWL

In Pink, crochet a circle from Basic pattern (Rnds 1–11, see page 23).

Rnds 12–17: 1 sc in every st of the prev rnd. (66 sts)
Rnd 18: 1 bpsc in every st of the prev rnd. (66 sts)

Change color to White.

Rnd 19: * 9 sc, dec 1 st *, rep from * to * 5 times more. (60 sts)
Rnd 20: 1 bpsc in every st of the prev rnd. (60 sts)
Rnds 21–26: 1 sc in every st of the prev rnd. (60 sts)
Rnd 27: * 8 sc, dec 1 st *, rep from * to * 5 times more. (54 sts)
Rnd 28: * 7 sc, dec 1 st *, rep from * to * 5 times more. (48 sts)
Rnd 29: * 6 sc, dec 1 st *, rep from * to * 5 times more. (42 sts)
Rnd 30: * 5 sc, dec 1 st *, rep from * to * 5 times more. (36 sts)
Rnd 31: * 4 sc, dec 1 st *, rep from * to * 5 times more. (30 sts)
Rnd 32: * 3 sc, dec 1 st *, rep from * to * 5 times more. (24 sts)
Rnd 33: * 2 sc, dec 1 st *, rep from * to * 5 times more. (18 sts)
Rnd 34: * 1 sc, dec 1 st *, rep from * to * 5 times more. (12 sts)
Rnd 35: Dec 1 st each, 6 times in all. (6 sts)

Rnd 36: * Skip 1 st, 1 sl-st *, rep from * to * 2 times more. (3 sts)

Break the working yarn, and secure the end.

Turn the white part into the pink part of the bowl, so that Rnds 18 and 19 form the rim of the bowl.

Sew the bowl onto the foot at a slight angle.

TIP: The instructions for the bowl can be used for crocheting a cereal dish and a mixing bowl. Experienced crocheters can modify the bowl to enlarge it by increasing the circumference of the beginning circle through working additional rounds.

ICE CREAM SCOOP

MATERIALS

- crochet hook, 2.5 mm (US B-1 or C-2)
- tapestry needle
- Schachenmayr Catania (100% cotton): 1 skein (1.75 oz/50 g) each in White (Weiß), Silver (Silber), and Violet (Violett)
- polyester fiberfill

INSTRUCTIONS

ICE CREAM SCOOP HEAD

In Silver, crochet a circle from Basic pattern (Rnds 1–7, see page 23).

Rnds 8–11: 1 sc in every st of the prev rnd. (42 sts)
Rnd 12: Working through the back loop of the st only: * 5 sc, dec 1 st *, rep from * to * 5 times more. (36 sts)
Rnd 13: 1 sc in every st of the prev rnd. (36 sts)

Change color to White.

Rnds 14 and 15: 1 sc in every st of the prev rnd. (36 sts)
Rnd 16: * 4 sc, dec 1 st *, rep from * to * 5 times more. (30 sts)
Rnd 17: * 3 sc, dec 1 st *, rep from * to * 5 times more. (24 sts)
Rnd 18: * 2 sc, dec 1 st *, rep from * to * 5 times more. (18 sts)
Rnd 19: * 1 sc, dec 1 st *, rep from * to * 5 times more. (12 sts)
Rnd 20: Dec 1 st each, 6 times in all. (6 sts)
Rnd 21: * Skip 1 st, 1 sl-st *, rep from * to * 2 times more. (3 sts)

Break the working yarn, and secure the end.

Press Rnds 13–21 into crocheted piece. Rnd 12 now forms the rim of the ice cream scoop head.

HANDLE

In White, crochet a circle from Basic pattern (Rnds 1–3, see page 23).

Rnds 4–6: 1 sc in every st of the prev rnd. (18 sts)

Change color to Violet.

Rnd 7: Working through the back loop of the st only: 1 sc in every st of the prev rnd. (18 sts)
Rnd 8: 1 sc in every st of the prev rnd. (18 sts)
Rnd 9: * 4 sc, dec 1 st *, rep from * to * 2 times more. (15 sts)
Rnd 10: 1 sc in every st of the prev rnd. (15 sts)
Rnd 11: 1 sc, dec 1 st, * 3 sc, dec 1 st *, rep from * to * once more, 2 sc. (12 sts)
Rnd 12: 1 sc in every st of the prev rnd. (12 sts)
Rnd 13: * 2 sc, dec 1 st *, rep from * to * 2 times more. (9 sts)
Rnds 14–18: 1 sc in every st of the prev rnd. (9 sts)
Rnd 19: * 2 sc, inc 1 st *, rep from * to * 2 times more. (12 sts)
Rnds 20 and 21: 1 sc in every st of the prev rnd. (12 sts)
Rnd 22: 1 bpsc in every st of the prev rnd. (12 sts)

Change color to Silver.

Rnd 23: Working through the back loop of the st only, 1 sc in every st of the prev rnd. (12 sts)
Rnds 24–26: 1 sc in every st of the prev rnd. (12 sts)
Rnd 27: 1 sl-st, 1 sc, 3 hdc, 1 sc, 1 sl-st. The remaining sts stay unworked. Chain 1 for turning, and turn work.
Row 28: Skip the first st (the last sl-st of the prev rnd), 1 sl-st, 4 sc, 1 sl-st.

Break the working yarn, and secure the end.

Stuff the handle with polyester fiberfill.

FINISHING

Sew on the handle in mattress stitch between Rnds 5 and 10 of the ice cream scoop head.

WRAPPED CANDY

MATERIALS

- crochet hook, 2.5 mm (US B-1 or C-2)
- tapestry needle
- Schachenmayr Catania (100% cotton) or similar yarn: about 0.5 oz (15 g) each in 2 colors of choice (A and B) for each wrapped candy
- polyester fiberfill

INSTRUCTIONS

Work in rounds. Begin every round with 1 chain, and end every round with 1 sl-st into the first stitch of the round. Do not turn work.

Rnd 1: In A, work 5 sc into an adjustable magic ring. (5 sts)
Rnd 2: Inc 1 st each, 5 times in all. (10 sts)
Rnd 3: 1 sc in every st of the prev rnd. (10 sts)
Rnd 4: * 4 sc, inc 1 st *, rep from * to * once more. (12 sts)
Rnd 5: 1 sc in every st of the prev rnd. (12 sts)
Rnd 6: 3 sc, dec 1 st, 4 sc, dec 1 st, 1 sc. (10 sts)

Rnd 7: 1 sc in every st of the prev rnd. (10 sts)

Stuff the candy with polyester fiberfill.

Rnd 8: Dec 1 st each, 5 times in all. (5 sts)
Rnd 9: * 1 sl-st, skip 1 st *, rep from * to * once more, 1 sl-st. (3 sts)

Break the working yarn and secure the end.

CANDY WRAPPER

Now, with the magic ring of the candy facing you, join new working yarn in B to the magic ring of the candy.

Work in rounds. Begin every round with 1 chain, and end every round with 1 sl-st into the first stitch of the round. Do not turn work.

Rnd 1: Work 2 sc in every st of the magic ring of the candy. (10 sts)
Rnd 2: Inc 1 st each 10 times in all. (20 sts)

Break the working yarn, and secure the end.

Join new working yarn in color B to Rnd 8 of the candy. You are looking from above at the last rnd. Work the 2 rnds for the candy wrapper as described above.

MATERIALS

- crochet hook, 2.5 mm (US B-1 or C-2)
- tapestry needle
- Schachenmayr Catania (100% cotton): 1 skein (1.75 oz/50 g) each in Creme and Cyclam, and 0.5 oz (15 g) each in Pastel Blue (Hellblau) and White (Weiß)
- cake pop stick

INSTRUCTIONS

Work in spiral rounds. Omit the chain at the beginning of the round, and at the end of the rnd, do not work a sl-st into the 1st st of the rnd. Important: The color change is not worked the usual way here, but instead by working parallel with 2 colors (i.e., sts in Cyclam are always crocheted into the sts in Creme from the prvious rnd, and the other way around). Every time when a stitch in one color is resting, pull the unused working loop longer, so as to prevent the work from unraveling.

Rnd 1: In Cyclam, work an adjustable magic ring, and work 3 sc into it. Pull the unused working loop of the last st longer, remove the hook, and let this stitch rest for now. Now, in Creme, work 3 more sc into the magic ring. (6 sts) You now have 2 spots in which you are working at the same time.
Rnd 2: Cyclam: inc 1 st each twice, Creme: inc 1 st each 3 times in all, Cyclam: inc 1 st. (12 sts)
Rnd 3: Cyclam: * 1 sc, inc 1 st *, rep from * to * once more, Creme:

*1 sc, inc 1 st *, rep from * to * 2 times more, in Cyclam: 1 sc, inc 1 st. (18 sts)
Rnd 4: Cyclam: * 2 sc, inc 1 st *, rep from * to * once more, Creme: * 2 sc, inc 1 st *, rep from * to * 2 times more, in Cyclam: 2 sc, inc 1 st. (24 sts)
Rnd 5: Cyclam: * 3 sc, inc 1 st *, rep from * to * once more, Creme: * 3 sc, inc 1 st *, rep from * to * 2 times more, Cyclam: 3 sc, inc 1 st. (30 sts)
Rnd 6: Cyclam: * 4 sc, inc 1 st *, rep from * to * once more, Creme: 1 sc, inc 1 st, 1 sc, 1 sl-st, Cyclam: 4 sc, inc 1 st.
Rnd 7: Cyclam: 5 sc, inc 1 st, 2 sc, 2 sl-st. The spiral ends here. To make a larger lollipop, continue working Rnds 1–5 in the same manner.

Break the working yarn, and secure the end.

Work a second circle following the instructions listed above. Place both pieces back to back, right sides facing out, and sew them together in Cyclam in running stitch along the outermost rnd. Leave a small opening through which to insert the cake pop stick.

BOW

In Pastel Blue, crochet a chain of 9. Work 1 hdc into the 4th chain from the hook, 1 sc, 1 sl-st, 1 sc, 1 hdc, 1 dc.

Break the working yarn, and secure the end.

Using white yarn, sew the bow to the front of the lollipop opposite the opening for the cake pop stick with a few stitches, wrapping the yarn around the center of the bow.

MATERIALS

- crochet hook, 2.5 mm (US B-1 or C-2)
- tapestry needle
- Chocolate 1 (with coffee bean): Schachenmayr Catania (100% cotton), about 0.5 oz (15 g) each in Cyclam, Soft Apricot, and Coffee (Kaffee)
- Chocolate 2: Schachenmayr Catania (100% cotton), about 0.5 oz (15 g) each in Anise (Anis) and Coffee (Kaffee)
- Chocolate 3: Schachenmayr Catania (100% cotton), about 0.5 oz (15 g) each in Coffee (Kaffee), Soft Apricot, and Sun (Sonne)
- Chocolate 4: Schachenmayr Catania (100% cotton), about 0.5 oz (15 g) each in Soft Apricot and Raspberry (Himbeer)
- polyester fiberfill

INSTRUCTIONS

CHOCOLATE 1 (WITH COFFEE BEAN)

Work in rounds. Begin every rnd with ch1, and end every rnd with 1 sl-st into the 1st st of the rnd. Do not turn work.

Rnd 1: In Soft Apricot, work 6 sc into an adjustable magic ring. (6 sts)
Rnd 2: Inc 1 st each, 6 times in all. (12 sts)
Rnd 3: Working through the back loop of the st only, 1 sc in every st of the prev rnd. (12 sts)
Rnd 4: * 2 sc, inc 1 st *, rep from * to * 3 times more. (16 sts)
Rnd 5: 1 bpsc in every st of the prev rnd. (16 sts)

Change color to Cyclam.

Rnd 6: * 2 sc, dec 1 st *, rep from * to * 3 times more. (12 sts)
Rnd 7: 1 sc in every st of the prev rnd. (12 sts)

Stuff the chocolate with polyester fiberfill.

Rnd 8: Dec 1 st each, 6 times in all. (6 sts)
Rnd 9: * Skip 1 st, 1 sl-st *, rep from * to * 2 times more. (3 sts)

Break the working yarn, and secure the end.

FINISHING

Hold the chocolate with the magic ring facing you. Now join new working yarn in Coffee between Rnds 8 and 9 of the chocolate, and work 6 sc in 1 rnd. Join into the round with 1 sl-st into the 1st st of the rnd.

Break the working yarn, and secure the end.

With the last rnd of the chocolate facing you, join new working yarn in Soft Apricot between Rnds 5 and 6 of the chocolate, and work 1 rnd of sc. Join into the round with 1 sl-st into the 1st st of the rnd.

Break the working yarn, and secure the end.

CHOCOLATE 2 (WITH PISTACHIO)

Work in rounds. Begin every round with 1 chain, and end every round with 1 sl-st into the first stitch of the round. Do not turn work.

Rnd 1: In Coffee, work 6 sc into an adjustable magic ring. (6 sts)
Rnd 2: Inc 1 st each, 6 times in all. (12 sts)
Rnd 3: * 1 sc, inc 1 st *, rep from * to * 5 times more. (18 sts)
Rnd 4: Working through the back loop of the st only, 1 sc in every st of the prev rnd. (18 sts)

Rnds 5 and 6: 1 sc in every st of the prev rnd. (18 sts)

Stuff the Chocolate with polyester fiberfill.

Rnd 7: Working through the back loop of the st only, * 1 sc, dec 1 st *, rep from * to * 5 times more. (12 sts)
Rnd 8: Dec 1 st each, 6 times in all. (6 sts)
Rnd 9: * Skip 1 st, 1 sl-st *, rep from * to * 2 times more. (3 sts)

Break the working yarn, and secure the end.

PISTACHIO:

Work in rounds. Begin every round with 1 chain, and end every round with 1 sl-st into the first stitch of the round. Do not turn work.

Rnd 1: In Anise, work 6 sc into an adjustable magic ring. (6 sts)
Rnds 2 and 3: 1 sc in every st of the prev rnd. (6 sts)
Rnd 4: 2 sc, dec 1 st, 2 sc. (5 sts)
Rnd 5: 1 sc, dec 1 st, 2 sc. (4 sts)

Break the working yarn, and secure the end.

Leave the pistachio unstuffed, and sew it to the chocolate at the magic ring.

CHOCOLATE 3 (DECORATED)

Work in rounds. Begin every round with 1 chain, and end every round with 1 sl-st into the first stitch of the round. Do not turn work.

Rnd 1: In Soft Apricot, crochet a chain of 5. Work 1 sc into the 2nd stitch from the hook, 2 sc, 4 sc into the last chain. Now work in the ch-sp, around the chain, without turning. 2 sc, 3 sc into the same stitch, into which the 1st st of the rnd had been worked earlier. (12 sts)
Rnd 2: * Inc 1 st, 2 sc *, rep from * to * 3 times more. (16 sts)

Change color to Coffee.

RASPBERRY CREAM   DECORATED
WITH PISTACHIO   WITH COFFEE BEAN

Rnd 3: Working through the back loop of the st only, 1 sc in every st of the prev rnd. (16 sts)
Rnd 4: * 6 sc, dec 1 st *, rep from * to * once more. (14 sts)
Rnd 5: 1 sc in every st of the prev rnd. (14 sts)
Rnd 6: * Dec 1 st, 2 sc, dec 1 st, 1 sc *, rep from * to * once more. (10 sts)

Break the yarn, leaving a long tail, and secure the end.

Stuff the chocolate with polyester fiberfill, and close the remaining opening lengthwise in whipstitch.

Join new working yarn in Sun to the Coffee-colored part at one end of

the chocolate, and surface-crochet a wavy line in sl-st.

Break the working yarn, and secure the end.

CHOCOLATE 4 (RASPBERRY CREAM)

Work in spiral rounds. Omit the chain at the beginning of the round, and do not join the round with a sl-st into the 1st st. Do not turn work.

Rnd 1: In Raspberry, work 6 sc into an adjustable magic ring. (6 sts)
Rnd 2: Working through the back loop of the st only, inc 1 st each, 6 times in all. (12 sts)
Rnds 3 and 4: Working through the back loop of the st only, 1 sc in every st of the prev rnd. (12 sts)

Stuff the chocolate with polyester fiberfill.

Rnd 5: Working through the back loop of the st only, dec 1 st each, 6 times in all. (6 sts)

Rnd 6: * Skip 1 st, 1 sl-st *, rep from * to * 2 times more. (3 sts)

Break the working yarn, and secure the end.

Holding the chocolate with the magic ring facing up, join new working yarn in Soft Apricot to the front loop of the 1st st of Rnd 2 of the chocolate. Now crochet 4 rnds, working 1 sl-st each through the front loop of every st.

Break the working yarn, and secure the end.

PINK LEMONADE BOTTLE

MATERIALS

- crochet hook, 2.5 mm (US B-1 or C-2)
- tapestry needle
- Schachenmayr Catania (100% cotton): 1 skein (1.75 oz/50 g) in Orchid (Orchidee), and 0.5 oz (15 g) each in White (Weiß), Silver (Silber), Anise (Anis), and Coffee (Kaffee)
- polyester fiberfill
- cake pop stick
- washi tape

INSTRUCTIONS

In Orchid, crochet a circle from Basic pattern (Rnds 1–6, see page 23).

Rnd 7: 1 bpsc in every st of the prev rnd. (36 sts)
Rnds 8–20: 1 sc in every st of the prev rnd. (36 sts)

Change color to White.

Rnds 21–24: 1 sc in every st of the prev rnd. (36 sts)

Change color to Orchid.

Rnds 25–27: 1 sc in every st of the prev rnd. (36 sts)
Rnd 28: * 4 sc, dec 1 st *, rep from * to * 5 times more. (30 sts)
Rnd 29: 1 sc in every st of the prev rnd. (30 sts)
Rnd 30: * 3 sc, dec 1 st *, rep from * to * 5 times more. (24 sts)
Rnd 31: 1 sc in every st of the prev rnd. (24 sts)
Rnd 32: * 2 sc, dec 1 st *, rep from * to * 5 times more. (18 sts)

Rnds 33 and 34: 1 sc in every st of the prev rnd. (18 sts)

Stuff the bottle with polyester fiberfill.

Rnd 35: * 1 sc, dec 1 st *, rep from * to * 5 times more. (12 sts)
Rnds 36–38: 1 sc in every st of the prev rnd. (12 sts)

Change color to Silver.

Rnds 39–43: 1 sc in every st of the prev rnd. (12 sts)

Now stuff the bottleneck with polyester fiberfill.

Rnd 44: Working through the back loop of the st only, dec 1 st each, 6 times in all. (6 sts)
Rnd 45: * Skip 1 st, 1 sl-st *, rep from * to * 2 times more. (3 sts)

Break the working yarn, and secure the end.

Holding the bottle with the bottle base (magic ring) facing you, join new working yarn in Silver to the front loop of the 1st st of Rnd 43, and work 1 hdc each through the front loop of every st of this rnd. Join into the round with 1 sl-st into the 1st st of the rnd.

LABEL

In White, crochet a circle from Basic pattern (Rnds 1–3, see page 23).

Change color to Anise.

Rnd 4: Working through the back loop of the st only: * 1 sl-st, 1 sl-st, ch3, 1 sl-st into the same st as the last sl-st had been worked *, rep from * to * 8 times more.
Break the working yarn, and secure the end.

FINISHING

Now sew the label centered onto the white band of the bottle in running stitch around Rnd 3.

In Coffee, embroider a curly letter L in backstitch onto the white part of the label.

Cut a piece of washi tape to the length of the cake pop stick, and affix it to the stick. Insert the stick through one of the sts of the last rnd—finished!

MATERIALS

- crochet hook, 2.5 mm (US B-1 or C-2)
- tapestry needle
- Schachenmayr Catania (100% cotton): 1 skein (1.75 oz/50 g) each in Freesia (Fresie) and Sun (Sonne)
- polyester fiberfill
- cake pop stick
- thin wooden dowel
- cardboard
- washi tape
- compass

INSTRUCTIONS

In Freesia, crochet a circle from Basic pattern (Rnds 1–5, see page 23).

Adjust the compass to the radius of the already completed part of the crocheted circle by inserting the compass needle centered into the magic ring and then extending the compass leg to the outer edge of the crocheted circle. Draw a circle of this size onto cardboard, and cut it out.

Rnd 6: 1 bpsc in every st of the prev rnd. (30 sts)

Now place the cardboard circle into the crocheted part.

Rnd 7: * 3 sc, dec 1 st *, rep from * to * 5 times more. (24 sts)

Rnd 8: 1 sc, dec 1 st, * 2 sc, dec 1 st *, rep from * to * 4 times more, 1 sc. (18 sts)

Rnd 9: 1 sc in every st of the prev rnd. (18 sts)

Rnd 10: * 4 sc, dec 1 st *, rep from * to * 2 times more. (15 sts)

Rnd 11: 1 sc, dec 1 st, * 3 sc, dec 1 st *, rep from * to * once more, 2 sc. (12 sts)

Rnd 12: * 1 sc, dec 1 st *, rep from * to * 3 times more. (8 sts)

Stuff the foot of the cocktail glass with polyester fiberfill.

Rnds 13–22: 1 sc in every st of the prev rnd. (8 sts)

Insert the thin wooden dowel into the crocheted piece, and stuff a small amount of additional polyester fiberfill around it.

Rnd 23: * 1 sc, inc 1 st *, rep from * to * 3 times more. (12 sts)

Rnd 24: 1 sc in every st of the prev rnd. (12 sts)

Rnd 25: Inc 1 st each, 12 times in all. (24 sts)

Rnd 26: 1 sc in every st of the prev rnd. (24 sts)

Rnd 27: * 2 bpsc, 1 fpsc *, rep from * to * 7 times more. (24 sts)

Rnd 28: 1 sc in every st of the prev rnd. (24 sts)

Rnd 29: * 3 sc, inc 1 st *, rep from * to * 5 times more. (30 sts)

Rnd 30: 1 bpsc in every st of the prev rnd. (30 sts)

Rnds 31–33: 1 sc in every st of the prev rnd. (30 sts)

Rnd 34: 1 bpsc in every st of the prev rnd. (30 sts)

Rnd 35: * 4 sc, inc 1 st *, rep from * to * 5 times more. (36 sts)

Rnd 36: 2 sc, inc 1 st, * 5 sc, inc 1 st *, rep from * to * 4 times more, 3 sc. (42 sts)

Rnd 37: Working through the front loop of the stitch only, 1 sc in every st of the prev rnd. (42 sts)

Rnd 38: 1 sc in every st of the prev rnd. (42 sts)

Break the working yarn, and secure the end.

Now join new working yarn in Sun through the back loop of the first st of Rnd 36 of the goblet, and continue as follows:

Rnd 37: Working through the back loop of the st only, * 5 sc, dec 1 st *, rep from * to * 5 times more. (36 sts)

Rnd 38: 2 sc, dec 1 st, * 4 sc, dec 1 st *, rep from * to * 4 times more, 2 sc. (30 sts)

Rnd 39: * 3 sc, dec 1 st *, rep from * to * 5 times more. (24 sts)

Stuff the remainder of the goblet with polyester fiberfill.

Rnd 30: * 2 sc, dec 1 st *, rep from * to * 5 times more. (18 sts)

Rnd 31: * 1 sc, dec 1 st *, rep from * to * 5 times more. (12 sts)

Rnd 32: Dec 1 st each, 6 times in all. (6 sts)

Rnd 33: * Skip 1 st, 1 sl-st *, rep from * to * 2 times more. (3 sts)

Break the working yarn, and secure the end.

For the drinking straw, cut a piece of washi tape to the length of the cake pop stick, and affix it to the stick. Insert the stick through one of the sts of the last rnd.

AT THE MOM-
AND-POP STORE

Children love to play grocery store! Here their first steps
as entrepreneurs are taken; wares are marketed and
sold. Service is, of course, always outstanding! A vast
array of merchandise is guaranteed: crochet fruit and
vegetables galore to let the register jingle!

CASH REGISTER

MATERIALS

- crochet hook, 2.5 mm (US B-1 or C-2)
- tapestry needle
- Schachenmayr Catania (100% cotton): 2 skeins (1.75 oz/50 g per skein) in Cyclam; 1 skein (1.75 oz/50 g) each in Anise (Anis), Pink (Rosa), Orchid (Orchidee), Apple (Apfel), and Pastel Blue (Hellblau), and 0.5 oz (15 g) each in Capri, White (Weiß), and Violet (Violett)
- polyester fiberfill
- pipe cleaners or craft wire

INSTRUCTIONS

Work in rows. At the end of the row, chain 1, and turn work.

SIDE PART (MAKE 2)

Row 1: In Cyclam, crochet a chain of 45. Work 1 sc into the 2nd chain from the hook, and 1 sc in every following ch. (44 sts)
Rows 2–11: 1 sc in every st of the prev row. (44 sts)
Row 12: Dec 1 st, 42 sc. (43 sts)
Row 13: 41 sc, dec 1 st. (42 sts)
Row 14: Dec 1 st, 40 sc. (41 sts)
Row 15: 39 sc, dec 1 st. (40 sts)
Rows 16 and 17: 1 sc in every st of the prev row. (40 sts)
Row 18: Dec 1 st, 38 sc. (39 sts)
Rows 19 and 20: 1 sc in every st of the prev row. (39 sts)
Row 21: 37 sc, dec 1 st. (38 sts)
Rows 22 and 23: 1 sc in every st of the prev row. (38 sts)
Row 24: Dec 1 st, 36 sc. (37 sts)

Rows 25 and 26: 1 sc in every st of the prev row. (37 sts)
Row 27: 35 sc, dec 1 st. (36 sts)
Row 28: 1 sc each every st of the prev row. (36 sts)
Row 29: 34 sc, dec 1 st. (35 sts)
Row 30: Dec 1 st, 33 sc. (34 sts)
Row 31: 32 sc, dec 1 st. (33 sts)
Row 32: Dec 1 st, 31 sc. (32 sts)
Row 33: 30 sc, dec 1 st. (31 sts)
Row 34: Dec 1 st, 29 sc. (30 sts)
Row 35: 20 sc. The remaining sts stay unworked. Chain 1, and turn work.
Rows 36–46: 1 sc in every st of the prev row. (20 sts)

Break the working yarn, and secure the end.

MIDDLE PART

Row 1 (WS): In Pink, crochet a chain of 37. Work 1 sc into the 2nd chain from the hook, and 1 sc in every following ch. (36 sts)
Rows 2–11: 1 sc in every st of the prev row. (36 sts)

Change color to Anise.

Row 12: Working through the back loop of the st only, 1 sc in every st of the prev row. (36 sts)
Rows 13–48: 1 sc in every st of the prev row. (36 sts)

Change color to Pink.

Row 49: Working through the front loop of the stitch only, 1 sc in every st of the prev row. (36 sts)
Rows 50–60: 1 sc in every st of the prev row. (36 sts)

Change color to Cyclam.

Row 61: Working through the front loop of the stitch only, 1 sc in every st of the prev row. (36 sts)
Rows 62–82: 1 sc in every st of the prev row. (36 sts)

Change color to Orchid.

Row 83: Working through the front loop of the stitch only, 1 sc in every st of the prev row. (36 sts)
Rows 84–128: 1 sc in every st of the prev row. (36 sts)

Change color to Pink.

Row 129: Working through the front loop of the stitch only, 1 sc in every st of the prev row. (36 sts)
Rows 130–181: 1 sc in every st of the prev row. (36 sts)

Break the working yarn, and secure the end.

Now wrong sides facing each other, sew the first and the last rnd of the middle part together in whipstitch.

In the next step, in Apple, you will crochet the side parts to the remaining openings of the middle part at the left and right. To do this, place the pieces together wrong sides facing each other, with the sts at the ends of the first 11 rows of the middle part exactly aligned with the sts at the ends of the first 11 rows of the respective side part. Hold the cash register so that you always look onto the middle part from above, and the respective side part is facing away from you. Now crochet the pieces together, working 1 sc in every end of the row of the middle part, while the color changes in the middle part optically mark the edges of the crocheted pieces. Stuff the cash register with polyester fiberfill, and crochet on the second side part the same way.

MICROPHONE

Work in spiral rounds.

Rnd 1: In Pastel Blue, work 6 sc into an adjustable magic ring. (6 sts)
Rnds 2–34: 1 sc in every st of the prev rnd. (6 sts)

Insert the pipe cleaner into the crocheted piece.

Change color to Capri.

Rnds 35–39: 1 hdc in every st of the prev rnd. (6 sts)
Rnd 40: * 2 hdc in 1 st *, rep from * to * 5 times more. (12 sts)
Rnds 41–44: 1 hdc in every st of the prev rnd. (12 sts)

Stuff the capri-colored part of the microphone with polyester fiberfill.

Rnd 45: [Hdc2tog] 6 times. (6 sts)
Rnd 46: * Skip 1 st, 1 sl-st *, rep from * to * 2 times more. (3 sts)

Break the working yarn, and secure the end.

KEYS (MAKE 9)

Work in rows. At the end of every row, chain 1, and turn work.

Row 1: In Violet, crochet a chain of 5. Work 1 sc into the 2nd chain from the hook. 1 sc in every following ch. (4 sts)
Rows 2–4: 1 sc in every st of the prev row. (4 sts)

Break the working yarn, and secure the end.

Sew the keys evenly spaced to the Anise-colored part of the cash register, and embroider digits 1–9 onto the keys with light-colored yarn remnants.

RECEIPT

Work in rows. At the end of every row, chain 1, and turn work.

Row 1: In White, crochet a chain of 15. Work 1 sl-st into the 2nd chain from the hook. 1 sc in every following ch. (14 sts)
Row 2: 12 sc, ch2, the last 2 sts of Row 1 stay unworked. Chain 1 for turning, turn. (14 sts)
Row 3: 1 sl-st into the 2nd chain from the hook, 1 sc into the next chain, 12 sc. (14 sts)
Row 4: Same as Row 2. (14 sts)
Row 5: Same as Row 3. (14 sts)

Row 6: Same as Row 2. (14 sts)

Row 7: Same as Row 3. (14 sts)

Break the working yarn, and secure the end.

Roll up the receipt by about 5 sts from the narrow straight edge, and sew it to the cash register with a few stitches. Sew the jagged end of the receipt to the main part of the cash register with a few stitches, too.

SCANNER

MATERIALS

- crochet hook, 2.5 mm (US B-1 or C-2)
- tapestry needle
- Schachenmayr Catania (100% cotton): 1 skein (1.75 oz/50 g) in Lavender (Lavendel), and about 0.5 oz (15 g) in Fuchsia and Signal Red (Signalrot)
- polyester fiberfill

INSTRUCTIONS

Work in rounds. Begin every rnd with ch1, and end every rnd with 1 sl-st into the 1st st of the rnd. Do not turn work. Gradually stuff with polyester fiberfill while you crochet the piece.

Rnd 1: In Fuchsia, crochet a chain of 13. Work 1 sc into the 2nd chain from the hook, 1 sc in each one of the next 10 chains, 5 sc into the last chain (from here on, work in the ch-sp, around the chain, without turning work), 10 sc, 4 sc into the same stitch into which the 1st st of the rnd had been worked earlier. Join into the round with 1 sl-st. (30 sts)

Change color to Lavender.

Rnd 2: * 12 sc, inc 1 st, 1 sc, inc 1 st *, rep from * to * once. (34 sts)

Rnd 3: 1 bpsc in every st of the prev rnd. (34 sts)

Rnd 4: 1 sc in every st of the prev rnd. (34 sts)

Rnd 5: 13 sc, dec 1 st, 16 sc, dec 1 st, 1 sc. (32 sts)

Rnd 6: 4 sc, dec 1 st each twice, 24 sc. (30 sts)

Rnd 7: 10 sc, dec 1 st, 16 sc, dec 1 st. (28 sts)

Rnd 8: Dec 1 st, 2 sc, dec 1 st, 2 sc, dec 1 st, 18 sc. (25 sts)

Rnd 9: 1 sc in every st of the prev rnd. (25 sts)

Rnd 10: 2 sc, dec 1 st each twice, 10 sc, 3 sc into the same st, 8 sc. (25 sts)

Rnd 11: 1 sc, dec 1 st each twice, 8 sc, inc 1 st, 3 sc, inc 1 st, skip 1 st, 6 sc. (24 sts)

Rnds 12 and 13: 1 sc in every st of the prev rnd. (24 sts)

Rnd 14: 7 sc, dec 1 st, 13 sc, dec 1 st. (22 sts)

Rnd 15: 1 sc, dec 1 st each twice, 17 sc. (20 sts)

Rnds 16 and 17: 1 sc in every st of the prev rnd. (20 sts)

Rnd 18: 2 sc, dec 1 st, 16 sc. (19 sts)

Rnds 19 and 20: 1 sc in every st of the prev rnd. (19 sts)

Rnd 21: 1 sc, dec 1 st each twice, 6 sc, inc 1 st, 1 sc, inc 1 st, 5 sc. (19 sts)

Rnds 22 and 23: 1 sc in every st of the prev rnd. (19 sts)

Rnd 24: 2 sc, dec 1 st, 8 sc, inc 1 st, 6 sc. (19 sts)

Rnd 25: 1 sc in every st of the prev rnd. (19 sts)

Rnd 26: 7 sc, dec 1 st, 8 sc, dec 1 st. (17 sts)

Rnd 27: Dec 1 st, 4 sc, dec 1 st each twice, 5 sc, dec 1 st. (13 sts)

Rnd 28: 2 sc, dec 1 st, 9 sc. (12 sts)

Rnd 29: Dec 1 st each, 6 times in all. (6 sts)

Rnd 30: * Skip 1 st, 1 sl-st *, rep from * to * 2 times more. (3 sts)

Break the working yarn, and secure the end.

In Signal Red, crochet a circle from the instructions on page 23 (Rnds 1 and 2) and sew centered onto the Fuchsia-colored part of the scanner.

MARKET BAG

MATERIALS

- crochet hook, 2.5 mm (US B-1 or C-2)
- tapestry needle
- Schachenmayr Catania (100% cotton): 1 skein (1.75 oz/50 g) each in Burgundy (Weinrot), Strawberry (Erdbeere), and Orchid (Orchidee)

INSTRUCTIONS

First, work dc in the round. At the beginning of every rnd, work ch3 to replace the first dc, and end every rnd with 1 sl-st into the 3rd ch of the ch3 replacing the first dc of the rnd. Do not turn work.

Rnd 1: In Burgundy, work 12 dc into an adjustable magic ring. (12 sts)

Rnd 2: [2 dc in 1 st] 12 times. (24 sts)

Rnd 3: * 1 dc, 2 dc in 1 st *, rep from * to * 11 times more. (36 sts)

Rnd 4: * 2 dc, 2 dc in 1 st *, rep from * to * 11 times more. (48 sts)

Rnd 5: * 3 dc, 2 dc in 1 st *, rep from * to * 11 times more. (60 sts)

From here on, continue in spiral rounds. Do not join the round with a sl-st into the 1st st of the rnd any more.

Rnd 6: Ch4, skip 3 sts, 1 sl-st into the 4th st of the prev rnd, * ch4, skip 2 sts, 1 sl-st *, rep from * to * 17 times more, ch4, skip 2 sts, 1 sl-st into the 1st ch-sp of the rnd (crocheting in the ch-sp instead of into the 1st st of the rnd creates the spiral effect). (100 sts)

Rnds 7–16: * Ch4, 1 sl-st in the next ch-sp *, rep from * to * 18 times more, ch4, 1 sl-st into the 1st ch-sp of the rnd. (100 sts)

Change color to Strawberry.

Rnds 17–20: * Ch4, 1 sl-st in the next ch-sp *, rep from * to * 18 times more, ch4, 1 sl-st into the 1st ch-sp of the rnd. (100 sts)

Change color to Orchid.

Rnds 21–23: * Ch4, 1 sl-st in the next ch-sp *, rep from * to * 18 times more, ch4, 1 sl-st into the 1st ch-sp of the rnd. (100 sts)

From here on, resume working regular rounds as usual. Begin every rnd with ch1, and end every rnd with 1 sl-st into the 1st st of the rnd. Do not turn work.

Rnd 24: * 3 sc in ch-sp *, rep from * to * 19 times more. (60 sts)

Rnd 25: 1 sc in every st of the prev rnd. (60 sts)

Rnd 26: 8 sc, ch14, skip 14 sts, 16 sc, ch14, skip 14 sts, 8 sc. (60 sts)

Rnd 27: 8 sc, 14 sc in ch-sp, 16 sc, 14 sc in ch-sp, 8 sc. (60 sts)

Break the working yarn, and secure the end.

MATERIALS

- crochet hook, 2.5 mm (US B-1 or C-2)
- tapestry needle
- sewing needle and thread
- Schachenmayr Catania (100% cotton): 1 skein (1.75 oz/50 g) in Peacock (Pfau), and 0.5 oz (15 g) each in Orchid (Orchidee, Apple (Apfel), Cyclam, and Lavender (Lavendel)
- For the coins: Schachenmayr Catania (100% cotton), 0.5 oz (15 g) each in Gold and Silver (Silber)
- 2 snaps

INSTRUCTIONS

Work in rounds. Begin every rnd with ch1, and end every rnd with 1 sl-st into the 1st st of the rnd. Do not turn work.

Rnd 1: In Peacock, work 6 sc into an adjustable magic ring. (6 sts)

Rnd 2: Inc 1 st each, 6 times in all. (12 sts)

Rnd 3: * 1 sc, inc 1 st *, rep from * to * 5 times more. (18 sts)

Rnd 4: * 2 sc, inc 1 st *, rep from * to * 5 times more. (24 sts)

Rnd 5: 1 sc, inc 1 st, * 3 sc, inc 1 st *, rep from * to * 4 times more, 2 sc. (30 sts)

Rnd 6: * 4 sc, inc 1 st *, rep from * to * 5 times more. (36 sts)

Rnd 7: 2 sc, inc 1 st, * 5 sc, inc 1 st *, rep from * to * 4 times more, 3 sc. (42 sts)

Rnd 8: Inc 1 st, 19 sc, inc 1 st each twice, 19 sc, inc 1 st. (46 sts)

Rnds 9–11: 1 sc each in every st of the prev rnd. (46 sts)

Rnd 12: Dec 1 st, 19 sc, dec 1 st each twice, 19 sc, dec 1 st. (42 sts)

Rnd 13: Dec 1 st, 17 sc, dec 1 st each twice, 17 sc, dec 1 st. (38 sts)

Rnd 14: 1 sc each in every st of the prev rnd. (38 sts)

Rnd 15: Dec 1 st, 15 sc, dec 1 st each twice, 15 sc, dec 1 st. (34 sts)

Change color to Orchid.

Rnds 16 and 17: 1 sc each in every st of the prev rnd. (34 sts)

Change color to Apple.

Rnd 18: Ch3 (replaces the first dc), 1 dc into the 2nd st, ch1, 1 dc into the same stitch into which the last dc had been worked earlier, skip 2 sts, * 1 dc, ch1, 1 dc into the same stitch into which the last dc had been worked earlier, skip 2 sts *, rep from * to * 9 times more. (This round will be joined with 1 sl-st into the 3rd chain of the ch3 replacing the 1st dc.)

Change color to Cyclam.

Rnd 19: Ch2 (counts as 1 hdc), 1 tulip-st into the 2nd st, ch1, skip 1 st (the chain between the two apple green dc's), 1 tulip-st, * 1 tulip-st, ch1, skip 1 st (the chain between the two apple green dc's), 1 tulip-st *, rep from * to * 9 times more.

Break the working yarn, and secure the end.

Join new working yarn in Lavender to the chain between the two first tulip-sts of Rnd 19, working not directly into the chain, but in the ch-sp instead:

Rnd 20: * Ch4, 1 sl-st in ch-sp between 2 tulip-sts of the prev rnd *, rep from * to * 10 times more.

Break the working yarn, and secure the end.

FINISHING

Now sew the two snaps to the orchid-colored area on the inside of the wallet.

COINS

In Gold (or Silver respectively), work 12 dc into an adjustable magic ring. Join into the round with 1 sl-st into the first stitch.

Break the working yarn, and secure the end.

HALF KIWI

MATERIALS

- crochet hook, 2.5 mm (US B-1 or C-2)
- tapestry needle
- Schachenmayr Catania (100% cotton): 1 skein (1.75 oz/50 g) in Tan (Taupe), and 0.5 oz (15 g) each in Anise (Anis), Mimosa (Mimose), Kiwi, and Coffee (Kaffee)
- polyester fiberfill

INSTRUCTIONS

Work in rounds. Begin every round with 1 chain, and end every round with 1 sl-st into the first stitch of the round. Do not turn work.

Rnd 1: In Mimosa, work 6 sc into an adjustable magic ring. (6 sts)

Change color to Kiwi.

Rnd 2: Inc 1 st each, 6 times in all. (12 sts)
Rnd 3: * 1 sc, inc 1 st *, rep from * to * 5 times more. (18 sts)

Change color to Anise.

Rnd 4: * 2 sc, inc 1 st *, rep from * to * 5 times more. (24 sts)
Rnd 5: 1 sc, inc 1 st, * 3 sc, inc 1 st *, rep from * to * 4 times more, 2 sc. (30 sts)

Change color to Tan.

Rnd 6: Working through the back loop of the st only, 1 sc each in every st of the prev rnd. (30 sts)
Rnds 7–9: 1 sc each in every st of the prev rnd. (30 sts)
Rnd 10: * 4 sc, dec 1 st *, rep from * to * 4 times more. (25 sts)
Rnd 11: 1 sc each in every st of the prev rnd. (25 sts)
Rnd 12: * 3 sc, dec 1 st *, rep from * to * 4 times more. (20 sts)
Rnd 13: 1 sc each in every st of the prev rnd. (20 sts)

Stuff the kiwi with polyester fiberfill.

Rnd 14: * 2 sc, dec 1 st *, rep from * to * 4 times more. (15 sts)
Rnd 15: * 1 sc, dec 1 st *, rep from * to * 4 times more. (10 sts)

Rnd 16: Dec 1 st each, 5 times in all. (5 sts)
Rnd 17: * 1 sl-st, skip 1 st *, rep from * to * once, 1 sl-st. (3 sts)

Break the working yarn, and secure the end.

FINISHING

In Coffee, embroider a circle in chain stitch between Rnds 15 and 16 of the half kiwi.

In Mimosa, embroider 7 satin stitches between Rnds 2 and 4, and then embroider 2 seeds each between these satin stitches, working 2 shorter satin stitches each in Coffee.

WHOLE APPLE

MATERIALS

- crochet hook, 2.5 mm (US B-1 or C-2)
- tapestry needle
- Schachenmayr Catania (100% cotton): 1 skein (1.75 oz/50 g) in Signal Red (Signalrot), and about 0.5 oz (15 g) in Coffee (Kaffee)
- polyester fiberfill
- stitch marker (optional)

INSTRUCTIONS

Work in spiral rounds. Do not turn work. Mark the beginning of the round with a stitch marker.

Rnd 1: In Signal Red, work 6 sc into an adjustable magic ring. (6 sts) Do not join into the round with 1 sl-st into the 1st st, just continue:

Rnd 2: Inc 1 st each, 6 times in all. (12 sts)

Rnd 3: * 1 sc, inc 1 st *, rep from * to * 5 times more. (18 sts)

Rnd 4: 1 sc in every st of the prev rnd. (18 sts)

Rnd 5: * 2 sc, inc 1 st *, rep from * to * 5 times more. (24 sts)

Rnd 6: * 3 sc, inc 1 st *, rep from * to * 5 times more. (30 sts)

Rnd 7: * 4 sc, inc 1 st *, rep from * to * 5 times more. (36 sts)

Rnds 8–11: 1 sc in every st of the prev rnd. (36 sts)

Rnd 12: * 5 sc, inc 1 st *, rep from * to * 5 times more. (42 sts)

Rnds 13–16: 1 sc in every st of the prev rnd. (42 sts)

Rnd 17: * 6 sc, skip 1 st *, rep from * to * 5 times more. (36 sts)

Rnd 18: 1 sc in every st of the prev rnd. (36 sts)

Rnd 19: * 5 sc, skip 1 st *, rep from * to * 5 times more. (30 sts)

Rnd 20: * 4 sc, skip 1 st *, rep from * to * 5 times more. (24 sts)

Rnd 21: * 3 sc, skip 1 st *, rep from * to * 5 times more. (18 sts)

Stuff the apple with polyester fiberfill.

Rnd 22: 1 sc in every st of the prev rnd. (18 sts)

Rnd 23: * 2 sc, skip 1 st *, rep from * to * 5 times more. (12 sts)

Rnd 24: 1 sc in every st of the prev rnd. (12 sts)

Rnd 25: * 1 sc, skip 1 st *, rep from * to * 5 times more. (6 sts)

Rnd 26: * Skip 1 st, 1 sl-st *, rep from * to * 2 times more. (3 sts)

Break the working yarn, and secure the end.

Stitch the tail through the center of the last round to the inside of the apple, so that the last few rounds turn inward.

Stitch the remainder of the tail to the magic ring the same way.

STEM

Work in spiral rounds. Do not turn work.

Rnd 1: In Coffee, work 6 sc into an adjustable magic ring. (6 sts) Do not join into the round with 1 sl-st into the 1st st, just continue:

Rnd 2: 1 sc, dec 1 st, 1 sc, dec 1 st. (4 sts)

Rnds 3–6: 1 sc in every st of the prev rnd. (4 sts)

Break the working yarn, and secure the end.

Sew the stem with a few stitches to the last round of the apple.

HALF APPLE

MATERIALS

- crochet hook, 2.5 mm (US B-1 or C-2)
- tapestry needle
- Schachenmayr Catania (100% cotton): 1 skein (1.75 oz/50 g) each in Signal Red (Signalrot) and White (Weiß), and about 0.5 oz (15 g) in Coffee (Kaffee)
- polyester fiberfill

INSTRUCTIONS

Work in rounds. Begin every round with 1 chain, and end every round with 1 sl-st into the first stitch of the round. Do not turn work. In dc rounds, begin with ch3 to replace the first dc, and end the round with 1 sl-st into the 3rd ch of the ch3 replacing the first dc.

Rnd 1: In White, work 13 dc into an adjustable magic ring. (13 sts)

Rnd 2: * 2 dc in 1 st of the prev rnd *, rep from * to * 12 times more. (26 sts)

Rnd 3: Ch3 (replaces first dc), 2 dc in 1 st, 1 dc, 2 dc in 1 st, 1 sl-st, 2 dc in 1 st, 1 dc, 2 dc in 1 st, 1 dc, * 1 sc, 2 sc in 1 st *, rep from * to * 3 times more, 1 sl-st, * 1 sc, 2 sc in 1 st *, rep from * to * 3 times more. (38 sts)

Change color to Signal Red.

Rnd 4: Working through the back loop of the st only, 6 sc, 1 sc worked below into the 5th st of Rnd 2, 18 sc, 1 sc worked below into the 18th st of Rnd 2, 12 sc. (38 sts)

From here on, only rounds in sc will be worked.

Rnds 5–7: 1 sc in every st of the prev rnd. (38 sts)

Rnd 8: * 1 sc, dec 1 st * rep from * to * once more, 2 sc, dec 1 st, * 1 sc, dec 1 st *, rep from * to * 4 times more, 2 sc, dec 1 st, * 1 sc, dec 1 st *, rep from * to * 2 times more. (26 sts)

Rnd 9: 1 sc in every st of the prev rnd. (26 sts)

Stuff the half apple with polyester fiberfill.

Rnd 10: * 1 sc, skip 1 st *, rep from * to * 12 times more. (13 sts)

Rnd 11: Skip 1 st, 1 sc in every following st of the prev rnd. (12 sts)

Rnd 12: Dec 1 st each, 6 times in all. (6 sts)

Rnd 13: * Skip 1 st, 1 sl-st *, rep from * to * 2 times more. (3 sts)

Break the working yarn, and secure the end.

In Coffee, embroider 4 apple seeds in lazy daisy stitch.

MATERIALS

- crochet hook, 2.5 mm (US B-1 or C-2)
- tapestry needle
- Schachenmayr Catania (100% cotton): 1 skein (1.75 oz/50 g) each in Sun (Sonne) and Soft Apricot, and about 0.5 oz (15 g) in Coffee (Kaffee)
- polyester fiberfill

INSTRUCTIONS

Work in rounds. Begin every round with 1 chain, and end every round with 1 sl-st into the first stitch of the round. Do not turn work.

Work Rnds 1–23 from the instructions for the Whole Banana, and then continue as follows:

Change color to Soft Apricot.

Rnd 24: Working through the back loop of the st only, 1 sc in every st of the prev rnd. (18 sts)
Rnd 25: Dec 1 st, 7 sc, inc 1 st, 8 sc. (18 sts)
Rnds 26–34: Work these rounds from the instructions for the Whole Banana.

Join new working yarn in Coffee between the magic ring and Rnd 1. Hold the banana with the magic ring facing away from you, and the other end of the banana facing you. Work 1 rnd of hdc. Join into the round with 1 sl-st into the 1st st.

Join new working yarn in Soft Apricot between Rnds 33 and 34, and work 1 rnd of hdc as described above.

Now join new working yarn in Sun to the front loop of the first stitch of Rnd 23 (the rnd in Sun), and continue in rows. End each row with ch1, and turn work.

BANANA PEEL

Row 1: 6 sc, ch1, turn work. The remaining sts will stay unworked for the time being.
Row 2: 1 sc in every st of the prev row. (6 sts)
Row 3: Dec 1 st, 2 sc, dec 1 st. (4 sts)
Rows 4–6: 1 sc in every st of the prev row. (4 sts)
Row 7: Dec 1 st each twice. (2 sts)
Rows 8 and 9: 1 sc in every st of the prev row. (2 sts)
Row 10: Dec 1 st. (1 st)

Break the working yarn, and secure the end.

Now join new working yarn in Sun to the front loop of the 7th st of Rnd 23, and repeat Rows 1–10 of the Banana Peel.

Break the working yarn, and secure the end.

Now join new working yarn in Sun to the front loop of the 13th st of Rnd 23, and again repeat Rows 1–10 of the Banana Peel. Chain 1, and then work sc edging around all 3 banana peels, working 1 sc in every end of the row, and 2 sc each into the sts of Row 10 of every individual peel. Finish by working 1 sl-st into the 1st st of the rnd.

Break the working yarn, and secure the end.

MATERIALS

- crochet hook, 2.5 mm (US B-1 or C-2)
- tapestry needle
- Schachenmayr Catania (100% cotton): 1 skein (1.75 oz/50 g) in Sun (Sonne), and about 0.5 oz (15 g) in Coffee (Kaffee)
- polyester fiberfill

INSTRUCTIONS

Work in rounds. Begin every round with 1 chain, and end every round with 1 sl-st into the first stitch of the round. Do not turn work.

Rnd 1: In Sun, work 6 sc into an adjustable magic ring. (6 sts)
Rnd 2: Inc 1 st each, 6 times in all. (12 sts)
Rnd 3: * 1 sc, inc 1 st *, rep from * to * 5 times more. (18 sts)
Rnds 4–10: 1 sc in every st of the prev rnd. (18 sts)
Rnd 11: Dec 1 st, 7 sc, inc 1 st, 8 sc. (18 sts)
Rnd 12: 1 sc in every st of the prev rnd. (18 sts)

Rnds 13–30: Alternatingly repeat Rnds 11 and 12. (18 sts)
Rnd 31: * 4 sc, dec 1 st *, rep from * to * 2 times more. (15 sts)

Stuff the banana with polyester fiberfill.

Rnd 32: * 3 sc, dec 1 st *, rep from * to * 2 times more. (12 sts)
Rnd 33: Dec 1 st each, 6 times in all. (6 sts)
Rnd 34: * Skip 1 st, 1 sl-st *, rep from * to * 2 times more. (3 sts)

Break the working yarn, and secure the end.

Join new working yarn in Coffee between the magic ring and Rnd 1. Hold the banana with the magic ring facing away from you, and the other end of the banana facing you. Work 1 rnd of hdc. Join into the round with 1 sl-st into the 1st st.

Join new working yarn in Coffee between Rnds 33 and 34, and work 1 rnd of hdc as described above.

WHOLE ORANGE

MATERIALS

- crochet hook, 2.5 mm (US B-1 or C-2)
- tapestry needle
- Schachenmayr Catania (100% cotton): 1 skein (1.75 oz/50 g) in Tangerine (Mandarine), and remnant in Golf Green (Golfgrün)
- polyester fiberfill

INSTRUCTIONS

In Tangerine, crochet a circle from Basic pattern (Rnds 1–7, see page 23).

Rnds 8–14: 1 sc in every st of the prev rnd. (42 sts)
Rnd 15: * 5 sc, dec 1 st *, rep from * to * 5 times more. (36 sts)
Rnd 16: * 4 sc, dec 1 st *, rep from * to * 5 times more. (30 sts)
Rnd 17: * 3 sc, dec 1 st *, rep from * to * 5 times more. (24 sts)

Stuff the orange with polyester fiberfill.

Rnd 18: * 2 sc, dec 1 st *, rep from * to * 5 times more. (18 sts)
Rnd 19: * 1 sc, dec 1 st *, rep from * to * 5 times more. (12 sts)
Rnd 20: Dec 1 st each, 6 times in all. (6 sts)
Rnd 21: * Skip 1 st, 1 sl-st *, rep from * to * 2 times more. (3 sts)

Break the working yarn, and secure the end.

In Golf Green, embroider a star in running stitch as stem base onto the magic ring.

CUT BLOOD ORANGE

MATERIALS

- crochet hook, 2.5 mm (US B-1 or C-2)
- tapestry needle
- sewing needle and beige sewing thread
- Schachenmayr Catania (100% cotton): 1 skein (1.75 oz/50 g) each in Tangerine (Mandarine) and Burgundy (Weinrot), and about 0.5 oz (15 g) in Soft Apricot
- polyester fiberfill

INSTRUCTIONS

Work in rounds. Begin every round with 1 chain, and end every round with 1 sl-st into the first stitch of the round. Do not turn work.

Rnd 1: In Soft Apricot, work 6 sc into an adjustable magic ring. (6 sts)

Change color to Burgundy.

Crochet a circle from Basic pattern (Rnds 2–7, see page 23).

Change color to Soft Apricot.

Rnd 8: 6 sc, 1 sc into the 7th st of the prev rnd and 1 spike stitch into the 6th st of Rnd 6, 6 sc, 1 sc into the 14th st of the prev rnd and 1 spike stitch into the 12th st of Rnd 6, 6 sc, 1 sc into the 21st st of the prev rnd and 1 spike stitch into the 18th st of Rnd 6, 6 sc, 1 sc into the 28th st of the prev rnd and 1 spike stitch into the 24th st of Rnd 6, 6 sc, 1 sc into the 35th st of the prev rnd and 1 spike stitch into the 30th st of Rnd 6, 6 sc, 1 sc into the 42nd st of the prev rnd and 1 spike stitch into the 36th st of Rnd 6. (48 sts)

Change color to Tangerine.

Rnd 9: 3 sc, inc 1 st, * 7 sc, inc 1 st *, rep from * to * 4 times more, 4 sc. (54 sts)
Rnd 10: 1 bpsc in every st of the prev rnd. (54 sts)
Rnds 11–13: 1 sc in every st of the prev rnd. (54 sts)
Rnd 14: * 7 sc, dec 1 st *, rep from * to * 5 times more. (48 sts)
Rnd 15: 3 sc, dec 1 st, * 6 sc, dec 1 st *, rep from * to * 4 times more, 3 sc. (42 sts)
Rnd 16: 1 sc in every st of the prev rnd. (42 sts)
Rnd 17: * 5 sc, dec 1 st *, rep from * to * 5 times more. (36 sts)
Rnd 18: 2 sc, dec 1 st, * 4 sc, dec 1 st *, rep from * to * 4 times more, 2 sc. (30 sts)
Rnd 19: * 3 sc, dec 1 st *, rep from * to * 5 times more. (24 sts)
Rnd 20: 1 sc in every st of the prev rnd. (24 sts)

Stuff the Cut Orange with polyester fiberfill.

Rnd 21: * 2 sc, dec 1 st *, rep from * to * 5 times more. (18 sts)
Rnd 22: * 1 sc, dec 1 st *, rep from * to * 5 times more. (12 sts)
Rnd 23: Dec 1 st each, 6 times in all. (6 sts)
Rnd 24: * Skip 1 st, 1 sl-st *, rep from * to * 2 times more. (3 sts)

Break the working yarn, and secure the end.

With sewing thread, embroider 1 satin stitch each between magic ring and every one of the 6 spike sts of Rnd 8.

TIP: For an individual orange segment, work Rnds 1–9 as for the Cut Orange. Fold the crocheted circle in half, and crochet both edges together in Tangerine in sl-st. Break the working yarn, and secure the end. Finally, embroider satin stitches as for the Cut Blood Orange.

PEAR

MATERIALS

- crochet hook, 2.5 mm (US B-1 or C-2)
- tapestry needle
- Schachenmayr Catania (100% cotton): 1 skein (1.75 oz/50 g) in Kiwi, and about 0.5 oz (15 g) in Coffee (Kaffee)
- polyester fiberfill

INSTRUCTIONS

Work in rounds. Begin every rnd with ch1, and end every rnd with 1 sl-st into the 1st st of the rnd. Do not turn work.

Rnd 1: In Kiwi, work 6 sc into an adjustable magic ring. (6 sts)
Rnd 2: Inc 1 st each, 6 times in all. (12 sts)
Rnd 3: 1 sc in every st of the prev rnd. (12 sts)
Rnd 4: * 1 sc, inc 1 st *, rep from * to * 5 times more. (18 sts)
Rnds 5–10: 1 sc in every st of the prev rnd. (18 sts)
Rnd 11: * 5 sc, inc 1 st *, rep from * to * 2 times more. (21 sts)
Rnd 12: 2 sc, inc 1 st, * 6 sc, inc 1 st *, rep from * to * once more, 4 sc. (24 sts)
Rnds 13 and 14: 1 sc in every st of the prev rnd. (24 sts)
Rnd 15: * 3 sc, inc 1 st *, rep from * to * 5 times more. (30 sts)
Rnds 16–21: 1 sc in every st of the prev rnd. (30 sts)
Rnd 22: * 3 sc, dec 1 st *, rep from * to * 5 times more. (24 sts)

Stuff the Pear with polyester fiberfill.

Rnd 23: * 2 sc, dec 1 st *, rep from * to * 5 times more. (18 sts)
Rnd 24: * 1 sc, dec 1 st *, rep from * to * 5 times more. (12 sts)
Rnd 25: Dec 1 st each, 6 times in all. (6 sts)
Rnd 26: * Skip 1 st, 1 sl-st *, rep from * to * 2 times more. (3 sts)

Break the working yarn, and secure the end.

STEM

Join new working yarn in Coffee to the magic ring of the pear. Crochet a chain of 5, work 1 sc into the 2nd stitch from the hook. Work into the remaining ch3: 1 sc and 2 sl-st. 1 sl-st into the magic ring of the pear.

Break the working yarn, and secure the end.

LEMON

MATERIALS

- crochet hook, 2.5 mm (US B-1 or C-2)
- tapestry needle
- Wolle Rödel Mille Fili (100% cotton): 1 skein (1.75 oz/50 g) in Neon Yellow (Neongelb)
- polyester fiberfill

INSTRUCTIONS

Work in rounds. Begin every rnd with ch1, and end every rnd with 1 sl-st into the 1st st of the rnd. Do not turn work.

Rnd 1: Work 6 sc into an adjustable magic ring. (6 sts)
Rnd 2: 1 sc in every st of the prev rnd. (6 sts)
Rnd 3: Inc 1 st each, 6 times in all. (12 sts)
Rnd 4: * 1 sc, inc 1 st *, rep from * to * 5 times more. (18 sts)
Rnd 5: * 5 sc, inc 1 st *, rep from * to * 2 times more. (21 sts)
Rnds 6 and 7: 1 sc in every st of the prev rnd. (21 sts)
Rnd 8: 3 sc, inc 1 st, * 6 sc, inc 1 st *, rep from * to * once more, 3 sc. (24 sts)
Rnds 9–11: 1 sc in every st of the prev rnd. (24 sts)
Rnd 12: * 6 sc, dec 1 st *, rep from * to * 2 times more. (21 sts)
Rnd 13: 1 sc in every st of the prev rnd. (21 sts)
Rnd 14: 2 sc, dec 1 st, * 5 sc, dec 1 st *, rep from * to * once more, 3 sc. (18 sts)

Stuff the Lemon with polyester fiberfill.

Rnd 15: * 1 sc, dec 1 st *, rep from * to * 5 times more. (12 sts)
Rnd 16: Dec 1 st each, 6 times in all. (6 sts)
Rnd 17: 1 sc in every st of the prev rnd. (6 sts)
Rnd 18: * Skip 1 st, 1 sl-st *, rep from * to * 2 times more. (3 sts)

Break the working yarn, and secure the end.

WATERMELON

MATERIALS

- crochet hook, 2.5 mm (US B-1 or C-2)
- tapestry needle
- Schachenmayr Catania (100% cotton): 1 skein (1.75 oz/50 g) each in Agave and Signal Red (Signalrot), and 0.5 oz (15 g) each in White (Weiß), Apple (Apfel), and Coffee (Kaffee)
- polyester fiberfill

INSTRUCTIONS

First, work in rows. End every row with ch1, and turn work.

BOWL

Row 1: In Agave, chain 2. Work 1 sc into the 2nd chain from the hook. (1 st)

Row 2: Inc 1 st. (2 sts)

Row 3: Inc 1 st each twice. (4 sts)

Row 4: 1 sc in every st of the prev row. (4 sts)

Row 5: Inc 1 st, 2 sc, inc 1 st. (6 sts)

Row 6: 1 sc in every st of the prev row. (6 sts)

Row 7: Inc 1 st, 4 sc, inc 1 st. (8 sts)

Rows 8–11: 1 sc in every st of the prev row. (8 sts)

Row 12: Inc 1 st, 6 sc, inc 1 st. (10 sts)

Row 13: 1 sc in every st of the prev row. (10 sts)

Row 14: Dec 1 st, 6 sc, dec 1 st. (8 sts)

Rows 15–18: 1 sc in every st of the prev row. (8 sts)

Row 19: Dec 1 st, 4 sc, dec 1 st. (6 sts)

Row 20: 1 sc in every st of the prev row. (6 sts)

Row 21: Dec 1 st, 2 sc, dec 1 st. (4 sts)

Row 22: 1 sc in every st of the prev row. (4 sts)

Row 23: Dec 1 st each twice. (2 sts)

Row 24: Dec 1 st. (1 st)

Break the working yarn, and secure the end.

PULP

Work in rounds. Begin every round with 1 chain, and end every round with 1 sl-st into the first stitch of the round. Do not turn work.

Rnd 1: In Signal Red, work 6 sc into an adjustable magic ring. (6 sts)

Rnd 2: Inc 1 st each, 6 times in all. (12 sts)

Rnd 3: * 1 sc, inc 1 st *, rep from * to * 5 times more. (18 sts)

Rnd 4: * 2 sc, inc 1 st *, rep from * to * 5 times more. (24 sts)

Rnd 5: 1 sc, inc 1 st, * 3 sc, inc 1 st *, rep from * to * 4 times more, 2 sc. (30 sts)

Rnd 6: * 4 sc, inc 1 st *, rep from * to * 5 times more. (36 sts)

Change color to White.

Rnd 7: 2 sc, inc 1 st, * 5 sc, inc 1 st *, rep from * to * 4 times more, 3 sc. (42 sts)

Change color to Apple.

Rnd 8: * 6 sc, inc 1 st *, rep from * to * 5 times more. (48 sts)

Break the working yarn, and secure the end.

Now, using yarn in Agave, sew the end-of-the-row sts of the rind to the sts of the last rnd of the pulp in whipstitch, always working through the back loop of the stitch only. Stuff the piece of watermelon with polyester fiberfill when three quarters of the seam have been completed, and then close up the remaining opening.

Finally, in Coffee, embroider seeds with French knots onto the red part of the watermelon.

CHERRIES

MATERIALS

- crochet hook, 2.5 mm (US B-1 or C-2)
- tapestry needle
- Schachenmayr Catania (100% cotton): 1 skein (1.75 oz/50 g) in Burgundy (Weinrot), and 0.5 oz (15 g) each in Coffee (Kaffee) and Apple (Apfel)
- polyester fiberfill

INSTRUCTIONS

CHERRY (MAKE 2)

Work in rounds. Begin every round with 1 chain, and end every round with 1 sl-st into the first stitch of the round. Do not turn work.

Rnd 1: In Burgundy, work 6 sc into an adjustable magic ring. (6 sts)

Rnd 2: Inc 1 st each, 6 times in all. (12 sts)

Rnds 3–5: 1 sc in every st of the prev rnd. (12 sts)

Stuff the cherry with polyester fiberfill.

Rnd 6: * 1 sc, dec 1 st *, rep from * to * 3 times more. (8 sts)

Rnd 7: 1 sc in every st of the prev rnd. (8 sts)

Rnd 8: Dec 1 st each, 4 times in all. (4 sts)

Break the working yarn, and secure the end.

STEM

Join new working yarn in Coffee to Rnd 8 of one of the two cherries, and chain 25. Work 1 sl-st into the Rnd 8 of the second cherry. Now work as follows into the just crocheted chain: 12 sl-st, 3 sc in 1 chain, 12 sl-st. Work an additional sl-st into the same stitch, to which you had joined the working yarn in Coffee.

Break the working yarn, and secure the end.

LEAVES

Join new working yarn in Apple to the second one of the 3 sc of the stem, and crochet a chain of 6. Continue as follows: 1 sl-st into the 2nd chain from the hook, 1 hdc, 2 dc, 1hdc. 1 sl-st into the same stitch to which you had joined the working yarn in Apple.

Again, chain 6, and work the second leaf the same way as the first. End with 1 sl-st into the same stitch to which you had joined the working yarn in Apple at the beginning.

Break the working yarn, and secure the end.

STRANBERRY

MATERIALS

- crochet hook, 2.5 mm (US B-1 or C-2)
- tapestry needle
- Schachenmayr Catania (100% cotton): 1 skein (1.75 oz/50 g) in Signal Red (Signalrot), and about 0.5 oz (15 g) in Mimosa (Mimose)
- Rico Design Essentials Cotton DK (100% cotton): about 0.5 oz (15 g) in Grass (Gras)
- polyester fiberfill

INSTRUCTIONS

Work in rounds. Begin every round with 1 chain, and end every round with 1 sl-st into the first stitch of round. Do not turn work.

Rnd 1: In Signal Red, work 5 sc into an adjustable magic ring. (5 sts)
Rnd 2: 1 sc in every st of the prev rnd. (5 sts)
Rnd 3: Inc 1 st each, 5 times in all. (10 sts)
Rnd 4: 1 sc in every st of the prev rnd. (10 sts)
Rnd 5: * 1 sc, inc 1 st *, rep from * to * 4 times more. (15 sts)
Rnd 6: 1 sc in every st of the prev rnd. (15 sts)

Rnd 7: * 4 sc, inc 1 st *, rep from * to * 2 times more. (18 sts)
Rnds 8 and 9: 1 sc in every st of the prev rnd. (18 sts)
Rnd 10: * 5 sc, skip 1 st *, rep from * to * 2 times more. (15 sts)

Stuff the Strawberry with polyester fiberfill.

Rnd 11: * 1 sc, dec 1 st *, rep from * to * 4 times more. (10 sts)
Rnd 12: Dec 1 st each, 5 times in all. (5 sts)
Rnd 13: * 1 sl-st, skip 1 st *, rep from * to * once more, 1 sl-st. (3 sts)

Break the working yarn, and secure the end.

STRAWBERRY LEAVES

Work in rounds. Begin every round with 1 chain, and end every round with 1 sl-st into the first stitch of the round. Do not turn work.

Rnd 1: In Grass, work 6 sc into an adjustable magic ring. (6 sts)
Rnd 2: Ch6, 1 sl-st into the 2nd chain from the hook, 1 sc, 1 hdc, 2 dc, skipping the 1st st of the magic ring, work 1 sl-st into the 2nd stitch of the prev rnd, * ch6, 1 sl-st into the 2nd chain from the hook, 1 sc, 1 hdc, 2 dc, 1 sl-st into the next st of the magic ring *, rep from * to * 3 times more, 1 sl-st into the 1st st of the rnd.

Break the working yarn, and secure the end.

Sew the strawberry leaf WS up centered onto Rnd 13 of the strawberry.

In Mimosa, embroider a few dots onto the strawberry for seeds with French knots.

RASPBERRY

MATERIALS

- crochet hook, 2.5 mm (US B-1 or C-2)
- tapestry needle
- Schachenmayr Catania (100% cotton): about 0.5 oz (15 g) in Cyclam

INSTRUCTIONS

Work in rounds. Begin every rnd with ch1, and end every rnd with 1 sl-st into the 1st st of the rnd. Do not turn work. The WS of the crocheted fabric will be on the outside of the raspberry.

Rnd 1: In Cyclam, work 6 sc into an adjustable magic ring. (6 sts)

Rnd 2: * 1 sc, inc 1 st *, rep from * to * 2 times more. (9 sts)
Rnd 3: 1 sc in every st of the prev rnd. (9 sts)
Rnd 4: * 2 sc, inc 1 st *, rep from * to * 2 times more. (12 sts)
Rnds 5 and 6: 1 sc in every st of the prev rnd. (12 sts)
Rnd 7: * 2 sc, dec 1 st *, rep from * to * 2 times more. (9 sts)
Rnd 8: * 1 sc, dec 1 st *, rep from * to * 2 times more. (6 sts)

Break the working yarn, and secure the end.

Pull the remaining tail through the middle of the last rnd, through the raspberry and the magic ring to let the last rnds of the raspberry turn inward.

CUCUMBER

MATERIALS

- crochet hook, 2.5 mm (US B-1 or C-2)
- tapestry needle
- Schachenmayr Catania (100% cotton): 1 skein (1.75 oz/50 g) in Agave, and about 0.5 oz (15 g) in Golf Green (Golfgrün)
- polyester fiberfill

INSTRUCTIONS

Work in rounds. Begin every round with 1 chain, and end every round with 1 sl-st into the first stitch of the round. Do not turn work.

Rnd 1: In Agave, work 6 sc into an adjustable magic ring. (6 sts)

Rnd 2: 1 sc in every st of the prev rnd. (6 sts)

Rnd 3: Inc 1 st each, 6 times in all. (12 sts)

Rnd 4: 1 sc in every st of the prev rnd. (12 sts)

Rnd 5: Inc 1 st each, 12 times in all. (24 sts)

Rnds 6–20: 1 sc in every st of the prev rnd. (24 sts)

Rnd 21: 8 sc, dec 1 st, 14 sc. (23 sts)

Rnds 22–24: 1 sc in every st of the prev rnd. (23 sts)

Rnd 25: 1 sc, dec 1 st, 20 sc. (22 sts)

Rnds 26–34: 1 sc in every st of the prev rnd. (22 sts)

Stuff the Cucumber with polyester fiberfill.

Rnd 35: * 3 sc, dec 1 st, 4 sc, dec 1 st *, rep from * to * once more. (18 sts)

Rnd 36: 1 sc in every st of the prev rnd. (18 sts)

Rnd 37: * 1 sc, dec 1 st *, rep from * to * 5 times more. (12 sts)

Rnd 38: Dec 1 st each, 6 times in all. (6 sts)

Rnd 39: * Skip 1 st, 1 sl-st *, rep from * to * 2 times more. (3 sts)

Break the working yarn, and secure the end.

In Golf Green, decorate the Cucumber with embroidered chain stitch lines from end to end.

PUMPKIN

MATERIALS

- crochet hook, 2.5 mm (US B-1 or C-2)
- tapestry needle
- Rico Design Essentials Cotton DK (100% cotton): 1 skein (1.75 oz/50 g) in Tangerine (Mandarine) (may be substituted with Schachenmayr Catania in Tangerine [Mandarine])
- Schachenmayr Catania (100% cotton): about 0.5 oz (15 g) in Agave
- polyester fiberfill

INSTRUCTIONS

Work in rounds. Begin every round with 1 chain, and end every round with 1 sl-st into the first stitch of the round. Do not turn work.

Rnd 1: In Tangerine, work 6 sc into an adjustable magic ring. (6 sts)
Rnd 2: Inc 1 st each, 6 times in all. (12 sts)
Rnd 3: * 1 sc, 3 sc in 1 st *, rep from * to * 5 times more. (24 sts)
Rnd 4: * 1 sc, inc 1 st *, rep from * to * 11 times more. (36 sts)
Rnd 5: * 1 sc, inc 1 st, 3 sc, inc 1 st *, rep from * to * 5 times more. (48 sts)
Rnd 6: * 1 sc, inc 1 st, 5 sc, inc 1 st *, rep from * to * 5 times more. (60 sts)
Rnd 7: * 1 sc, inc 1 st, 7 sc, inc 1 st *, rep from * to * 5 times more. (72 sts)
Rnd 8: * 1 sc, inc 1 st, 9 sc, inc 1 st *, rep from * to * 5 times more. (84 sts)

Rnds 9–23: 1 sc in every st of the prev rnd. (84 sts)
Rnd 24: 2 sc, skip 1 st, * 13 sc, skip 1 st *, rep from * to * 4 times more, 11 sc. (78 sts)
Rnd 25: 1 sc, skip 1 st, * 12 sc, skip 1 st *, rep from * to * 4 times more, 11 sc. (72 sts)
Rnd 26: * 11 sc, skip 1 st *, rep from * to * 5 times more. (66 sts)
Rnd 27: * 10 sc, skip 1 st *, rep from * to * 5 times more. (60 sts)
Rnd 28: * 9 sc, skip 1 st *, rep from * to * 5 times more. (54 sts)
Rnd 29: * 8 sc, skip 1 st *, rep from * to * 5 times more. (48 sts)
Rnd 30: * 1 sc, dec 1 st (by sc2tog) *, rep from * to * 15 times more. (32 sts)

Stuff the Pumpkin with polyester fiberfill.

Rnd 31: 1 sc in every st of the prev rnd. (32 sts)
Rnd 32: Dec 1 st each, 16 times in all. (16 sts)
Rnd 33: 1 sc in every st of the prev rnd. (16 sts)

Add a little more polyester fiberfill.

Rnd 34: * 2 sc, dec 1 st *, rep from * to * 3 times more. (12 sts)
Rnd 35: Dec 1 st each, 6 times in all. (6 sts)
Rnd 36: * Skip 1 st, 1 sl-st *, rep from * to * 2 times more. (3 sts)

Break the working yarn, and secure the end.

STEM

Work in rounds. Begin every round with 1 chain, and end every round with 1 sl-st into the first stitch of the round. Do not turn work. Work this piece WS facing out.

Rnd 1: In Agave, work 4 sc into an adjustable magic ring. (4 sts)
Rnds 2–4: 1 sc in every st of the prev rnd. (4 sts)

Rnd 5: * 1 sc, inc 1 st *, rep from * to * once more. (6 sts)
Rnd 6: 1 sc in every st of the prev rnd. (6 sts)
Rnd 7: * 1 sc, inc 1 st *, rep from * to * 2 times more. (9 sts)
Rnd 8: 1 sc in every st of the prev rnd. (9 sts)
Rnd 9: 1 sc, inc 1 st each twice, 6 sc. (11 sts)
Rnd 10: 1 sc in every st of the prev rnd. (11 sts)
Rnd 11: 2 sc, inc 1 st, 8 sc. (12 sts)
Rnd 12: Inc 1 st each, 12 times in all. (24 sts)

Break the working yarn, and secure the end.

To shape the grooves, using a tapestry needle, thread a piece of working yarn in Tangerine from top to bottom through the center of the crocheted sphere. Then bring the yarn around the outside of the Pumpkin, and insert the tapestry needle on the opposite side again. Pull the yarn taut. Wind the yarn around the Pumpkin the same way 5 more times, dividing the Pumpkin into 6 sections.

FINISHING

Sew the stem centered onto Rnd 1 of the Pumpkin, and stuff the lower part of the stem lightly with polyester fiberfill while sewing it on.

CARROT

MATERIALS

- crochet hook, 2.5 mm (US B-1 or C-2)
- tapestry needle
- Schachenmayr Catania (100% cotton): 1 skein (1.75 oz/50 g) in Mandarine (Tangerine), and about 0.5 oz (15 g) in Apple (Apfel)
- polyester fiberfill

INSTRUCTIONS

CARROT

Work in rounds. Begin every rnd with ch1, and end every rnd with 1 sl-st into the 1st st of the rnd. Do not turn work. Gradually stuff with polyester fiberfill.

Rnd 1: In Tangerine, work 6 sc into an adjustable magic ring. (6 sts)
Rnd 2: Inc 1 st each, 6 times in all. (12 sts)
Rnd 3: * 1 sc, inc 1 st *, rep from * to * 5 times more. (18 sts)
Rnds 4–7: 1 sc in every st of the prev rnd. (18 sts)
Rnd 8: * 4 sc, dec 1 st *, rep from * to * 2 times more. (15 sts)
Rnds 9–12: 1 sc in every st of the prev rnd. (15 sts)
Rnd 13: * 3 sc, dec 1 st *, rep from * to * 2 times more. (12 sts)
Rnds 14–18: 1 sc in every st of the prev rnd. (12 sts)
Rnd 19: 1 sc, dec 1 st, 9 sc. (11 sts)
Rnds 20 and 21: 1 sc in every st of the prev rnd. (11 sts)
Rnd 22: 5 sc, dec 1 st, 4 sc. (10 sts)
Rnds 23 and 24: 1 sc in every st of the prev rnd. (10 sts)
Rnd 25: 3 sc, dec 1 st, 5 sc. (9 sts)

Rnds 26–29: 1 sc in every st of the prev rnd. (9 sts)
Rnd 30: Dec 1 st, 7 sc. (8 sts)
Rnds 31 and 32: 1 sc in every st of the prev rnd. (8 sts)
Rnd 33: 3 sc, dec 1 st, 3 sc. (7 sts)
Rnds 34 and 35: 1 sc in every st of the prev rnd. (7 sts)
Rnd 36: 1 sc, dec 1 st, 4 sc. (6 sts)
Rnd 37: 1 sc in every st of the prev rnd. (6 sts)
Rnd 38: 4 sc, dec 1 st. (5 sts)
Rnd 39: 1 sc, dec 1 st, 2 sc. (4 sts)

Break the working yarn, and secure the end.

Do not weave in the remaining tail, instead leave a short end out when breaking the yarn.

CARROT TOPS

Join new working yarn in Apple to a stitch of the magic ring of the Carrot, and work as follows: Ch14, 1 sl-st into the 2nd chain from the hook, 2 sl-sts, ch4, 1 sl-st into the 2nd chain from the hook, 2 sl-sts, ch4, 1 sl-st into the 2nd chain from the hook, 2 sl-sts, ch4, 1 sl-st into the 2nd chain from the hook, 2 sl-st.

Now work back again over the already crocheted sts of the carrot top: * 1 sl-st into the next st, ch4, 1 sl-st into the 2nd chain from the hook, 2 sl-st *, rep from * to * 2 times more, 1 sl-st each into the remaining chains.

Work 1 sl-st into the next st of the magic ring, and repeat the instructions from the first asterisk. Work the steps 3 times more, creating a total of 5 carrot tops.

Break the working yarn, and secure the end.

PEAPOD

MATERIALS

- crochet hook, 2.5 mm (US B-1 or C-2)
- tapestry needle
- Schachenmayr Catania (100% cotton): 1 skein (1.75 oz/50 g) in Golf Green (Golfgrün), and about 0.5 oz (15 g) in Kiwi
- polyester fiberfill

INSTRUCTIONS

PEA (MAKE 3)

Work in rounds. Begin every rnd with ch1, and end every rnd with 1 sl-st into the 1st st of the rnd. Do not turn work.

Rnd 1: In Kiwi, work 7 hdc into an adjustable magic ring. (7 sts)
Rnds 2–4: 1 hdc in every st of the prev rnd. (7 sts)

Stuff lightly with polyester fiberfill.

Rnd 5: * Skip 1 st, 1 sl-st *, rep from * to * 2 times more, skip 1 st. (3 sts)

Break the working yarn, and secure the end.

POD

Work in rows. At the end of every row, ch1, and work 1 sl-st into the 1st st of the row. Turn work.

Row 1: In Golf Green, work 4 sc into an adjustable magic ring. (4 sts)
Row 2: 1 sc in every st of the prev row. (4 sts)
Row 3: * 1 sc, inc 1 st *, rep from * to * once more. (6 sts)
Row 4: 1 sc in every st of the prev row. (6 sts)
Row 5: * 1 sc, inc 1 st *, rep from * to * 2 times more. (9 sts)
Row 6: 6 sc. The remaining 3 sts stay unworked. (6 sts)
Rows 7–13: 1 sc in every st of the prev row. (6 sts)
Row 14: 6 sc, ch3. (9 sts)
Row 15: * Dec 1 st, 1 sc *, rep from * to * 2 times more. (6 sts)
Row 16: 1 sc in every st of the prev row. (6 sts)
Row 17: * 1 sc, dec 1 st *, rep from * to * once more. (4 sts)
Row 18: 1 sc in every st of the prev row. (4 sts)

Break the working yarn, and secure the end.

FINISHING

Sew the 3 peas to the inside of the pod.

CORNCOB

MATERIALS

- crochet hook, 2.5 mm (US B-1 or C-2)
- tapestry needle
- Schachenmayr Catania (100% cotton): 1 skein (1.75 oz/50 g) in Sun (Sonne), and about 0.5 oz (15 g) in Raffia (Bast)
- polyester fiberfill

INSTRUCTIONS

Work in rounds. Begin every rnd with ch1, and end every rnd with 1 sl-st into the 1st st of the rnd. Do not turn work.

Rnd 1: In Raffia, work 6 sc into an adjustable magic ring. (6 sts)
Rnd 2: Inc 1 st each, 6 times in all. (12 sts)

Change color to Sun.

Rnd 3: Working through the back loop of the st only: * 1 tulip-st, (1 tulip-st and 1 sc) in 1 st *, rep from * to * 5 times more. (18 sts)

Rnds 4–15: 1 tulip-st in every st of the prev rnd. (18 sts)
Rnd 16: Skip 1 st, 1 tulip-st in every following st of the prev rnd. (17 sts)
Rnds 17 and 18: 1 tulip-st in every st of the prev rnd. (17 sts)
Rnd 19: Skip 1 st, 1 tulip-st in every following st of the prev rnd. (16 sts)
Rnd 20: 1 tulip-st in every st of the prev rnd. (16 sts)
Rnd 21: Skip 1 st, 1 tulip-st in every following st of the prev rnd. (15 sts)
Rnd 22: 1 tulip-st in every st of the prev rnd. (15 sts)

Stuff the corncob with polyester fiberfill.

Change color to Raffia.

Rnd 23: Working through the back loop of the st only: * 1 sc, dec 1 st *, rep from * to * 5 times more. (12 sts)
Rnd 24: Dec 1 st each, 6 times in all. (6 sts)
Rnd 25: * Skip 1 st, 1 sl-st *, rep from * to * 2 times more. (3 sts)

Break the working yarn, and secure the end.

POTATO

MATERIALS

- crochet hook 2.5 mm [US B-1 or C-2, UK/Can 12]
- tapestry needle
- Schachenmayr Catania (100% cotton): 1 skein (1.75 oz/50 g) in Gold, about 0.5 oz (15 g) in Tan (Taupe)
- polyester fiberfill

INSTRUCTIONS

In Gold, crochet a circle from Basic pattern (Rnds 1–4, see page 23).

Rnds 5 and 6: 1 sc in every st of the prev rnd. (24 sts)
Rnd 7: 3 sc, inc 1 st, 10 sc, dec 1 st, 8 sc. (24 sts)
Rnd 8: 5 sc, inc 1 st, 9 sc, dec 1 st, 7 sc. (24 sts)
Rnd 9: 3 sc, inc 1 st, 3 sc, inc 1 st, 6 sc, dec 1 st, 1 sc, dec 1 st, 5 sc. (24 sts)
Rnd 10: 5 sc, inc 1 st, 10 sc, dec 1 st, 6 sc. (24 sts)
Rnd 11: 12 sc, inc 1 st, 4 sc, inc 1 st, 2 sc, inc 1 st, 3 sc. (27 sts)

Rnd 12: 20 sc, inc 1 st, 2 sc, inc 1 st, 3 sc. (29 sts)
Rnd 13: 21 sc, inc 1 st, 7 sc. (30 sts)
Rnd 14: 1 sc in every st of the prev rnd. (30 sts)
Rnd 15: 1 sc in every st of the prev rnd. (30 sts)
Rnd 16: 5 sc, dec 1 st, 4 sc, dec 1 st, 17 sc. (28 sts)
Rnd 17: 7 sc, dec 1 st, 1 sc, dec 1 st, 16 sc. (26 sts)
Rnd 18: 5 sc, dec 1 st, 1 sc, dec 1 st, 16 sc. (24 sts)

Stuff the potato with polyester fiberfill.

Rnd 19: * 2 sc, dec 1 st *, rep from * to * 5 times more. (18 sts)

Rnd 20: * 1 sc, dec 1 st *, rep from * to * 5 times more. (12 sts)
Rnd 21: Dec 1 st each, 6 times in all. (6 sts)
Rnd 22: * Skip 1 st, 1 sl-st *, rep from * to * 2 times more. (3 sts)

Break the working yarn, and secure the end.

In Tan, embroider a few dots onto the Potato with French knots.

BROCCOLI

MATERIALS

- crochet hook, 2.5 mm (US B-1 or C-2)
- tapestry needle
- Schachenmayr Catania (100% cotton): 1 skein (1.75 oz/50 g) each in Kiwi and Agave
- polyester fiberfill

INSTRUCTIONS

In Kiwi, crochet a circle from Basic pattern (Rnds 1–3, see page 23).

Rnd 4: Working through the back loop of the st only, 1 sc in every st of the prev rnd. (18 sts)

Rnd 5: 2 sc, dec 1 st, 6 sc, dec 1 st, 6 sc. (16 sts)

Rnd 6: 1 sc in every st of the prev rnd. (16 sts)

Rnd 7: Inc 1 st, 9 sc, dec 1 st, 4 sc. (16 sts)

Rnds 8 and 9: 1 sc in every st of the prev rnd. (16 sts)

Rnd 10: 6 sc, dec 1 st, 6 sc, inc 1 st, 1 sc. (16 sts)

Rnd 11: 1 sc in every st of the prev rnd. (16 sts)

Rnd 12: * 4 sc, dec 1 st *, rep from * to * once more, 4 sc. (14 sts)

Rnds 13–15: 1 sc in every st of the prev rnd. (14 sts)

Rnd 16: 8 sc, dec 1 st, 4 sc. (13 sts)

Rnd 17: 3 sc, dec 1 st, 8 sc. (12 sts)

Rnd 18: Inc 1 st each, 12 times in all. (24 sts)

Stuff the stem with polyester fiberfill.

Rnd 19: * 2 sc, inc 1 st *, rep from * to * 2 times more, inc 1 st, 4 sc, inc 1 st, 1 sc, inc 1 st, 3 sc, inc 1 st, 1 sc, inc 1 st, 1 sc. (32 sts)

Rnd 20: * Inc 1 st, 1 sc *, rep from * to * 15 times more. (48 sts)

Rnd 21: 1 sc in every st of the prev rnd. (48 sts)

Change color to Agave.

Rnd 22: Working through the back loop of the st only, 2 sc, 3 sc into the same st, 2 sc, inc 1 st, 3 sc, inc 1 st, 3 sc, inc 1 st, 1 sc, dec 1 st, 2 sc, inc 1 st, 1 sc, 3 sc into the same st, 3 sc, dec 1 st, 4 sc, inc 1 st each twice, 3 sc, dec 1 st each twice, 3 sc, inc 1 st, 1 sc, sc3tog. (53 sts)

Rnd 23: 1 sc in every st of the prev rnd. (53 sts)

Rnd 24: 1 sc, 1 bb (bobble, see page 16), 6 sc, 1 bb, 4 sc, 1 bb, 4 sc, 1 bb, 2 sc, dec 1 st, 2 sc, 1 bb, 2 sc, 1 bb, 2 sc, dec 1 st, 5 sc, 1 bb, 1 sc, 1 bb, 2 sc, dec 1 st, 1 sc, dec 1 st, 2 sc, 1 bb, 2 sc. (49 sts)

Rnd 25: 4 sc, dec 1 st each twice, 2 sc, dec 1 st, 7 sc, skip 1 st, 2 sc, dec 1 st, 5 sc, dec 1 st each twice, 7 sc, dec 1 st, 7 sc. (41 sts)

Rnd 26: 3 sc, 1 bb, 5 sc, 1 bb, 3 sc, 1 bb, 3 sc, inc 1 st, 3 sc, dec 1 st, 4 sc, inc 1 st, 1 bb, 2 sc, inc 1 st, 4 sc, 1 bb, 4 sc. (43 sts)

Rnd 27: 5 sc, 1 bb, 10 sc, 1 bb, 2 sc, dec 1 st, 1 sc, 1 bb, 3 sc, 1 bb, 6 sc, 1 bb, 7 sc, 1 bb, 1 sc. (42 sts)

Rnd 28: 1 sc, 1 bb, 9 sc, 1 bb, 3 sc, 1 bb, 5 sc, inc 1 st, 1 sc, 1 bb, 3 sc, 1 bb, 7 sc, 1 bb, 2 sc, 1 bb, 3 sc. (43 sts)

Rnd 29: 7 sc, dec 1 st, 10 sc, 1 bb, 11 sc, 1 bb, 11 sc. (42 sts)

Rnd 30: 3 sc, 4 dc in 1 st, 4 sc, 4 dc in 1 st, 7 sc, 4 dc in 1 st, 4 sc, 3 dc in 1 st, 6 sc, 3 dc in 1 st, 6 sc, 2 dc in 1 st, 4 sc, 3 dc in 1 st, 1 sc. (58 sts)

Stuff the crown with polyester fiberfill.

Rnd 31: 3 sc, sc4tog, 4 sc, sc4tog, 5 sc, dec 1 st, sc4tog, 4 sc, sc3tog, 2 sc, dec 1 st, 2 sc, sc3tog, 1 sc, dec 1 st, 3 sc, dec 1 st, 1 sc, dec 1 st, 1 sc, sc3tog, 1 sc. (38 sts)

Rnd 32: Dec 1 st, 2 sc, dec 1 st each twice, 1 sc, dec 1 st, 2 sc, dec 1 st, 2 sc, dec 1 st, 2 sc, dec 1 st, 2 sc, dec 1 st, 1 sc, dec 1 st, 3 sc, dec 1 st, 2 sc, dec 1 st, 3 sc. (28 sts)

Rnd 33: * 2 sc, dec 1 st *, rep from * to * 6 times more. (21 sts)

Rnd 34: * 1 sc, dec 1 st *, rep from * to * 6 times more. (14 sts)

Rnd 35: Skip 1 st, 1 bb, dec 1 st, skip 1 st, 1 bb, dec 1 st each twice, skip 1 st, 1 bb, dec 1 st. (7 sts)

Rnd 36: * Skip 1 st, 1 sl-st *, rep from * to * 2 times more, skip 1 st. (3 sts)

Break the working yarn, and secure the end.

Hide the tail by pulling it through the last rnd to the opposite side of the Broccoli.

STEM LEAVES

With stem side of Broccoli facing you, join new working yarn in Kiwi to any spot of the stem. Work: 1 hdc, 2 hdc in 1 st, 1 sl-st.

Break the working yarn, and secure the end.

Repeat these steps in two other spots.

GARLIC

MATERIALS

- crochet hook, 2.5 mm (US B-1 or C-2)
- tapestry needle
- Schachenmayr Catania (100% cotton): 1 skein (1.75 oz/50 g) in Creme, and about 0.5 oz (15 g) in Soft Apricot
- Schachenmayr Brazilia Color (100% polyester): about 0.5 oz (15 g) in Ruby Red (Rubin-Braun) (or any other eyelash yarn)
- polyester fiberfill

INSTRUCTIONS

First, work in the round. Begin every round with 1 chain, and end every round with 1 sl-st into the first stitch of the round. Do not turn work.

Rnd 1: In Soft Apricot, work 6 sc into an adjustable magic ring. (6 sts)

Change color to Creme.

Rnd 2: Working through the back loop of the st only, inc 1 st each, 6 times in all. (12 sts)

Rnd 3: Inc 1 st each, 12 times in all. (24 sts)

Rnd 4: * 3 sc, inc 1 st *, rep from * to * 5 times more. (30 sts)

Rnds 5 and 6: 1 sc in every st of the prev rnd. (30 sts)

Rnd 7: * 3 sc, dec 1 st *, rep from * to * 5 times more. (24 sts)

Rnd 8: * 2 sc, dec 1 st *, rep from * to * 5 times more. (18 sts)

Rnd 9: 1 sc in every st of the prev rnd. (18 sts)

Rnd 10: * 4 sc, dec 1 st *, rep from * to * 2 times more. (15 sts)

Rnd 11: * 3 sc, dec 1 st *, rep from * to * 2 times more. (12 sts)

Stuff the Garlic bulb with polyester fiberfill.

Rnd 12: * 1 sc, dec 1 st *, rep from * to * 3 times more. (8 sts)

Rnd 13: 1 sc in every st of the prev rnd. (8 sts)

Rnd 14: 6 sc, dec 1 st. (7 sts)

Rnd 15: 5 sc, dec 1 st. (6 sts)

Rnd 16: 1 sc in every st of the prev rnd. (6 sts)

Rnd 17: 4 sc, dec 1 st. (5 sts)

Break the working yarn, and secure the end.

Don't stuff the stem of the Garlic.

FINISHING

In Ruby Red, embroider a circle in backstitch between Rnds 1 and 2 of the Garlic bulb.

In Soft Apricot, starting from the back loop of the st in Rnd 1 (magic ring), from each one of the 6 sts, embroider a long vertical stitch toward the top to Rnd 6, pulling the yarn taut after every stitch.

SCALLION

MATERIALS

- crochet hook, 2.5 mm (US B-1 or C-2)
- tapestry needle
- Schachenmayr Catania (100% cotton): 1 skein (1.75 oz/50 g) each in White (Weiß), Anise (Anis), Apple (Apfel), and Agave, and 0.5 oz (15 g) each in Golf Green (Golfgrün), Tan (Taupe), and Raffia (Bast)
- polyester fiberfill

INSTRUCTIONS

Work in rounds. Begin every rnd with ch1, and end every rnd with 1 sl-st into the 1st st of the rnd. Do not turn work. Gradually stuff the scallion with polyester fiberfill as you go.

Rnd 1: In Tan, work 6 sc into an adjustable magic ring. (6 sts)

Change color to Raffia.

Rnd 2: Inc 1 st each, 6 times in all. (12 sts)

Change color to White.

Rnd 3: * 1 sc, inc 1 st *, rep from * to * 5 times more. (18 sts)
Rnd 4: * 5 sc, inc 1 st *, rep from * to * 2 times more. (21 sts)
Rnds 5 and 6: 1 sc in every st of the prev rnd. (21 sts)
Rnd 7: * 1 sc, dec 1 st *, rep from * to * 6 times more. (14 sts)
Rnd 8: 10 sc, dec 1 st, 2 sc. (13 sts)
Rnd 9: 9 sc, dec 1 st, 2 sc. (12 sts)
Rnd 10: 2 sc, change color to Anise: 2 sc, inc 1 st, change color to

White: 1 sc, inc 1 st, 1 sc, dec 1 st, 2 sc. (13 sts)
Rnd 11: 1 sc, change color to Anise: 6 sc, change color to White: 6 sc. (13 sts)

Change color to Anise.

Rnd 12: Dec 1 st, 4 sc, dec 1 st each 3 times, 1 sc. (9 sts)
Rnd 13: Dec 1 st, 2 sc, dec 1 st, 3 sc. (7 sts)
Rnds 14–18: 1 sc in every st of the prev rnd. (7 sts)
Rnd 19: 4 sc, inc 1 st, 2 sc. (8 sts)
Rnds 20–22: 1 sc in every st of the prev rnd. (8 sts)

Change color to Apple.

Rnd 23: * 1 sc, 1 sc worked below *, rep from * to * 3 times more. (8 sts)
Rnds 24 and 25: 1 sc in every st of the prev rnd. (8 sts)

From here on, work the inner leaves in rows. End every row with ch1, and turn work.

Row 26: Working through the back loop of the st only, 4 sc. The remaining sts will stay unworked for the time being.
Rows 27–31: 1 sc in every st of the prev row. (4 sts)

Change color to Golf Green.

Row 32: * 1 sc, 1 spike stitch *, rep from * to * once more. (4 sts)
Rows 33–39: 1 sc in every st of the prev row. (4 sts)

Change color to Agave.

Row 40: * 1 sc, 1 spike stitch *, rep from * to * once more. (4 sts)
Rows 41–51: 1 sc in every st of the prev row. (4 sts)

Break the working yarn, and secure the end.

Now join new working yarn in Apple to the 5th st of Rnd 25, and work 1 sc each through the back loop only of the 4 remaining sts. Continue as for the first inner leaf, repeating Rows 27–51.

Break the yarn, leaving a long tail, and secure the end.

OUTER LEAVES

Join new working yarn in Apple to the front loop of the 3rd st of Rnd 25, and continue in rows (ch1, and turn at end of row) as follows:

Row 26: Working through the front loop of the stitch only, 4 sc. (4 sts) The remaining sts will stay unworked for the time being.
Row 27: 1 sc in every st of the prev row. (4 sts)

Change color to Agave.

Rows 28–51: 1 sc in every st of the prev row. (4 sts)

Break the working yarn, and secure the end.

Now join new working yarn in Apple to the front loop of the 7th st of Rnd 25, and work 1 sc each through the back loop only of the 4 remaining sts. Continue as for the first outer leaf, repeating Rows 27–51.

Break the working yarn, and secure the end.

FINISHING

Using the long tail in Agave, sew the respective outer edges of the inner leaves together in running stitch, starting at the last row, up to the color change to Golf Green, causing the leaf to curl.

Sew the outer leaves together the same way, starting at the last row, and ending at Row 33.

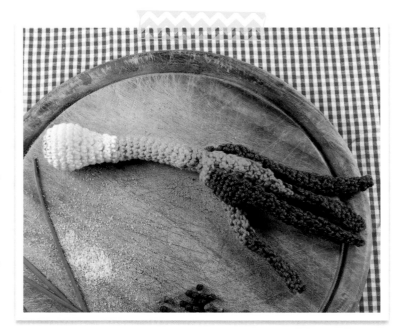

TOMATO ON THE VINE

MATERIALS

- crochet hook, 2.5 mm (US B-1 or C-2)
- tapestry needle
- Schachenmayr Catania (100% cotton): 1 skein (1.75 oz/50 g) in Signal Red (Signalrot), and about 0.5 oz (15 g) in Agave
- polyester fiberfill

INSTRUCTIONS

TOMATO

Using Signal Red, crochet a circle from Basic pattern (Rnds 1–5, see page 23).

Rnds 6–8: 1 sc in every st of the prev rnd. (30 sts)
Rnd 9: * 3 sc, dec 1 st *, rep from * to * 5 times more. (24 sts)
Rnd 10: * 2 sc, dec 1 st *, rep from * to * 5 times more. (18 sts)

Stuff the tomato—not too firm—with polyester fiberfill.

Rnd 11: * 1 sc, dec 1 st *, rep from * to * 5 times more. (12 sts)
Rnd 12: 1 sc in every st of the prev rnd. (12 sts)
Rnd 13: Dec 1 st each, 6 times in all. (6 sts)
Rnd 14: * Skip 1 st, 1 sl-st *, rep from * to * 2 times more. (3 sts)

Break the working yarn, and secure the end.

Sew the remainder of the tail through the center of the last rnd of the tomato, and exit the needle on the other side of the tomato through the magic ring, so that the last 3 rnds of the tomato turn slightly inward.

TOMATO GREENS

Rnd 1: In Agave, work 6 sc into an adjustable magic ring. (6 sts)
Rnd 2: Ch6, 1 sl-st into the 2nd chain from the hook, 4 sc, 1 sl-st into the 2nd stitch of the prev rnd, * ch6, 1 sl-st into the 2nd chain from the hook, 4 sc, 1 sl-st into the next st of the prev rnd *, rep from * to * 3 times more, ch6, 1 sl-st into the 2nd chain from the hook, 4 sc, 1 sl-st into the 1st st of the magic ring (prev rnd).

Break the working yarn, and secure the end.

FINISHING

Sew the tomato greens WS facing up centered onto the last rnd of the tomato.

TIP: Do you want to crochet a whole tomato vine? For the vine, in Agave, crochet a chain of the desired length, and then work back over the chain in sc. Break the working yarn, and secure the end. Now attach the tomato to the vine by joining new working yarn in Agave to the center of the tomato. Ch5, and join with a sl-st to any st of the stem.

JALAPEÑO PEPPER

MATERIALS

- crochet hook, 2.5 mm (US B-1 or C-2)
- tapestry needle
- Schachenmayr Catania (100% cotton): 1 skein (1.75 oz/50 g) in Anise (Anis)
- Rico Design Essentials Cotton DK (100% cotton): about 0.5 oz (15 g) in Grass (Gras)
- polyester fiberfill

INSTRUCTIONS

Work in rounds. Begin every round with 1 chain, and end every round with 1 sl-st into the 1st st of the rnd. Do not turn work. Gradually stuff the Jalapeño Pepper with polyester fiberfill as you go.

Rnd 1: In Anise, work 6 sc into an adjustable magic ring. (6 sts)
Rnd 2: Inc 1 st each, 6 times in all. (12 sts)
Rnd 3: Inc 1 st each, 12 times in all. (24 sts)
Rnd 4: 1 sc in every st of the prev rnd. (24 sts)
Rnd 5: * 2 sc, dec 1 st *, rep from * to * 5 times more. (18 sts)
Rnd 6: * 1 sc, dec 1 st *, rep from * to * 5 times more. (12 sts)
Rnds 7–11: 1 sc in every st of the prev rnd. (12 sts)
Rnd 12: 1 sc, dec 1 st, 4 sc, dec 1 st, 3 sc. (10 sts)
Rnd 13: 1 sc in every st of the prev rnd. (10 sts)
Rnd 14: 1 sc, dec 1 st, 7 sc. (9 sts)
Rnd 15: 2 sc, dec 1 st, 3 sc, inc 1 st, 1 sc. (9 sts)
Rnds 16 and 17: 3 sc, dec 1 st, 2 sc, inc 1 st, 1 sc. (9 sts)
Rnd 18: 1 sc in every st of the prev rnd. (9 sts)
Rnd 19: 2 sc, dec 1 st, 5 sc. (8 sts)
Rnd 20: 1 sc in every st of the prev rnd. (8 sts)
Rnd 21: 2 sc, dec 1 st, 4 sc. (7 sts)
Rnd 22: 1 sc in every st of the prev rnd. (7 sts)
Rnd 23: 1 sc, dec 1 st, 4 sc. (6 sts)
Rnd 24: 1 sc in every st of the prev rnd. (6 sts)
Rnd 25: 1 sc, dec 1 st, 3 sc. (5 sts)
Rnds 26 and 27: 1 sc in every st of the prev rnd. (5 sts)
Rnd 28: Dec 1 st, 3 sc. (4 sts)

Break the working yarn, and secure the end.

STEM

Rnd 1: In Grass, work 6 sc into an adjustable magic ring. (6 sts)
Rnd 2: Ch3, 1 sl-st into the 2nd chain from the hook, 1 sc, skipping the 1st st of the magic ring, 1 sl-st into the next st of the magic ring, * 1 sl-st, ch3, 1 sl-st into the 2nd chain from the hook, 1 sc, 1 sl-st into the next st of the magic ring *, rep from * to * once.

Break the working yarn, and secure the end.

Sew the stem to the magic ring of the Jalapeño Pepper with a few stitches.

Join new working yarn in Grass to the magic ring of the stem, and crochet a chain of 8.

Break the working yarn, and secure the end.

RADISH

MATERIALS

- crochet hook, 2.5 mm (US B-1 or C-2)
- tapestry needle
- Schachenmayr Catania (100% cotton): 1 skein (1.75 oz/50 g) in Strawberry (Erdbeere), and 0.5 oz (15 g) each in Kiwi, Anise (Anis), and Creme
- polyester fiberfill

INSTRUCTIONS

In Strawberry, crochet a circle from Basic pattern (Rnds 1–3, see page 23).

Rnds 4–7: 1 sc in every st of the prev rnd. (18 sts)
Rnd 8: * 4 sc, dec 1 st *, rep from * to * 2 times more. (15 sts)

Stuff the Radish with polyester fiberfill.

Rnd 9: * 3 sc, dec 1 st *, rep from * to * 2 times more. (12 sts)
Rnd 10: 1 sc in every st of the prev rnd. (12 sts)
Rnd 11: Dec 1 st each, 6 times in all. (6 sts)
Rnd 12: 1 sc in every st of the prev rnd. (6 sts)

Change color to Creme.

Rnd 13: Dec 1 st each, 3 times in all. (3 sts)

Break the working yarn, and secure the end.

GREENS WITH LEAVES

Join new working yarn in Kiwi to one of the 6 sts of the magic ring of the Radish, and continue as follows: * ch17 (the last 4 chains of which replace the first treble), 3 tr into the 5th st from the hook, ch4 (these replace the last treble), 1 sl-st into the same stitch into which the 3 tr had been worked earlier, 12 sl-st into the remaining chains, 1 sl-st into the magic ring. Work 1 additional sl-st *, rep from * to * 2 times more.

Break the working yarn, and secure the end.

Now join working yarn in Anise to one of the leaves in the 4th chain of the chains replacing the first tr, and work into the 5 sts of the trebles: 1 sc, 1 hdc, 1 dc, 1 hdc, 1 sl-st.

Break the working yarn, and secure the end.

Repeat this step for the two other leaves.

EGGPLANT

MATERIALS

- crochet hook, 2.5 mm (US B-1 or C-2)
- tapestry needle
- Schachenmayr Catania (100% cotton): 1 skein (1.75 oz/50 g) in Violet (Violett)
- Wolle Rödel Mille Fili (100% cotton): about 0.5 oz (15 g) in Kiwi (may be substituted with Schachenmayr Catania in Apple [Apfel])
- polyester fiberfill

INSTRUCTIONS

EGGPLANT

In Violet, crochet a circle from Basic pattern (Rnds 1–6, see page 23).

Rnds 7–10: 1 sc in every st of the prev rnd. (36 sts)
Rnd 11: 3 sc, dec 1 st, 31 sc. (35 sts)
Rnd 12: 2 sc, dec 1 st, 31 sc. (34 sts)
Rnd 13: 1 sc, dec 1 st, 2 sc, dec 1 st, 27 sc. (32 sts)
Rnd 14: Dec 1 st, 3 sc, dec 1 st, 20 sc, dec 1 st, 3 sc. (29 sts)
Rnd 15: 3 sc, dec 1 st, 19 sc, dec 1 st, 3 sc. (27 sts)
Rnd 16: 1 sc in every st of the prev rnd. (27 sts)
Rnd 17: 1 sc, dec 1 st, 3 sc, dec 1 st, * 4 sc, dec 1 st *, rep from * to * 2 times more, 1 sc. (22 sts)
Rnd 18: 1 sc in every st of the prev rnd. (22 sts)
Rnd 19: 2 sc, dec 1 st, 15 sc, dec 1 st, 1 sc. (20 sts)
Rnd 20: 1 sc in every st of the prev rnd. (20 sts)
Rnd 21: Dec 1 st, 2 sc, dec 1 st, 14 sc. (18 sts)
Rnd 22: 2 sc, dec 1 st, 14 sc. (17 sts)

Stuff the Eggplant with polyester fiberfill.

Rnd 23: 7 sc, dec 1 st, 2 sc, dec 1 st, 4 sc. (15 sts)
Rnd 24: * 3 sc, dec 1 st *, rep from * to * 2 times more. (12 sts)

If needed, add more polyester fiberfill.

Rnd 25: Dec 1 st each, 6 times in all. (6 sts)
Rnd 26: * Skip 1 st, 1 sl-st *, rep from * to * 2 times more. (3 sts)

Break the working yarn, and secure the end.

STEM

Work in rounds. Begin every round with 1 chain, and end every round with 1 sl-st into the first stitch of the round. Do not turn work.

Rnd 1: In Kiwi, work 6 sc into an adjustable magic ring. (6 sts)
Rnd 2: Working through the back loop of the st only, 1 sc in every st of the prev rnd. (6 sts)
Rnd 3: Skip 1 st, 5 sc. (5 sts)
Rnd 4: 1 sc in every st of the prev rnd. (5 sts)
Rnd 5: Inc 1 st each, 5 times in all. (10 sts)
Rnd 6: Inc 1 st each, 10 times in all. (20 sts)
Rnd 7: Ch3 (replaces the first dc), 2 dc into the 1st st, 1 hdc, 1 sl-st, 1 hdc, * 3 dc in 1 st, 1 hdc, 1 sl-st, 1 hdc *, rep from * to * 3 times more. (30 sts)

Break the working yarn, and secure the end.

Sew the stem to the last round of the Eggplant.

HALF AVOCADO

MATERIALS

- crochet hook, 2.5 mm (US B-1 or C-2)
- tapestry needle
- Schachenmayr Catania (100% cotton): 1 skein (1.75 oz/50 g) each in Mimosa (Mimose) and Agave, and 0.5 oz (15 g) each in Kiwi and Apple (Apfel)
- polyester fiberfill

INSTRUCTIONS

Work in rounds. Begin every rnd with ch1, and end every rnd with 1 sl-st into the 1st st of the rnd. Do not turn work.

Rnd 1: In Mimosa, work 6 sc into an adjustable magic ring. (6 sts)
Rnd 2: Inc 1 st each, 6 times in all. (12 sts)
Rnd 3: 1 sc in every st of the prev rnd. (12 sts)
Rnd 4: * 1 sc, inc 1 st *, rep from * to * 5 times more. (18 sts)
Rnd 5: * 2 sc, inc 1 st *, rep from * to * 5 times more. (24 sts)
Rnds 6 and 7: 1 sc in every st of the prev rnd. (24 sts)
Rnd 8: Working through the back loop of the st only: * 3 sc, inc 1 st *, rep from * to * 5 times more. (30 sts)
Rnd 9: 1 sc, inc 1 st, 5 sc, inc 1 st, * 4 sc, inc 1 st *, rep from * to * 3 times more, 2 sc. (36 sts)

Continue in rows. At the end of every row, chain 1, and turn work.

Row 1: Dec 1 st, 6 sc, dec 1 st. (8 sts) The remaining sts will stay unworked for the time being.

Row 2: Dec 1 st, 4 sc, dec 1 st. (6 sts)
Rows 3 and 4: 1 sc in every st of the prev row. (6 sts)
Row 5: 2 sc, dec 1 st, 2 sc. (5 sts)
Rows 6 and 7: 1 sc in every st of the prev row. (5 sts)
Row 8: 1 sc, dec 1 st, 1 sc. (3 sts) Change color to Kiwi. Chain 1, turn work.

Resume working in the round.

Rnd 1: Crochet an edging around the piece, working 1 sc in every st (each end of the row counts as 1 st). (45 sts)

Change color to Apple.

Rnd 2: 1 sc, inc 1 st, 7 sc, dec 1 st, 4 sc, inc 1 st, * 6 sc, inc 1 st *, rep from * to * 2 times more, dec 1 st, 6 sc. (48 sts)

Change color to Agave.

Rnd 3: 13 sc, inc 1 st, * 7 sc, inc 1 st *, rep from * to * 2 times more, 10 sc. (52 sts)
Rnd 4: 1 bpsc in every st of the prev rnd. (52 sts)
Rnd 5: 1 sc in every st of the prev rnd. (52 sts)
Rnd 6: 2 sc, dec 1 st, 18 sc, dec 1 st, 3 sc, dec 1 st, 3 sc, dec 1 st, 18 sc. (48 sts)
Rnd 7: Skip 1 st, 2 sc, dec 1 st, 5 sc, dec 1 st, 12 sc, dec 1 st each twice, 11 sc, dec 1 st, 5 sc, dec 1 st. (41 sts)
Rnd 8: 1 sc, dec 1 st, 1 sc, dec 1 st, 13 sc, dec 1 st, 1 sc, dec 1 st, 15 sc, dec 1 st. (36 sts)
Rnd 9: 2 sc, dec 1 st each twice, 10 sc, dec 1 st, 1 sc, dec 1 st, 13 sc, dec 1 st. (31 sts)
Rnd 10: 1 sc, dec 1 st each 3 times, 18 sc, dec 1 st each 3 times. (25 sts)

Now stuff the Avocado with polyester fiberfill, keeping in mind that the first 7 rnds will be pressed into the crocheted piece, and should not bulge outward.

Rnd 11: * 3 sc, dec 1 st *, rep from * to * 4 times more. (20 sts)

Rnd 12: * 2 sc, dec 1 st *, rep from * to * 4 times more. (15 sts)

Rnd 13: * 1 sc, dec 1 st *, rep from * to * 4 times more. (10 sts)

Rnd 14: Dec 1 st each, 5 times in all. (5 sts)

Rnd 15: * 1 sl-st, skip 1 st *, rep from * to * once more, 1 sl-st. (3 sts)

Break the working yarn, and secure the end.

TEMPLATES

PORTABLE CROCHET KITCHEN
Page 32

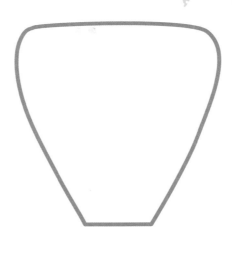

SPATULA
Page 36

EGG CUP
Page 46

THANK YOU

This book would not have been possible without the dedicated support of my husband, Andreas. Thank you for all the outings on which you took the children to free up time for me to work on this book, for your tireless commitment to housework, and for all the relaxing neck massages, without which I would have despaired at the laptop.

A big thank you goes to my three wonderful children, whose imagination and passion for playing have substantially contributed to the creation of this book. In case of doubt, you always come up with another idea for what else could be crocheted.

A heartfelt thank you to my parents and parents-in-law.

Many thanks to my editor, Charlotte May, and the whole team at Edition Michael Fischer for bringing this book to life.

Last but not least, I would like to sincerely thank all readers of my blog. Your comments and emails are always a delight!

Heartfelt thanks to our models, Coco, Niklas, and Mathilda—without you, the book would have been only half the fun!

ABOUT THE AUTHOR

Lucia Förthmann lives with her husband and three children in the suburbs of Hamburg, Germany. She discovered her passion for crocheting during her first pregnancy and has been creating her own crochet patterns with great enthusiasm ever since. The results of this labor of love are presented on Instagram @LuciaFoerthmann.